The beginnings of railway development in Russia

The beginnings of railway development in Russia in the reign of Nicholas I, 1835–1842

Richard Mowbray Haywood

Duke University Press   Durham, North Carolina   1969

Printed in the U.S.A. by the Seeman Printery, Inc.

To my parents

Preface

For a long time nineteenth-century Russian history has been viewed largely as a study in the development of a revolution. The history of the reign of Nicholas I has only recently been studied in detail in some of its other aspects. Although several works in the last few years have dealt with other features of the period and have looked at events through eyes other than those of men who rebelled against the tyranny of Nicholas I's autocratic rule, much remains to be done. The present study deals with one more aspect of the reign and by throwing additional light on it may help in giving a less one-sided picture.

Nicholas I's theory of government was not suited to nineteenth-century Russia, and he died knowing that his reign had been largely a failure, but his failure grew not out of a lack of good will or intelligence but from a rigid and emotional adherence to guiding principles that had become inappropriate. Had Nicholas I ruled a smaller and more manageable realm before the French Revolution, he might have gone down in history as the benevolent despot he wanted to be. But he did not live a hundred years earlier, and his conception of the ideal government, rooted in the eighteenth century, which had an entirely different conception of the state and sovereignty from that coming to be held in Western Europe, led him into the anachronistic behavior that has called down on his head so much abuse from historians.

Just as accounts of Nicholas I's arbitrary behavior and oppressive measures sometimes obscure the fact that he had some very real good qualities, so the lack of political progress during his reign has tended to blind the historian to the economic and social progress that there was. The term "Frozen Russia" for Nicholas' realm is spoken with the political situation in mind. Economically there was movement. The population was growing, and standards of living were rising. There were the beginnings of economic specialization, and considerable growth in both internal and external trade. The number of factory workers was increasing, and somewhat more of them were free labor. Compared to that of Western Europe, Russia's progress was slow, but there was progress. True, government policies in general were passive; there were no programs to reorganize established economic processes, and Count Kankrin, the minister of finance until 1844, if competent, was ultracautious and ultraconservative, although his two successors were somewhat more liberal. The government can, in truth, be given very little credit for the modest progress of Russia's economic life.

Yet Nicholas did oppose Kankrin on occasion, as in the case of railways. The Tsar listened to friends and foes of railways alike and then had the courage to act as appeared best to him in what seemed to most a dangerously uncertain undertaking. In the matter of railways he was open-minded. In this he showed himself not at all afraid of the new. He would listen on economic matters, about which he knew that he was not well informed and concerning which, except where engineering or building entered into the situation, he had rather little natural interest. He feared changes, but it was political changes he feared or social changes which might give rise to political changes, not economic ones.

There was some little social progress, too, under Nicholas. The intelligentsia of the 1840's differed from that of the 1820's in including men not of the nobility. Education under Nicholas I had reached down to the middle class and was responsible for the change. Unfortunately for Nicholas even the wider diffusion of education which he had allowed must have seemed to him to be rising to plague him since these educated men so often evinced opposition to his principles of government.

The attention of this intelligentsia was fixed on the lot of the peasant, but few seemed to realize that rapid economic growth and any real betterment in conditions for the peasant must go hand in hand. With the exception of a few men such as A. S. Khomiakov, who had a mechanical bent, the intelligentsia was not interested in railways. It could not guess that the coming of railways to Russia would have more effect on the lot of the peasant than all its talk and all its writing. Serfdom seemed the root of the peasants' troubles, but emancipation alone could have had little tangible result, except perhaps over a very long period of time, had it not been for railways. Not only did industrialization wait upon better means of transport, but the development of agriculture waited as well. In view of the immensity of the economic and social revolution that the construction of railways brought to Russia, it is surprising that while so much attention has been given to intellectual history, the history of Russian railways has yet to be written.

The time with which the present work deals, 1835–1842, the period in which events led up to the authorization of the construction of the St. Petersburg–Moscow Railway, was critical for Russian railways, for during these years it was decided that Russia should enter the Railway Age at this, for a backward country, early date. Precisely because Russia was to fall behind in the years that followed for a number of reasons—the high cost of railway building in Russia, high military expenditures, lack of vision—its start was important, but it is to be hoped that the complete history of Russian railways, of which this work is meant to be a beginning, will be written in the not too distant future.

It seemed desirable, since many of the sources for this early period are rare and therefore difficult of access, to recount what happened in some detail, but it should perhaps be remarked that the building of railways eventually led to questions concerning labor, finance, and government policy not exhaustively dealt with here. The comments made are not an attempt at discussion of any of these problems as they developed later. An account of how the early problems presented themselves and were dealt with is all that has been undertaken. During these early years no plan was made in advance; there were only responses to current problems. The importance of some economic and military considerations, so obvious later, was not readily apparent at this early stage.

The few works dealing at all with the history of Russian railways before 1855 tend to pass very quickly over the period before the authorization of the St. Petersburg–Moscow Railway in January, 1842. While there are quite a few books dealing with the pioneer period in other countries, the only secondary work, either Russian or non-Russian, dealing exclusively with the early Russian period, is the relatively short, semipopular work of V. S. Virginskii, *Vozniknovenie zheleznykh dorog v Rossii do nachala 40-ykh godov XIX veka.* Unfortunately Professor Virginskii, writing in the late 1940's at the height of the *Zhdanov-*

shchina, purposely underestimated the role of the Russian government, especially the Tsar, and of non-Russians in railway development.

Professor Virginskii used archival material from the Central State Historical Archives in Leningrad (TsGIAL). The great majority of documents used by him, and many that were not, have been printed in *Krasnyi Arkhiv*, and of these the writer has availed himself as well as of non-Russian archival sources. The works of Franz Anton von Gerstner have been extensively used. There is ample epistolary and memoir material, files of contemporary newspapers and periodicals are generally available in some of the Western libraries, and there are, of course, published laws and papers of some of the administrative institutions.

I have used printed sources from the following libraries: Columbia University Library, the New York Public Library, the Library of Congress (the Exchange and Gift Division of which was especially helpful in obtaining many valuable microfilms of printed matter from the Soviet Union), the Widener Library of Harvard University, the Yale University Library, the University of Michigan Library, the British Museum Library (which has valuable collections of Russian journals and newspapers otherwise unobtainable outside the Soviet Union), the Library of the University of Helsinki, the Saltykov-Shchedrin Library in Leningrad, and the Österreichische Nationalbibliothek in Vienna. To the members of the staffs of these institutions who more than once gave me unusual help I am grateful.

I would also like to express my thanks to Professor Walter M. Pintner of Cornell University, who lent me microfilms of some rare Russian printed works and of some archival material which he obtained in the Soviet Union. I have also used unprinted materials from the National Archives, Washington; the Manuscript Division of the New York Public Library; the Public Record Office, London; and the Österreichisches Haus-, Hof-, und Staatsarchiv, Vienna.

I am indebted to my colleagues at Eastern Michigan University, Professors Charles Helppie and Harold Simmons, for a number of helpful suggestions, and to Miss Janice Guerriero of the Department of Geography at the University of Michigan, who prepared the two maps for this work. My warmest gratitude goes to my wife and my parents, who have given valuable criticism and helped with much typing and editing. I would also like to thank Eastern Michigan University and Mr. Dean M. Warren for their generosity in providing funds to make publication of this work possible.

R. M. H.

Ypsilanti, Michigan
March, 1968

Contents

Maps

(following page 230)

Principal transportation facilities in Russia, 1842

St. Petersburg and environs, 1842

Russian measures, money, dates, and transliteration

1 vershok	equals	1.75 inches
1 arshin	"	28 inches
1 sazhen	"	7 feet
1 verst	"	0.67 miles
1 desiatin	"	2.7 acres
1 pood	"	36.1 pounds

All prices in Russian currency are quoted in paper ("assignat") rubles, unless specifically quoted in silver rubles. (One silver ruble was equal to approximately 3.5 paper rubles at this time.)

All dates referring to events in Russia are given according to the Julian calendar (Old Style), unless otherwise indicated. (The Julian calendar lagged behind the Gregorian calendar by twelve days in the nineteenth century.)

Transliterations have been done according to the system in use at the Library of Congress, slightly simplified, except for names commonly used in English.

Introduction

The countries pioneering in railway building during the seven years between 1835 and 1842—England, the United States, Belgium, France, Germany, and Austria, in addition to Russia[1]— were faced with many of the same problems, while they argued the usefulness of railways as opposed to canals, saw the construction of their first railways, debated where railways should be built and what their government's relationship to railways should be, especially in relation to assuring the provision of the necessary capital. Even in minor details there were many correspondences from country to country. Yet although most of the problems in their broad outlines were common to every pioneering country, the variations in geographic, economic, and political conditions meant that each country's approach to the problems had unique features. Russia's circumstances differed from those of most of the others largely because of its size, its greater economic backwardness, and the extremely autocratic and paternalistic nature of its government. England, where railways began, was at the opposite pole from Russia in all three respects.

All or almost all the problems of early railway building arose in connection with the decisions to build Russia's first railway, the Tsarskoe Selo Railway, and the St. Petersburg–Moscow Railway. How these problems were dealt with is the subject of this study. Successive chapters will deal with (1) the previously existing transportation system and its adequacy in relation to felt needs; (2) the state of technology as shown by the earliest native attempts at railway construction; (3) government reaction to early projects for public railways submitted by private individuals; (4) the problems of construction and operation of the first short railway; (5) the likelihood of the financial success and usefulness of the railways that were suggested in further projects; and (6) the proper role of the government in railway building, especially in relation to the gathering of capital.

1. Railways, but ones so short as to be of no real significance, had also been built in Holland and Italy.

The transportation system before the coming of railways is described in detail, since no account of it can be found elsewhere. Contemporaries could plainly see that economic changes were putting pressure on transportation facilities, but it was difficult for most not to think that rivers, canals, and seacoast must always be depended upon for the main movement of heavy goods. This assumption and the resulting desire to spend public funds to increase the number and capabilities of canals retarded the acceptance of railways as a governmental responsibility in Russia, as in most countries.

Some attention has been given to the work of Russians before 1835 in building factory railways and steam locomotives. Although these accomplishments were outside the main stream of events, a history of early Russian railways should mention them, if for no other reason than that they show, as the Soviet historian V. S. Virginskii strives so hard to prove, that railway building in this period was not completely dependent upon foreign initiative.

A description of the steps in getting the government's permission and help and enough capital for building the first railway follows. The government, faced for the first time by the question of its proper relation to railways, had many questions to decide in addition to whether a privilege should be granted. Especially important were the questions of how much aid should be extended and whether the railway should remain private property indefinitely.

Since it has proved possible to construct in some detail the story of the building and the operation of Russia's first railway, a rather full account is offered here. Projects suggested for further railways and the resultant discussion of the usefulness and financial feasibility of various proposed lines and of whole networks are discussed, and the influence of persons who favored and opposed railways is assessed. Finally, the steps that led to the ordering and the building of the St. Petersburg–Moscow Railway at the expense of the state are analyzed.

The reader will find that consideration of these matters led in Russia to increasing government participation in railway building as it did in the other pioneering countries on the Continent. The size of railway undertakings and a growing realization of their importance would naturally lead to this result in countries with a tradition of government interference in economic matters and government responsibility for transportation. It is interesting to note that other countries took as long as Russia to assume a great deal of responsibility for railways. Of course, the larger or more backward the country, the more necessary government assistance and encouragement became.

Within the topical and chronological arrangement used here at least partial answers may be found to questions which naturally arise. First of all, why was an economically backward country like Russia one of the pioneers of railway building? The first steam railway in Russia was opened to the public in 1837, the first in France in 1832, the first in Germany in 1835, and the first in Austria in 1837. In January, 1842, Russia made the decision that railways were sufficiently desirable to warrant sacrifices by the government to build them, a decision just being reached also in France, Prussia, and Austria. Why was Russia in the forefront both in building her first railway and in making a decision as to a policy of governmental support?

Second, what was Nicholas I's attitude toward railways? Contradictory statements have been made concerning his feeling toward railway building. B. H. Sumner says that Nicholas I "shared the aversion to railways felt by most of his advisers, largely on the ground that they would involve the dependence of Russia on foreign capital and equipment." M. A. Polievktov, on the other hand, remarks that Count P. A. Kleinmichel was a favorite with the Tsar because of Kleinmichel's early enthusiasm for railways. What does the evidence show about Nicholas I's attitude?

Finally, why with an early start did Russia so soon fall behind other pioneering countries in the number of versts of railway built, not only in relation to its size, but in the absolute as well? Although the whole answer to this question must be sought in the history of the period after 1842, part of the answer falls within the period with which this study deals.

But, to begin with, the history of early railways must concern itself with the reasons for any railway building, namely, the inadequacies of already existing means of transport, which is the subject of the first chapter of this volume.

The beginnings of railway development in Russia

Chapter I. Transportation in Russia before the advent of railways

Part 1. Waterways in Russia before 1835

In the 1830's and 1840's the most pressing need for better transportation, which many hoped that railways could fill, arose primarily, of course, from the facts of geography, but the building of the very first railways grew out of the new industrial needs and was not in those nations whose geography made transportation most difficult. In fact, in England, where railways began, geography made transportation easy. Until the coming of railways commerce had been largely water-borne because not many products could stand the cost of being carried over long distances by land. England's small size and extensive coastline meant that distances were short, not just to the nearest canal or river, but to the sea, and gave her great commercial advantage. Russia, with little usable coastline and a large land mass which, despite some magnificent rivers, included vast expanses with no reasonable access to either a river or a canal, was at the other extreme. From the standpoint of geography Russia needed railways much more than England. Economically speaking, however, England—with growing specialization of labor, shortage of wood but abundance of coal, and relatively dense population—felt need for transport, as Russia because of its backwardness did not. The other pioneering countries lay somewhere between, both in their geographic and their economic needs.

But if the first railways were built in the very countries where transportation was superior, for the specific purposes of carrying cotton from Liverpool to Manchester and coal from Stockton to Darlington or out of the coal fields of the Loire, the fact remains that basically the greatest need for railways was where nature had not supplied good means of communication. By the 1840's, when the success of railways was becoming apparent, some governments awakened to the possibility of overcoming geographic disadvantages by means of the railway, and comprehensive planning began to appear, if sometimes, as in Austria, for only part of the country.

3

Russia took part in this general movement as it had taken part in canal building in the "canal era" and as it had taken part in building one of the earliest railways.[1] By the 1840's Russia also was beginning to think of geographic lacks in relation to railways. The needs that grew out of Russian topography combined with Russia's economic necessities, and the canals and roads that had been built to meet these needs are the subject of this chapter. From the standpoint of geography it was Russia's size that made the greatest need for transportation, but neither this nor Russia's lack of adequate natural means of communication by water nor its harsh climate would have mattered if it had been entirely a nation of self-sufficient communities with undeveloped mineral resources and with domestic handicraft industries whose products were consumed locally or sent to the yearly Nizhnii Novgorod Fair. This was not exactly the case. Some of Russia's ancient river cities had grown to a considerable size, it was inconveniently divided into forest and steppe zones that needed to complement each other, and the products that the country depended upon for foreign trade often originated far from any port. Furthermore, when railways were being considered, the inadequacy of the efforts which the nation had made to cope with transportation needs was as important a consideration as topography.

What is described here is the whole picture of transportation which the people of the 1830's and 1840's knew and grew up with. To understand their points of view it is necessary to see the picture as they saw it, not with the hindsight of over a hundred years later. To them, canals were of first importance. The discussion of the wisdom of railway building always seemed to concern the known capabilities of canals as opposed to the unknown advantages of railways. The years just before the coming of railways had seen a greatly increased concern with canals and increased building of them, and since in most countries canal

1. It may seem remarkable that Russia started building a railway, the Tsarskoe Selo, as early as 1836, when there was no specific compelling reason as in Lancashire or the region of the Loire, but there were other early suburban railways. King Ludwig of Bavaria was passionately interested and was responsible for the opening in 1835 of the first German railway, the line from Nuremberg to Fürth. And Emil Pereire started to build the line from Paris to St. Germain in 1835, having wrested permission from a skeptical Parliament, with the express idea of awakening the people of Paris to the railway's possibilities.

interests were private these new interests naturally fought railways through legislative bodies or through the bureaucracy, as the case might be. In Russia the government had built the canals, but those responsible for them fought for them as against railways and the struggle was no less real than elsewhere. Twenty years later, when it was plain what railways could do to develop agriculture, or forty years later, to develop industry, geographical considerations were of a different nature. During this early period rivers and the capabilities of roads and canals, but especially canals, were always in the background of people's thinking as they considered railways.

Before describing Russia's transport on the eve of railway building, a reminder may be in order that if Russia's roads and waterways must be described as primitive, so also would those of most other countries, especially where no Roman roads were present as a basis. For example, although Austria had started to repair its deficiencies in roads in the decades preceding the building of its first railway, there had been only one road between Vienna and Prague and that not a good one at the time of the ending of the Napoleonic Wars. And in the 1830's eastern Prussia was so poorly equipped with roads that a large section of Pomerania did not contain one made road.

From the very beginning of Russia's history, its rivers and lakes, navigable over great distances, had been the natural means of communication between the various parts of the country. Little was done to improve these natural waterways until the time of Peter the Great, during whose reign the first real attempts were made to build artificial constructions on them. The main impetus for improving waterways was the transfer of the capital to St. Petersburg. Since Moscow and the surrounding area remained important commercially, Peter the Great considered it important to unite the two areas by water and, now that Russia had access to the Baltic Sea, to give the interior the advantage of that access and encourage the use of St. Petersburg as a port instead of Archangel.[2] To link St. Petersburg with rivers of the interior, Peter the Great had the so-called Vyshnii Volochek System built.

2. K. A. Oppengeim, *Rossiia v dorozhnom otnoshenii* (Moscow, 1920), p. 6.

The necessary technical knowledge, lacking in Old Muscovy, was gained from Europe, and European engineers were brought to Russia.[3] Although Peter the Great made plans for other similar systems, lack of funds prevented the realization of such schemes until the reign of Paul I, when work was started on the Mariinskii System and the Tikhvinskii System was planned. They were opened to traffic in 1810 and 1811, respectively, during the reign of Alexander I.[4]

Work on these two systems occupied hydraulic engineers during all the first years of Alexander I's reign, but when they were completed St. Petersburg was linked to the interior of Russia by three water systems, in the eyes of contemporaries a notable achievement.[5] Beside this, Alexander I founded the Institute of Transport Engineers (Institut Inzhenerov Putei Soobshcheniia) which was meant to provide Russia with skilful engineers to serve in the also newly formed Corps of Transport Engi-

3. *Kratkii istoricheskii ocherk razvitiia vodianykh i sukhoputnykh soobshchenii i torgovykh portov v Rossii* (St. Petersburg, 1900), p. 105.
4. Although final work on the Tikhvinskii System was not completed until 1814, it was put into service in 1811 because of the imminence of the war with Napoleon (*ibid.*, pp. 167-169; Otto Baron von Wittenheim, *Über Russlands Wasserverbindungen, wie solche bis zum Jahre 1830 bestanden, und seitdem bis jetzt vermehrt oder verändert worden* [Mittau, 1842], pp. 71-73).
5. The Vyshnii Volochek System began near Tver and went along the Tvertsa River to the Vyshnii Volochek Canal. From there it went for a short distance through the river Tsna and Lake Mstino to the river Msta, then through the Msta River and the Sievers Canal. From there it went for a longer distance through the Volkhov River, then through the Ladoga Canal which emptied into the Neva River near Schlüsselburg (V. F. Meien, *Rossiia v dorozhnom otnoshenii* [St. Petersburg, 1902], I, 120-121; *Kratkii istoricheskii ocherk razvitiia vodianykh i sukhoputnykh soobshchenii*, pp. 116, 153; cf. Wittenheim, p. 27). The Mariinskii System started in the river Sheksna near Rybinsk and continued through Beloozero, the river Kovzha, the Mariinskii Canal, the river Vytegra, Lake Onega, part of which was avoided by the Onega Canal, the river Svir', and thence through the Svir' Canal, the Sias' Canal, and the Ladoga Canal, into the Neva (Meien, I, 122-123; "Istoricheskoe obozrenie putei soobshcheniia i publichnykh zdanii s 1825 po 1850 g.," *Sbornik Imperatorskogo Russkogo Istoricheskogo Obshchestva* [hereafter referred to as *SIRIO*], XCVIII [1896], 537; cf. Wittenheim, pp. 11, 66-67). The Tikhvinskii System began where the Mologa River joined the Volga near Rybinsk and continued along the Mologa and Chagodoshcha rivers to the river Somina and thence to the Tikhvinskii Canal, to the Tikhvina River, to the Sias' River, and finally to the Sias' and Ladoga Canals (Meien, I, 122-123; Wittenheim, pp. 68, 73).

6

neers (Korpus Inzhenerov Putei Soobshcheniia).[6] After the Napoleonic Wars increasingly ambitious canals were undertaken. In the years 1818–1820 the Onega Canal, 19 versts (1 verst = 0.67 miles) long, was built along the southern shore of Lake Onega to allow boats to avoid a part of the usually stormy trip along that lake when passing through the Mariinskii System.[7] In 1823 the Kirilov Canal was begun to unite the Mariinskii System—and thereby St. Petersburg or the Volga—with the Northern Dvina and Archangel. When it was completed, in 1828, Nicholas I commanded that henceforth the canal should be called "the Canal of Duke Alexander von Württemberg" after the head of the Main Administration of Transport (Glavnoe Upravlenie Putiami Soobshcheniia).[8]

Most ambitious of all was the project conceived at the end of the reign and undertaken in 1825 to connect Moscow with the Vyshnii Volochek System and St. Petersburg by a more direct route to the Volga than the roundabout route by way of the Moskva and Oka rivers. A canal was to be dug to connect the Istra and Sestra rivers, near Klin, thereby establishing a link between the Moskva River and the Middle Volga.[9] Nicholas I must have considered this project of great importance, for, though an extremely religious man, on May 1, 1826, he informed the Duke of Württemberg that 300,000 rubles assigned to the building of the Church of Christ the Savior near Moscow were to be applied to the building of this canal.[10] Work was stopped, however, in 1844. At that time it was considered too costly to continue work, and it was felt that the St. Petersburg–Moscow Railway, then under construction, would compete too successfully for goods sent from Moscow to St. Petersburg.[11]

Except for carrying on the work of these last two canals and the construction in the years 1826–1836 of the Visherskii Canal, 14.5 versts long, on the Vyshnii Volochek System to make a con-

6. E. Sokolovskii, *Piatidesiatiletie Instituta i Korpusa Inzhenerov Putei Soobshcheniia* (St. Petersburg, 1859), pp. 4, 10-11.
7. "Istoricheskoe obozrenie," *SIRIO*, XCVIII (1896), 537; Wittenheim, p. 11.
8. N. Dubrovin (ed.), *Sbornik istoricheskikh materialov, izvlechennykh iz Arkhiva Sobstvennoi Ego Imperatorskogo Velichestva Kantseliarii* (St. Petersburg, 1876–1917), VII, 67–68.
9. Wittenheim, pp. 118-120.   10. Dubrovin, VII, 13.
11. "Istoricheskoe obozrenie," *SIRIO*, XCVIII (1896), 541.

7

nection[12] between the rivers Msta and Vishera near Novgorod,[13] most of the work done during the early years of Nicholas I's reign (before he became seriously interested in railways) was on facilities already in existence. He was always especially concerned that the facilities connecting St. Petersburg with the interior be kept in good order so that the provisioning of the city should proceed in an uninterrupted manner.

On the Tikhvinskii System the reservoir system was considerably improved and new towpaths were constructed.[14] On the Mariinskii System effort was chiefly directed toward improving the artificial constructions on the Vytegra and Kovzha rivers, thereby reducing the time necessary to navigate the system by over ten days. The river Svir' was cleared of stones and provided with a towpath.[15]

But it was on the oldest of the three Volga-Neva water systems, the Vyshnii Volochek System, and on the Ladoga Canal that the greatest amount of work was done in the years 1822–1833. Some of the works carried out on the Vyshnii Volochek System were so ingenious and original that they aroused the interest of hydraulic engineers in foreign countries. Engineers came even from America to see them.[16] For example, on the river Msta there were dangerous rapids, especially at Borovitsa, where the rapids were 30 versts in length with a drop of 30 sazhens (1 sazhen = 7 feet). Boats customarily covered the distance in three hours or less. Because of this great speed and the winding nature of the river, many boats were broken against the rocky shore. To make navigation easier and safer, so-called *zaplyvy* were built. They were resilient wooden beams held by ropes along the shores of the river, especially at sharp turns, and were meant to keep boats in the proper channel.[17]

Also on the Vyshnii Volochek System reservoirs were im-

12. The Sievers Canal, built under Paul I, had already made a connection in order to avoid Lake Il'men.
13. "Istoricheskoe obozrenie," *SIRIO*, XCVIII (1896), 533.
14. *Kratkii istoricheskii ocherk razvitiia vodianykh i sukhoputnykh soobshchenii*, p. 182.
15. "Istoricheskoe obozrenie," *SIRIO*, XCVIII (1896), 535-536.
16. V. A. Panaev, "Vospominaniia," *Russkaia Starina*, LXXX (1893), 399.
17. "Istoricheskoe obozrenie," *SIRIO*, XCVIII (1896), 534.

proved, especially after the dry summer of 1826. An important part of the work was that the capacity of the Zavodskii Reservoir at Vyshnii Volochek, the highest point of the system, was increased.[18] Also the Tvertsa River was cleared of stones and the channel of the river was deepened. A towpath was built along its banks. The Msta River was also dredged and its banks shored up.

Improvements made on the Ladoga Canal and the Neva were especially important, since all three water systems linking St. Petersburg with the interior met at the Ladoga Canal to gain access to the Neva.[19] New granite sluices were built at both ends. The canal was dredged, and new towpaths were built. Reservoirs were improved, and steam pumping engines were introduced to raise the level of the canal. The "waterfalls" in the Neva, that is, shallows with stones, were cleared by 1830.[20] In 1826 Nicholas I approved a plan for dredging and deepening the canals and rivers of St. Petersburg.[21]

The remarks on the canals made here should not imply that there were not canals existing or planned outside the area discussed. Thinking and discussion about the first railways in Russia was largely centered, however, on the area of the three great Volga-Neva systems. The interest and effort of three emperors had been concentrated on them as the chief means of transportation of goods, if not of passengers, from the Volga to the Baltic. These waterways were especially important for the transportation of bulk commodities such as grain, iron, flax, and hemp, which, along with animal products, were the main items of Russia's internal and external trade.

During Nicholas I's reign the three water systems showed themselves to be inadequate. The population of St. Petersburg was growing, and Russia was undergoing the beginning of a very gradual change from a natural to a market economy. At the same time in Western Europe the demands of early industrialization

18. *Kratkii istoricheskii ocherk razvitiia i deiatel'nosti Vedomstva Putei Soobshcheniia za sto let ego sushchestvovaniia* (1798-1898) (St. Petersburg, 1898), p. 64; Wittenheim, p. 37.

19. See *Biblioteka dlia Chteniia*, XXIII (1837), Sec. V, 44-45.

20. Wittenheim, pp. 28, 47.

21. *Polnoe Sobranie Zakonov Rossiiskoi Imperii* (hereafter referred to as PSZ), 2nd ser., I, No. 474 (July 15, 1826); Dubrovin, VII, 21-22.

and of a growing population resulted in increased needs for food and raw materials, part of which Russia was called upon to supply. This increase in domestic and foreign trade meant additional demands upon Russia's waterways, so that in spite of efforts by the Russian government to improve them, the three waterways proved unable to handle the new traffic satisfactorily. The three water systems were always intensively used. In 1838, as an example, they supplied St. Petersburg from the interior with 60 million poods (1 pood = 36.1 pounds) of goods worth 143 million rubles, and in 1839 with 81 million poods worth 197 million rubles.[22] This commerce was of vital importance for the provisioning of the city—which in the late 1830's had nearly 500,-000 inhabitants[23] and especially required grain, most of which had to come by water from a great distance.

Also the port of St. Petersburg had the major share of the trade of many commodities exported by Russia. Seventy to 80 per cent of Russia's iron exports, and 90 per cent of its copper exports went through the port of St. Petersburg.[24] Animal products, especially tallow and hides, from the south of Russia and from the Central Provinces were another important Russian export, and the port of St. Petersburg had 80 to 90 per cent of this trade.[25] Next to cereal culture and the raising of domestic animals, the culture of hemp and flax, both as textile plants and oleaginous grains, was the most important part of Russian agriculture. Hemp and flax and products derived from them were exported in great quantities, especially to England.[26] St. Petersburg was the main port of export for hemp and was second in importance (the first being Riga) for the export of flax.[27] The only important item of Russia's export trade that was not exported in any significant amount through St. Petersburg was

22. "Donesenie Nikolaiu I komissii po ustroistvu zheleznoi dorogi mezhdu Peterburgom i Moskvoi, 15 sentiabria 1841 g.," *Krasnyi Arkhiv*, LXXVI (1936), 142. For an itemization of the various kinds of goods brought to St. Petersburg, see N. Atreshkov (Otreshkov-Tarasenko), *Ob ustroenii zheleznykh dorog v Rossii* (St. Petersburg, 1835), p. 42.
23. *Severnaia Pchela*, May 30, 1838, p. 475.
24. G. P. Nebol'sin, *Statisticheskoe obozrenie vneshnei torgovli Rossii* (St. Petersburg, 1850), II, 217, 236.
25. *Ibid.*, pp. 114-115, 265.
26. *Ibid.*, pp. 2-3; Ludwik Tengoborskii, *Commentaries on the Productive Forces of Russia* (London, 1855), I, 340, 342.
27. Nebol'sin, II, 7-8.

grain. Other Baltic ports such as Riga and, in ever increasing measure, southern Russian ports such as Odessa had a greater share of the grain export trade than did St. Petersburg.[28] The port of St. Petersburg was of great significance also for Russia's import trade. About 80 per cent of Russia's imports came through the Baltic ports, and of this import trade St. Petersburg had by far the greatest share.[29]

Because of the nature of these exports and the need for grain to provision the city, the goods transported along two of the three systems, the Vyshnii Volochek and the Mariinskii, were mainly raw materials of a bulky nature. On the Vyshnii Volochek System in the years 1824–1828, grain and grain products, iron, and hemp in that order were the chief items carried.[30] But at Novgorod, from which the trip by water to St. Petersburg normally took only ten to fourteen days,[31] some manufactured wares, military supplies, and perishable provisions such as fruits and vegetables bound for the markets of St. Petersburg were also loaded.[32] Similarly, on the Mariinskii System the chief products carried were grain, lumber, and metal products, but there were also some manufactured articles and, especially from landings on the River Svir' near St. Petersburg, some perishable foodstuffs.[33]

The predominance of bulky and relatively inexpensive raw materials in the goods carried by these two systems was connected with the fact that these two were the longer of the three water systems and took the greatest amount of time to traverse but were the least expensive. The Vyshnii Volochek System was 1,187 versts from Rybinsk to St. Petersburg,[34] and under good conditions the journey took about three months.[35] By way of the Mariinskii System the trip between Rybinsk and St. Petersburg, a distance of 1,088 versts,[36] generally took about two months.[37]

Since the goods carried on these two systems were largely meant either to be exported or to be used for the basic food re-

28. *Ibid.*, I, 9-31.   29. *Ibid.*, II, 452.
30. Wittenheim, p. 43.
31. *Severnaia Pchela*, May 30, 1838, p. 476.
32. Wittenheim, pp. 55-56.   33. *Ibid.*, pp. 91, 93.
34. *Ibid.*, p. 84.
35. *Severnaia Pchela*, May 30, 1838, p. 479.
36. Wittenheim, p. 83.
37. A. I. Chuprov, *Zheleznodorozhnoe khoziaistvo* (Moscow, 1910), I, 11.

quirements of the city, both the amount and value of goods carried in the direction of St. Petersburg exceeded by many times the amount and value of the goods carried from St. Petersburg toward the interior on both the Vyshnii Volochek and the Mariinskii systems. In the year 1828, which was a fairly good year without any unusual dry spells or early freezes, 8,841 loaded and 275 empty barges were sent to St. Petersburg on the Vyshnii Volochek System, but only 280 loaded and 2,231 empty barges made the return journey. In the same year, 2,280 loaded and 151 empty barges were sent to St. Petersburg on the Mariinskii System.[38] Statistics for barges making the return journey are lacking for 1828, but judging from previous years, 1824–1826, the number of barges, especially loaded barges, was proportionately about the same as on the Vyshnii Volochek System.[39]

The Tikhvinskii System was shorter than either of the other systems. The distance between St. Petersburg and Rybinsk via the Tikhvinskii System was only 847 versts,[40] and the journey took only about a month.[41] However, the Tikhvinskii System was the most expensive of the three water systems.[42] Since it was narrow and shallow, barges used on it had to be smaller and could carry less; but because it was the fastest route, the traffic could bear higher charges. Accordingly, it was the Tikhvinskii System that carried the greatest amount of more expensive and less bulky goods, especially wares imported by way of the port of St. Petersburg or manufactured in St. Petersburg and its suburbs. These goods were customarily transported to the interior along the Tikhvinskii System, mostly to Moscow or to the Nizhnii Novgorod Fair, although many goods were also transported by road.[43] Therefore traffic from St. Petersburg in the direction of the interior was especially important on the Tikhvinskii System,[44] again in contrast to the other two. Products of a nature similar to those carried by the Vyshnii Volochek and the Mariinskii

38. After the Württemberg Canal was opened in 1828 traffic on the Mariinskii System notably increased.
39. Wittenheim, pp. 43, 80-81.   40. *Ibid.*, p. 83.
41. "Donesenie," *Krasnyi Arkhiv*, LXXVI (1936), 139.
42. *Ibid.*
43. V. P. Gur'ev, "Mysli o pervoi kompanii zimnikh dorog v Rossii," *Biblioteka dlia Chteniia*, XXXI (1838), Sec. IV, 13.
44. Wittenheim, p. 74.

systems as well as products of value were carried on the Tikh-vinskii System toward St. Petersburg.[45]

That the Tikhvinskii System carried as many goods as it did, in spite of its relatively high rates, showed the need for a rapid form of transportation for high-priced goods such as manufactured articles and for perishables. But the greater part of Russian trade consisted of goods of the type carried by the Vyshnii Volochek and Mariinskii systems, that is, bulky, low-priced raw materials. The question that arose was whether the advantages of speed and uninterrupted communication afforded by a railway would outweigh the fact that rates on the Vyshnii Volochek and Mariinskii systems were low and would attract enough traffic to allow the railway to make a profit.

Traffic was fed into these three partly artificial systems by the great natural waterway of the Volga and its two large tributaries, the Kama and Oka rivers, with their tributaries. The Volga, one of the longest commercial arteries in the world, which with the help of the canal systems carried goods to the sea, was also the main route for Russia's internal trade. It was navigable over almost its entire length from Astrakhan and its mouths in the Caspian Sea to a point where the River Gzhat emptied into it in Tver Province. At the Volga landings, of which the main ones were Astrakhan, Kazan, Nizhnii Novgorod, Rybinsk, and Tver, goods worth 50–60 million silver rubles were loaded yearly during the 1830's.[46]

From the Lower Volga and its tributaries came those products of nearby southern grain-producing provinces which were not consumed locally or exported by way of the Caspian and Black seas. Besides various sorts of grain, such products as tallow and potash were transported along the Lower Volga to the north.[47]

Great contributions to the Volga traffic were made by its more northerly tributaries. One the most important of these, along with its tributaries, the Viatka and Belaia, was the Kama

45. *Ibid.*, p. 92.
46. E. Ziablovskii, *Rossiiskaia Statistika* (2nd ed.; St. Petersburg, 1842), II, 156; Wittenheim, p. 105. Statistics on the amount of traffic handled on Russia's waterways should be considered only as approximations, since there is considerable doubt as to their accuracy.
47. Nebol'sin, II, 114, 307.

River, which emptied into the Volga at a point about sixty versts below Kazan. The products of Perm, Kazan, Viatka, and Orenburg provinces, consisting mostly of metals, salt, lumber, and grain, were shipped to the Volga by way of these rivers. The most important of the products were the metals from the Urals. The chief landing on the Kama River was at Perm, where the metals, mainly iron and copper, were collected for shipment to the Volga and beyond. Iron from the Urals, loaded on "caravans" of boats at foundry landings on the tributaries of the Kama, traveled to Perm and from there on larger craft along the Kama to the Volga. Some iron went directly to St. Petersburg; all the rest was unloaded at Nizhnii Novgorod for the fair,[48] for which about 3.5 million poods of iron were shipped yearly. One-seventh of this amount was bought for use in Nizhnii Novgorod Province for manufacturing. The rest was bought to be sent to the South or along the Oka River to Moscow and Tula or to the Riazan and Tambov provinces or to St. Petersburg and places between such as Yaroslavl, Tver, and Novgorod.[49]

Salt from the large deposits in Perm Province was also a very important item of commerce along the Kama and was mostly transported to the storehouses in Nizhnii Novgorod.[50] The traffic included only a relatively small amount of grain, mostly rye and oats from Perm and Viatka provinces.[51] The Kama was also the main route of transport for goods imported from China and from other Asiatic lands.[52]

Near Nizhnii Novgorod, a little farther up the Volga, the river Oka entered the Volga. It was by means of the Oka and its

48. Every year during the month of August Nizhnii Novgorod was the scene of a fair which was the largest not only in Russia but also in Europe. Because of the difficulties of communication and the lack of credit facilities fairs had an importance in Russia which they did not have in other countries. Goods from all parts of Russia, Europe, and the Orient were brought to Nizhnii Novgorod to be bought and sold. Nizhnii Novgorod was very well situated to play an important role in the internal commerce of Russia, since goods could come into it from southern Russia by way of the Volga and from the Urals by way of the Kama and goods could be sent from it either to St. Petersburg by way of Rybinsk and one of the canal systems or to Moscow and the Central Provinces by way of the Oka and its tributaries (Tengoborskii, II, 156-157).

49. Nebol'sin, II, 213.

50. Ferdinand H. Mueller, *Historisch-geographische Darstellung des Stromsystems der Wolga* (Berlin, 1839), p. 375; Ziablovskii, I, 24.

51. Nebol'sin, I, 30.   52. Wittenheim, p. 114.

tributaries that Moscow and the Central Provinces were connected to St. Petersburg and the rest of Russia. The Oka, flowing in a northeasterly direction, was navigable from a point near Orel to the Volga, a distance of nearly 500 versts.

The Oka had several important tributaries. One of these was the Susha River, on which the most important landing was Mtsensk, which, like Orel, supplied St. Petersburg with some quantities of grain.[53] Farther to the north was the Upa River, on which was located the manufacturing town of Tula. Perhaps the most important tributary of the Oka was the river Tsna,[54] whose main landing was Morshansk, in Tambov Province. Morshansk was especially important for the grain trade, since grain to supply St. Petersburg, consisting mainly of rye flour, oats, and buckwheat, was brought there from surrounding areas and provinces to the south.[55]

The Oka and its tributaries transported not only the products of the provinces through which they flowed but also to a certain extent those from provinces to the south like Voronezh and Saratov. From these provinces, poor in water communications, goods were brought by land, mostly by "winter road." They were carried by the Oka either to Moscow by way of the Moskva River or to St. Petersburg over a very roundabout route more than 2,300 versts long and taking four months to traverse by way of Nizhnii Novgorod, Rybinsk, and the Vyshnii Volochek System.[56]

Moscow was connected by water with the rest of the empire by means of the Oka and by the Moskva River, which was navigable for 160 versts of its length, but which had the disadvantage of low water, especially in summer.[57] River traffic was much heavier to Moscow than from Moscow, but in 1828 only 1,720 boats carrying goods worth 16.3 million rubles were sent to Moscow and a mere 78 boats carrying goods worth 0.9 million rubles from Moscow.[58] Goods sent from Nizhnii Novgorod and the

53. Nebol'sin, I, 16.
54. This river Tsna should not be confused with the river Tsna in Tver Province which formed part of the Vyshnii Volochek System.
55. Nebol'sin, I, 30; *Kratkii istoricheskii ocherk razvitiia vodianykh i sukhoputnykh soobshchenii,* p. 193.
56. "Donesenie," *Krasnyi Arkhiv,* LXXVI (1936), 138.
57. Wittenheim, p. 107.   58. *Ibid.,* p. 109.

Lower Volga landings to Moscow were only a small fraction of those sent to St. Petersburg. Also, of the goods originating from the Oka landings, Orel to Riazan, less than two-thirds went to Moscow, and of the goods originating from the Tsna landings and those of its tributary the Moksha less than one-half went to Moscow. In both cases the remainder was shipped along the Oka to Nizhnii Novgorod and thence to Rybinsk and St. Petersburg.[59]

There were several reasons why Moscow had less river traffic than St. Petersburg. For one thing, in the early 1830's Moscow had a smaller population than St. Petersburg. Also, Moscow was not a seaport and therefore did not have an export trade. Furthermore, it was in the midst of a centrally located agricultural and industrial area and could be supplied by road, either from the environs or from the Ukraine (whereas St. Petersburg was at the edge of the empire, far from its sources of supply, especially of foodstuffs), while navigation on the Moskva was constantly hindered by low water, to such an extent, in fact, that the Austrian engineer von Gerstner in the summer of 1836 proposed as one of the first railways a railway linking Moscow with Kolomna, where the Moskva River joined the Oka.

Moscow could have had a far greater share of transit trade of goods coming from the South and the East and destined for St. Petersburg if there had been any direct water route to the northwest, such as the water system linking Moscow with the Volga that has been mentioned as under construction in the early 1830's but completed only under Stalin. Since the Moscow *Chaussée* was not adequate for transporting large quantities of bulk goods, either a water system or another improved form of transportation, such as a railway, was badly needed. When the route of Russia's first major railway was being considered, a railway between St. Petersburg and Moscow was an obvious choice.

But a railway between St. Petersburg and Rybinsk was also seriously thought of, for important as Nizhnii Novgorod was from its handling most of the trade that came from the South and down the Kama and Oka rivers to the Volga, Rybinsk, the nearest landing above it on the Volga, was perhaps the most important

59. "Donesenie," *Krasnyi Arkhiv*, LXXVI (1936), 138.

landing on the whole river or indeed in the whole empire. It not only fed the three systems leading to St. Petersburg but allowed products imported by way of St. Petersburg and products from northern Russia around and below Archangel to reach the interior. These latter goods moved by way of the Northern Dvina, the Württemberg Canal, and the river Sheksna. V. P. Gur'ev rightly stated that Rybinsk stood commercially in the same relation to the capitals as the port of Liverpool did to the manufacturing center of Manchester in England.[60] Yet this most important junction had only slightly over three thousand inhabitants. It was at Rybinsk that the Volga became much shallower, so that goods moving toward St. Petersburg were reloaded there from the larger Volga boats into smaller ones, either to continue along the Middle Volga to Tver and thence to the Vyshnii Volochek System, or to enter the Tikhvinskii or Mariinskii systems.[61]

Although the Volga and its great tributaries, the Kama and Oka, were the main carriers of trade to St. Petersburg, minor commerce with the city was carried on by means of the Middle Volga between Rybinsk and Tver and the Upper Volga above Tver. In 1838–1839, goods sent to St. Petersburg from the Middle Volga amounted to about 4.5 million poods yearly, consisting mainly of tallow, flour, grain, and iron.[62] On the Upper Volga above Tver there were several landings of commercial significance, from which goods were sent to St. Petersburg by way of the Vyshnii Volochek System and which at that time supplied the system with 25–33 per cent of its traffic.[63] In the late 1830's the yearly average of goods sent to St. Petersburg from landings on the Upper Volga and on the Gzhat River, a tributary, was 7 million poods, valued at 36.5 million rubles.[64] From these landings some grain and other food supplies, brought by "winter road" from surrounding provinces, were sent to St. Petersburg, but the amount of grain shipped was small compared to other items

60. V. P. Gur'ev, *Ob uchrezhdenii tortsovykh dorog i sukhoputnykh parokhodov v Rossii posredstvom kompanii* (St. Petersburg, 1837), p. 50.
61. Wittenheim, pp. 123–124; "Istoricheskoe obozrenie," *SIRIO*, XCVIII (1896), 546.
62. "Donesenie," *Krasnyi Arkhiv*, LXXVI (1936), 137.
63. *Severnaia Pchela*, May 30, 1838, p. 475.
64. "Donesenie," *Krasnyi Arkhiv*, LXXVI (1936), 136.

such as hides and tallow, butter and flax, and especially hemp. Goods coming from beyond Rybinsk and from the Middle and Upper Volga landings entered the Vyshnii Volochek System at Tver. The journey by water from Tver to St. Petersburg was 1,060 versts long and took from one and a half to two months to complete.[65] Tver had better communications with St. Petersburg by water than did Moscow, but Tver was less than 500 versts from St. Petersburg by road, one-half the distance by water, so that it is not surprising that Tver's location and commercial importance, as well as that of Moscow, was a factor in the decision to build the St. Petersburg–Moscow Railway.

Goods on all these Russian rivers moved slowly, since the means of transportation and locomotion on the waterways of Russia were extremely primitive. Goods were carried in crudely constructed barges built in the forests at their place of origin. The largest of these was the flat-bottomed *lad'ia* built in the forests along the Kama and Volga rivers. The *lad'ia* was often over 30 sazhens long and 8 sazhens wide, with a capacity of 100,000–110,000 poods. Since river barges were propelled commonly by manpower and for every 1,000 poods of load about three and a half boatmen were needed, a boat like the *lad'ia* needed a crew of up to three hundred men.[66]

Boatmen (*burlaki*) either pulled a boat along a towpath, or if there was no towpath, as was often the case, and the terrain was too rough or if the channel was too far away from the shore, the *burlaki* rode on the barge, using anchors in a process known as kedging. A boat would have three or four anchors, each of which in turn was carried ahead by a smaller boat, from which the anchor would be thrown into the water. While the *burlaki* were pulling the boat toward the anchor, another small boat with another anchor would go forward, and the whole process would be repeated.[67] Sails were sometimes used but were dangerous, especially since the crews were usually not skilled enough to manage them. A sudden shift of wind would often capsize a

65. *Ibid.*, p. 138; "Istoricheskoe obozrenie," *SIRIO*, XCVIII (1896), 535.
66. Mueller, p. 375; *Kratkii istoricheskii ocherk razvitiia i deiatel'nosti Vedomstva Putei Soobshcheniia*, p. 53.
67. Mueller, p. 377.

boat. Horse traction was occasionally used for boats along canals and some rivers like the Moskva and Oka, but the use of horses as a means of traction was much less frequent than that of *burlaki*.[68]

In 1810, a French engineer employed in Russia invented a simple and inexpensive machine whereby horse power could replace *burlaki* in turning the capstan which drew a river barge to its anchor.[69] The use of these machines meant that only one-fifth as many *burlaki* as were formerly needed were required on a barge. Even so, this invention represented only a minor improvement compared to the steamboats which were about to come.

Steamboats were introduced into Russia in the second decade of the nineteenth century. The policy of the Russian government toward them in many ways paralleled its later policy toward railways. The government, wishing to see a potentially useful invention introduced into Russia, but not wishing to take the initiative and risks itself, issued a ukase in December, 1813, by which the American inventor Robert Fulton, who had launched his famous steamship *Clermont* on the Hudson River in 1807, was granted a fifteen-year privilege to build and operate steamboats between St. Petersburg and Kronstadt, and on the rivers of Russia, on the condition that if no steamboats were operating within three years the privilege would be revoked. Fulton promised to have a steamboat running between St. Petersburg and Kronstadt by 1815. But neither he nor his assistants appeared in Russia, and in 1815 Fulton died.[70]

The first man in Russia to build an operational steamboat was the Scottish mechanic Charles Baird, who also built industrial steam engines. In the summer of 1815 Baird fitted a balance steam engine of the Watt system on an ordinary Tikhvinskii barge and thereby introduced the first steamboat into Russia. Such a

68. V. S. Virginskii, *Vozniknovenie zheleznykh dorog v Rossii do nachala 40-ykh godov XIX veka* (Moscow, 1949), p. 41.

69. "Mashina vymyshlennaia g. inzhener-mekhanikom Puadebardom dlia vzvozki sudov s velikim gruzom vverkh protiv techeniia bol'shikh rek," *Syn Otechestva*, XV (1814), 63.

70. *Kratkii istoricheskii ocherk razvitiia vodianykh i sukhoputnykh soobshchenii*, pp. 174-176; "Stimbot na Neve," *Syn Otechestva*, XXIV (1815), 210-211.

steamboat could be used to carry passengers or freight or to tow other barges.[71]

In the summer of 1817, Baird, convinced that steamboats could be operated successfully on most of the chief waterways of Russia, petitioned the Russian government for a ten-year privilege giving him the exclusive right to build and operate steamboats on all of Russia's waterways. The Russian government on October 30, 1817, granted him such a privilege. Baird's steamboats were to observe all rules of traffic on the waterways on which they operated and were not to damage other boats or hinder traffic. If Baird failed to take steps to introduce steamboats on any specific waterway within three years, the privilege would be considered terminated for that waterway. The government reserved for itself the right to build and operate steamboats without reference to Baird's privilege.[72] The Russian government was willing to authorize the introduction of an apparently useful technological innovation and to aid it by granting an exclusive privilege for a term of years, but it did not give any concession such as freedom from taxation, nor did it promise any form of direct financial aid. The Russian government was also careful to make sure that Baird's exclusive privilege would not prevent other private companies from introducing steamboat service after a period of three years in the event of nonfeasance by Baird or impair the unrestricted right of the government to do so.

Baird, having received his privilege, formed a company to build and operate steamboats, but it soon failed.[73] Other at-

71. "Stimbot," *Syn Otechestva*, XXIV (1815), 211-214. This first steamboat in Russia, named the *Elizaveta*, made its first run from St. Petersburg to Kronstadt on November 3, 1815, taking two and three-fourths hours for the journey at an average speed of 8.75 versts per hour ("Pervaia poezdka na parokhode iz Peterburga v Kronshtadt i obratno v 1815 g.," *Syn Otechestva*, XXVI [1815], 37-39). By 1820 four steamboats built by Baird, carrying both passengers and freight, were plying between St. Petersburg and Kronstadt (*Kratkii istoricheskii ocherk razvitiia vodianykh i sukhoputnykh soobshchenii*, p. 176). These steamboats continued to operate until the 1840's (A. Brandt, *Ocherk istorii parovoi mashiny i primeneniia parovykh dvigatelei v Rossii*, vol. XXIII of *Sbornik Instituta Inzhenerov Zheleznodorozhnogo Transporta* [St. Petersburg, 1892], p. 61).

72. For the full text of this privilege, see *PSZ*, 1st ser., XXXIV, No. 27120 (October 30, 1817).

73. *Kratkii istoricheskii ocherk razvitiia vodianykh i sukhoputnykh soobshchenii*, p. 179. Later, however, Baird's steamboat service between St. Petersburg and Kronstadt became very profitable.

tempts to build and operate steamboats during the 1820's likewise met with limited success.[74]

By 1832, there were only seventeen steamboats operating in Russia, eleven on the Gulf of Finland and the Neva River, three on the Caspian Sea and the Volga River, and three on the Black Sea.[75] The steamboats were slow, heavy, and relatively expensive to build. They also broke down frequently, and there was a lack of mechanics to repair them. In some areas there was a lack of fuel.[76] The use of steamboats did not become widespread until the late 1840's and early 1850's. There were 16 steamboats in 1840, 99 in 1850, and 339 in 1860, the majority of which operated on the Volga.[77] However, even in 1860 the number of steamboats was very small compared to the number of boats still propelled by conventional means.

Part 2. Roads in Russia before 1835

Russia's roads were less developed than its waterways. Although previous Tsars had built roads in Russia,[1] Alexander I

74. For these other attempts, see Brandt, pp. 54-57; *Kratkii istoricheskii ocherk razvitiia i deiatel'nosti Vedomstva Putei Soobshcheniia*, p. 54; and *Kratkii istoricheskii ocherk razvitiia vodianykh i sukhoputnykh soobshchenii*, pp. 179, 183.
The Russian government also operated steamboats on a limited scale during these years. For this, see Brandt, p. 49, and *PSZ*, 2nd ser., V, No. 4150 (November 29, 1830).

75. V. Pel'chinskii, *O sostoianii promyshlennykh sil Rossii do 1832 g.* (St. Petersburg, 1833), p. 85.

76. A. Pravdin, *O zheleznykh i tortsovykh dorogakh v Rossii* (Moscow, 1838), pp. 31-32; Brandt, p. 57.

77. Brandt, p. 61; M. K. Rozhkova (ed.), *Ocherki ekonomicheskoi istorii Rossii pervoi poloviny XIX veka: Sbornik statei* (Moscow, 1959), p. 271.

1. Peter the Great, though more interested in waterways than in roads, built a winding dirt road between Moscow and his new capital, which was 750 versts in length and went via Novgorod, Valdai, Vyshnii Volochek, and Tver. This road was often unsatisfactory because of mud and broken bridges. Travel was extremely slow, so that even foreign ambassadors were known to take as much as five weeks to travel between St. Petersburg and Moscow, although in 1768 a traveler managed to cover the distance "easily" in thirteen days (Vasilii Kliuchevskii, *Peter the Great*, trans. Liliana Archibald [New York, 1961], p. 150; Johann Peter Falk, *Beiträge zur topographischen Kenntnis des russischen Reichs* [St. Petersburg, 1785–1786], I, 5). Peter the Great also started the so-called *perspektivnaia doroga*, a corduroy road between St. Petersburg and Moscow. Peter wished this road to be at least a hundred versts shorter than the 750-verst length of his earlier road.

was the first to make a well-organized effort to unify and improve the administration of roads[2] and to go ahead systematically with the construction of new ones. He had work started in 1817 on the St. Petersburg–Moscow *Chaussée*, a hard-surface road such as those already existing between St. Petersburg and Peterhof, Pavlovsk, and Gatchina.[3] *Chaussées*, like railways later, were constructed first for the short distances in the vicinity of St. Petersburg; then the first major project was to link the capitals. But by 1825 the Moscow *Chaussée* had been finished only from St. Petersburg to Novgorod, a distance of 180 versts.[4]

The reign of Tsar Nicholas I saw an increased interest in the development of Russia's roads. In the years 1825–1835 the future importance of railways had not yet been foreseen, but the concern over the improvement of roads shows that the time had come for a better form of land transportation than had previously existed.[5] Perhaps the Tsar took greater interest in roads than in waterways because he traveled extensively on roads on his frequent and rapid inspection trips to various parts of the empire, or perhaps, since military affairs so interested him, because a

It was built with logs and bundles of sticks (*fashiny*) which made the road so rough that when completed in 1746 carriage travel was impossible; sledges had to be used even in summer, and the road soon fell into disuse (V. S. Virginskii, *Vozniknovenie zheleznykh dorog v Rossii do nachala 40-ykh godov XIX veka* [Moscow, 1949], p. 29). During the reign of Catherine the Great, the Georgian Military Road between Vladikavkaz and Tiflis, a distance of 203 versts was completed (K. A. Oppengeim, *Rossiia v dorozhnom otnoshenii* [Moscow, 1920], p. 35). In 1781 the Siberian Military Road was begun, to link the capitals with Tobolsk and Irkutsk, a distance of over 6,000 versts (Oscar Matthesius, "Verkehrswesen und Verkehrspolitik in Russland bis zum Jahre 1835," *Archiv für Eisenbahnwesen*, No. 5 [1903], p. 935).

2. See *Kratkii istoricheskii ocherk razvitiia vodianykh i sukhoputnykh soobshchenii i torgovykh portov v Rossii* (St. Petersburg, 1900), p. 340, and V. F. Meien, *Rossiia v dorozhnom otnoshenii* (St. Petersburg, 1902), I, 21.

3. *Kratkii istoricheskii ocherk razvitiia i deiatel'nosti Vedomstva Putei Soobshcheniia za sto let ego sushchestvovaniia* (1798-1898) (St. Petersburg, 1898), p. 46.

4. "Istoricheskoe obozrenie putei soobshcheniia i publichnykh zdanii s 1825 po 1850 g.," *Sbornik Imperatorskogo Russkogo Istoricheskogo Obshchestva*, XCVIII (1896), 555; *Kratkii istoricheskii ocherk razvitiia vodianykh i sukhoputnykh soobshchenii*, p. 341.

5. S. M. Seredonin, *Istoricheskii obzor deiatel'nosti Komiteta Ministrov* (St. Petersburg, 1902-1905), II, part 2, 152.

good system of roads would have a military value for the rapid transportation of troops and supplies, which waterways could not have.

Nicholas showed great interest in technological innovations in road construction, just as he would later in railways. And, as was later the case with railways, he was not always supported by his ministers in the introduction of these innovations. An incident in the 1820's illustrates the contrasting attitudes of the Tsar and some of his ministers. In 1824 Prince D. V. Golitsyn had become military governor general of Moscow and had found the roads of his province in very bad condition. He wished to improve them gradually by using a new method of construction. Roads were to be divided into three sections, with the middle section meant for carriages and the two outside sections for carts and cattle. The middle section was to be drained and paved with gravel. These proposals found the approval of the Tsar, and work began. By 1827, having rebuilt 227 versts of road at a cost of 1.5 million rubles, Golitsyn asked permission to have a special committee formed to supervise further construction of this sort. The Committee of Ministers would not approve his request, stating that too much money had already been spent on roads. Count Kankrin, agreeing with the conclusion of the committee, added that he felt that such roads as Prince Golitsyn advocated were "useless" and that it was better either to keep roads in their previous condition or to use the tried and proven methods such as the *chaussée*.[6]

The Tsar's reply to this was that he had found the roads improved by Golitsyn much better than those left in their original condition, and he suggested that the Committee of Ministers then set about finding the best method of improving roads at reasonable expense, a matter he considered extremely important. However, in 1830, the Committee of Ministers, under Kankrin's influence, reaffirmed its opinion concerning Golitsyn's innovations.[7]

During the years 1829-1833 Nicholas I often concerned himself with the condition and maintenance of roads and bridges over which he had traveled and which were in disrepair.[8] His

6. *Ibid.*, pp. 154-156. 7. *Ibid.*, pp. 156-158.
8. *Polnoe Sobranie Zakonov Rossiiskoi Imperii*, 2nd ser., IV, No. 3017

observations and directives for work to be done often went into the minutest detail, which was typical of Nicholas, who liked to direct in this meticulous way everything he could that went on in the empire, and who also fancied himself a good engineer in his own right. Early in 1833, the Tsar formed a committee to study the best overall long-range plan for providing Russia with a network of good roads, especially *chaussées*. By a law of March 24, 1833, a general plan for building a network of major roads was promulgated. All the roads of the empire were to be divided into five classes and improved gradually by the central, provincial, and local authorities as funds and labor became available.[9] Here was a comprehensive plan to give Russia a network of roads that would have been equal to those of the more advanced western European countries. But because of the lack of funds, of a sufficient number of skilled engineers, and of an adequate supply of labor, the gap between what was planned and what was actually done was large.[10]

During the first ten years of Nicholas I's reign some progress was made in the further construction of *chaussées*. From 1825 on relatively short *chaussées* continued to be built around major centers such as St. Petersburg.[11] But the Tsar's main efforts were directed toward accelerating construction of the Moscow *Chaussée*, originally scheduled for completion by the mid-1840's.[12] This road, which was completed in 1834, was 677.5 versts in length and cost 22.5 million rubles, that is about 33,500 rubles per verst.[13] The St. Petersburg–Moscow Railway, completed nearly twenty years later (1851) was about 70 versts shorter. The *chaussée* did not go in a straight line as did the railway,

(July 22, 1829); N. Dubrovin (ed.), *Sbornik istoricheskikh materialov, izvlechennykh iz Arkhiva Sobstvennoi Ego Imperatorskogo Velichestva Kantseliarii* (St. Petersburg, 1876-1917), VIII, 4, 8, 10, 11, 12-13, 20, 21, 22.

9. See PSZ, 2nd ser., VIII, No. 6076 (March 24, 1833).
10. Matthesius, *Archiv für Eisenbahnwesen*, No. 5 (1903), p. 937.
11. Dubrovin, VII, 42.
12. *Kratkii istoricheskii ocherk razvitiia i deiatel'nosti Vedomstva Putei Soobshcheniia*, p. 65.
13. "Istoricheskoe obozrenie," *SIRIO*, XCVIII (1896), 555; N. Atreshkov (Otreshkov-Tarasenko), *Ob ustroenii zheleznykh dorog v Rossii* (St. Petersburg, 1835), p. 32.

but went through Novgorod and through Torzhok in Tver Province.[14]

Just like the St. Petersburg–Moscow Railway later, the Moscow *Chaussée* was substantially built.[15] Many fine bridges were built on the *chaussée*, with one or two having a length of more than 100 sazhens.[16] These bridges were often built of granite and had iron railings ornamented with the imperial coat of arms. The verst-posts were of marble and had the Tsar's initials. There were even benches on which foot-travelers could rest.[17] At regular intervals there were well-maintained posthouses, usually kept by Germans. These posthouses were generally large and well furnished. Every public room had a portrait of the Tsar, and special apartments were reserved for his use.[18]

Travel over the *chaussée* could be rapid. Maxwell estimates that the average speed of travel for a passenger was 8 to 10 miles per hour, while Custine states that 4.5 to 5 leagues (or about 11 to 12 miles) could be covered in an hour and that the Tsar was reputed to cover 7 leagues (about 17 miles) in an hour.[19]

Though the Moscow *Chaussée* was completed in 1834, large-scale construction of other *chaussées* did not take place until the 1840's and 1850's. During each of these two decades slightly over 2,500 versts of *chaussées* were constructed.[20] However, even by 1860 Russia had less mileage in *chaussées* by far, both in proportion to its area and in the absolute, than did England and especially France.[21]

Most of the main and secondary roads in Russia were still

14. Oppengeim, p. 38.

15. For a brief description of construction methods, see "Istoricheskoe obozrenie," *SIRIO*, XCVIII (1896), 559-560; *Kratkii istoricheskii ocherk razvitiia vodianykh i sukhoputnykh soobshchenii*, p. 363, n.*.

16. *Kratkii istoricheskii ocherk razvitiia vodianykh i sukhoputnykh soobshchenii*, p. 367; E. Sokolovskii, *Piatidesiatiletie Instituta i Korpusa Inzhenerov Putei Soobshcheniia* (St. Petersburg, 1859), p. 130.

17. John S. Maxwell, *The Czar, His Court, and People* (New York, 1848), p. 182; Marquis de Custine, *Russia* (2nd ed.; London, 1854), II, 230.

18. Maxwell, p. 193; Custine, II, 242.

19. Maxwell, p. 183; Custine, II, 232.

20. M. K. Rozhkova (ed.), *Ocherki ekonomicheskoi istorii Rossii pervoi poloviny XIX veka: Sbornik statei* (Moscow, 1959), p. 269. For a list of *chaussées* completed or under construction in 1850 see "Istoricheskoe obozrenie," *SIRIO*, XCVIII (1896), 555-556.

21. Oppengeim, p. 39.

unimproved dirt roads, as they had been from time immemorial. After 1822 there were in theory two types of dirt roads in Russia, the narrow(5–10 sazhens) and the wide (30 sazhens).[22] Sometimes landowners or peasants would seize part of the right of way for plowing, with the result that roads were often narrowed down to a width of 2 sazhens, so that two carts could pass each other only with difficulty.[23] A main road, which was often bordered by two rows of birches and drainage ditches, consisted usually of a main path in the middle and one or two side paths, all of which were covered with a layer of sand.[24]

Although the network of these dirt roads extended over the whole empire, the two capitals were the main road centers, just as later they were to be the main railway centers.[25] Five main roads radiated from St. Petersburg. From Moscow there were eight major roads, including the old Peterburgskii Trakt, the original road between Moscow and St. Petersburg built by Peter the Great, which was still in use after completion of the *chaussée*. It was still of commercial significance because it connected Moscow with river landings from which goods could go by water to St. Petersburg.[26]

Land transport—by cart in summer and by sledge in winter—had advantages over water transport for goods high in value and low in bulk which had to be transported rapidly. Goods could be carried between the capitals via the Moscow *Chaussée* in sixteen days, or even in ten days.[27] A large part of the goods imported via the port of St. Petersburg or manufactured in that city and its environs was transported by road to the interior.[28]

Although most goods coming to St. Petersburg from the interior were of a bulky nature and were brought by water, there was also a considerable number of carts and sledges bringing

22. Seredonin, I, 513.
23. P. I. Rudchenko, *Guzhevye i vodnye puti* (St. Petersburg, 1904), p. 10.
24. Matthesius, *Archiv für Eisenbahnwesen*, No. 5 (1903), pp. 939-940.
25. For further details see V. S. Virginskii, *Voznikovenie*, p. 243.
26. Matthesius, *Archiv für Eisenbahnwesen*, No. 5 (1903), p. 938.
27. "Donesenie Nikolaiu I komissii po ustroistvu zheleznoi dorogi mezhdu Peterburgom i Moskvoi, 15 sentiabria 1841 g.," *Krasnyi Arkhiv*, LXXVI (1936), 136.
28. V. P. Gur'ev, "Mysli o pervoi kompanii zimnikh dorog v Rossii," *Biblioteka dlia Chteniia*, XXXI (1838), Sec. IV, 13.

goods, especially perishables, by road. For instance, 500,000 carts of vegetables entered St. Petersburg yearly.[29] Moscow, because it had poor water connections with the rest of Russia, was a road center, a focal point for the carting industry. Especially in winter, the city was provisioned by road from the Ukraine and the southern part of Russia. Perishable goods were also brought to Moscow from the South to be forwarded to St. Petersburg.[30] Even though the small capacity of carts and sledges made such transport expensive, bulk goods, too, had to be transported by land if there were no water communications between two points.[31] The carting industry employed many thousands of peasants. According to V. P. Gur'ev it engaged 800,000 men in summer and 3 million in winter.[32] Metal products of the Urals often had to be transported hundreds of versts to reach the nearest landing on the Kama or on one of its tributaries.[33] Because of the lack of navigable waterways in the Central Provinces south of the Oka and Tsna landings, most goods were brought to these landings by road. Peasants from overpopulated Smolensk Province would earn money in winter taking their sledges to the black-soil areas, especially around Orel, and transporting grain to the nearest river landing.[34] The peak period of travel was the months from November to March. During this period there was often as much road traffic as during the other eight months of the year.[35]

"Winter roads" had a number of advantages. A horse could pull a larger load at a greater speed on a good "winter road" than on a dirt road in summer, especially if that road were badly built and maintained. Also "winter roads" could go in a direct line over frozen swamps and lakes.[36] Furthermore, in the

29. Atreshkov, p. 42.
30. *Severnaia Pchela*, June 1, 1838, p. 483.
31. G. P. Nebol'sin, *Statisticheskoe obozrenie vneshnei torgovli Rossii* (St. Petersburg, 1850), I, 187.
32. V. P. Gur'ev, *Ob uchrezhdenii tortsovykh dorog i sukhoputnykh parokhodov v Rossii posredstvom kompanii* (St. Petersburg, 1837), p. 15.
33. Matthesius, *Archiv für Eisenbahnwesen*, No. 5 (1903), p. 945.
34. *Ibid.*, p. 947.
35. "Donesenie," *Krasnyi Arkhiv*, LXXVI (1936), 142.
36. A. I. Chuprov, *Zheleznodorozhnoe khoziaistvo* (Moscow, 1910), I, 11; A. Pravdin, *O zheleznykh i tortsovykh dorogakh v Rossii* (Moscow, 1838), p. 9, n.*.

winter more peasant carters were available, since there was no work to be done in the fields, and consequently transport in the winter was less expensive than in summer. To transport a pood of goods by road between the capitals, the rates were 60 to 70 kopecks in winter, but 2 to 2.5 rubles in summer.[37] Many agricultural products were held after the harvest and were transported to river landings during the winter so that they could be transported further by water when the ice melted the following spring, thereby having a full season of navigation in which to reach their destination. Goods which had accumulated during the time when autumn rains had made road transport impossible were also carried by "winter road." As soon as the first snows of winter had fallen, goods could be transported.[38]

Before the coming of railways to Russia, roads were also important as the means of transportation best suited to travelers. They could travel in a variety of ways. One could travel *na dolgikh*, i.e., with his own carriage and horses. Generally only the well-to-do could afford to travel in this manner. One could also travel *na volnykh*, i.e., by hiring a carriage or cart from a private person.[39]

There was also travel *na pochtovykh*. Since the end of the fifteenth century, the Russian government had maintained post stations along many of the roads of the empire. These were run either by peasants who provided post horses in return for exemption from other obligations[40] or, increasingly in the early nineteenth century, by private individuals under contract to the government and compensated by the revenue from an extra tax placed on the local population.[41] By 1800 there were 3,222 post stations, with 37,840 horses, serving most roads between major centers of the empire and enabling mail and parcels to be forwarded and persons with the necessary credentials to travel. To use the facilities of the post stations, the traveler had to have a document (*podorozhnaia*) giving him the right to do so and stating the route of his journey, its purpose, and the number and kind of horses to which he was entitled, a matter determined by

37. Atreshkov, p. 59.
38. Matthesius, *Archiv für Eisenbahnwesen*, No. 5 (1903), p. 947.
39. K. V. Vasilevich, *Pochta v Rossii v XIX veke* (Moscow, 1927), p. 42.
40. Meien, I, 12.   41. Vasilevich, p. 36.

the traveler's rank. He also had to pay a charge (*poverstnye den'gi*).[42]

Passenger traffic was aided by the introduction in the 1820's of diligences, or public stagecoaches. Diligences in many ways may be considered the precursors of railways. Also, the course of their development in many respects was similar to that of railways later, as was often the policy of the Russian government concerning them.

In 1820 the first stock company was formed to operate diligences, the Obshchestvo Uchreditelei Dilizhansov po Moskovskomu Traktu (Company of the Founders of Diligences on the Moscow Highway). Early that year a group of investors, including many influential members of the nobility, presented a plan to form a stock company to operate diligences between St. Petersburg and Moscow to the head of the Post Department. By a law of June 15, 1820, the Russian government granted the requests of the founders of the Obshchestvo Dilizhansov: (1) a ten-year privilege, during which no other company could operate diligences between St. Petersburg and Moscow; (2) permission to use post horses without payment of the *poverstnye den'gi*;[43] (3) an agreement that the Obshchestvo Dilizhansov be taken under the protection (*pokrovitel'stvo*) of the Post Department, and the St. Petersburg post director become the chairman of a committee formed to administer the company.[44] The Obshchestvo Dilizhansov received its privilege finally on August 30, 1820.[45]

Operations of the Obshchestvo Dilizhansov, which began on September 1, 1820, were successful from the beginning, even though at first dividends on the company's stock seem to have been very small.[46]

The trip between the capitals usually took four to four and a half days except during the time of the *rasputitsa*, or season

42. *Ibid.*, pp. 8, 42.
43. This concession would cost the government nearly 27,000 rubles yearly, since post horses used for diligences sent three times a week between the capitals would cost that amount (*ibid.*, p. 51).
44. For the full text see *PSZ*, 1st ser., XXXVII, No. 28317 (June 15, 1820).
45. *Ibid.*, 2nd ser., III, No. 1992 (April 24, 1828).
46. "A. A." [A. V. Abaza], *Mysli moskovskogo zhitelia o vozmozhnosti uchredit' obshchestvo na aktsiiakh dlia sooruzheniia zheleznoi dorogi ot S. Peterburga do Moskvy* (St. Petersburg, 1838), p. 24, n.*.

of bad roads. In each diligence four passengers could travel at a fare of 120 rubles each, and in summer an additional two passengers could travel on the outside of the vehicle at a fare of 60 rubles. At first, diligences made the trip between the capitals twice a week, but soon daily trips began to be made, as the public became more interested. In the first ten years of its existence, the Obshchestvo Dilizhansov carried 33,603 passengers.[47]

During the 1820's other Russians applied for and received authorization to operate diligences along various routes. In each case the Russian government was willing to help the enterprise by granting a ten-year exclusive privilege for any route on which diligences were not yet in operation. But the government showed an increasing reluctance to allow post horses to be used free of charge. Diligence companies had either to use their own horses or to pay the full charge for post horses. Also, it was generally stipulated that diligence companies might not carry letters, money, or parcels if this would deprive already existing government postal services of revenue. In other words, the government was in favor of diligence companies and was willing to help them— if the government did not lose financially thereby. These principles were embodied in a law of July 22, 1830, which stated the bases on which private diligence companies might be founded in the future.[48]

In spite of the less liberal policy of the government, the Obshchestvo Dilizhansov after the expiration of its original ten-year exclusive privilege in 1830 prospered more and more. By 1832, four or five diligences were often sent daily between the capitals.[49] The dividends on the stock of the company, relatively small during the first years of its operation, grew to 40 per cent on the ruble.[50] Other diligence companies began to flourish both on the St. Petersburg–Moscow route and elsewhere and were aided by the gradual introduction of *chaussées*. By 1832 one Baron von Müller was running express diligences between the capitals which made the trip in fifty hours, using his own horses.[51] By the middle of the decade there were six diligence

47. V. Pel'chinskii, *O sostoianii promyshlennykh sil Rossii do 1832 g.* (St. Petersburg, 1833), p. 86; Vasilevich, pp. 50-51.
48. For full text see *PSZ*, 2nd ser., V, No. 3814 (July 22, 1830).
49. Pel'chinskii, p. 86.   50. Abaza, p. 24, n.*.
51. *PSZ*, 2nd ser., VII, No. 5447 (June 21, 1832).

companies running between the capitals and several others running on other routes, all of them profitable.[52]

After some earlier unsuccessful attempts, in 1840 the Russian government, convinced by the increasing profitableness and expansion of private diligence companies that it need not fear lack of passengers, decided to go into the diligence business itself. The Department of Post Coaches (Otdelenie Pochtovykh Karet i Brik) was set up, with headquarters in St. Petersburg. The department ran carriages of various types carrying mail and two to four passengers on a very strict schedule between the two capitals.[53] By the early 1850's there were seven government routes with a total length of 10,425 versts.[54]

The 1850's marked the high point for diligences, however. When railways became widespread, the need for diligences declined, and the Department of Post Coaches was finally closed in 1863.[55]

Part 3. Evaluation of Russia's Transportation System before 1835

Beginning with Peter the Great, the Russian government had from time to time expended great amounts of money and made great efforts to build and improve waterways. Contemporary authorities sometimes wrote with praise of these waterways, which they considered among the best in Europe. They were said to be extensive, well constructed, and able to transport large amounts of goods.[1] It was pointed out that these goods could be transported relatively cheaply and that a horse could pull a load fifty to a hundred times greater along waterways than he could along even the best of *chaussées*.[2]

Other authorities, however, pointed out that, although Russia did possess rivers with slow, regular courses, these rivers suffered from a lack of water. There were not enough mountains, the melting snows of which would have provided Russia's rivers

52. Abaza, p. 24, n.*.   53. Vasilevich, pp. 53-54.
54. *Ibid.*, p. 56.   55. *Ibid.*

1. See, for example, V. Pel'chinskii, *O sostoianii promyshlennykh sil Rossii do 1832 g.* (St. Petersburg, 1833), p. 107; E. Ziablovskii, *Rossiiskaia Statistika* (2nd ed.; St. Petersburg, 1842), II, 153-154.
2. A. I. Chuprov, *Zheleznodorozhnoe khoziaistvo* (Moscow, 1910), I, 6; A. Pravdin, *O zheleznykh i tortsovykh dorogakh v Rossii* (Moscow, 1838), p. 7.

with a steady supply of water. On Russia's flat terrain the winter snows melted all at once, which meant that the period of high water was of short duration.[3] It was pointed out that there were also such hindrances to navigation as shallows, shifting channels, and rapids, as well as swift currents in some places which made navigation upstream difficult if not impossible.[4] In addition, waterways were frozen for a good part of the year. Because of all these limitations, fewer goods could be transported by water in Russia than in many other European countries.[5]

The lack of water was, indeed, one of the greatest drawbacks to Russian water transport. If during the "navigation," that is, the season of navigation, there was unusually low water, barges on rivers and canals frequently were stranded or had to be unloaded and reloaded to negotiate a place of shallow water. Often, if it became known at Rybinsk that further on toward St. Petersburg there was exceptionally low water, merchants would unload their wares and store them on the shore, to wait for the "navigation" of the next year.[6] Both the Vyshnii Volochek and Tikhvinskii systems were rendered much less navigable by a dry season.

The main channel of the Volga below Nizhnii Novgorod did not suffer from low water enough to hinder navigation, even in the driest summers,[7] but between Nizhnii Novgorod and Rybinsk and even more between Rybinsk and Tver the depth of the Volga became much less, so that in dry summers it was almost impassable.[8] Navigation on the Moskva and on the Tsna, on which was situated the important landing of Morshansk, was limited mainly to the spring during the period of high water.[9]

3. Ludwik Tengoborskii, *Commentaries on the Productive Forces of Russia* (London, 1855), I, 13; Gersevanov, "O vodianykh i sukhoputnykh soobshcheniiakh v Rossii," *Syn Otechestva*, IX (1839), Sec. III, 129.

4. Pel'chinskii, p. 107; Pravdin, p. 7.

5. "Donesenie Nikolaiu I komissii po ustroistvu zheleznoi dorogi mezhdu Peterburgom i Moskvoi, 15 sentiabria 1841 g.," *Krasnyi Arkhiv*, LXXVI (1936), 142.

6. *Severnaia Pchela*, May 30, 1838, p. 475.

7. Otto Baron von Wittenheim, *Über Russlands Wasserverbindungen wie solche bis zum Jahre 1830 bestanden und seitdem bis jetzt vermehrt oder verändert worden* (Mittau, 1842), p. 100.

8. *Severnaia Pchela*, November 20, 1839, p. 1052.

9. G. P. Nebol'sin, *Statisticheskoe obozrenie vneshnei torgovli Rossii* (St. Petersburg, 1850), I, 186; Wittenheim, p. 107.

There was ample reason, too, for the complaint concerning other natural hindrances. Rapids caused the foundering of many barges which either capsized or were dashed against the rocks of the shore;[10] storms, especially on lakes, often made passage hazardous;[11] and frequently a "caravan" of barges would hit a shoal because of the shifting from that spring's period of high water and be wrecked and block the river channel for days.[12]

Perhaps the greatest disadvantage of water transport was that Russia's waterways were free of ice for only part of the year. In the southern part of Russia, waterways were frozen three to four months of the year, in the central part four to six months, and in the northern part six to seven months.[13] Navigation on the three Volga-Neva water systems was generally possible between the middle of April and the end of October. However, there could be exceptionally severe winters, for instance in 1829 when navigation lasted only from the middle of May until the end of September.[14] Also some parts of a waterway would be blocked with ice earlier and free from ice later than other parts. Lake Onega was such a hindrance to navigation on the Mariinskii System.[15] Goods in barges forced to winter at places along the way, such as Nizhnii Novgorod, Rybinsk, and Tver, were often damaged or completely ruined.[16]

A general disadvantage of water transport was its slowness even under good conditions. A boat pulled upstream along the Volga by *burlaki* could often not go faster than 1 verst per hour.[17] It has been estimated that the average rate of progress along the Volga was at most 10 versts per day.[18] On the Vyshnii

10. Wittenheim, p. 48.

11. V. P. Gur'ev, *Ob uchrezhdenii tortsovykh dorog i sukhoputnykh parokhodov v Rossii posredstvom kompanii* (St. Petersburg, 1837), p. 48.

12. P. P. Mel'nikov, "Poezdka na Volgu," ed. M. Krutikov, *Krasnyi Arkhiv*, LXXXIX–XC (1938), 313, 318-319.

13. Oscar Matthesius, "Verkehrswesen und Verkehrspolitik in Russland bis zum Jahre 1835," *Archiv für Eisenbahnwesen*, No. 5 (1903), p. 946; V. F. Meien, *Rossiia v dorozhnom otnoshenii* (St. Petersburg, 1902), I, 112.

14. Wittenheim, p. 44.

15. *Severnaia Pchela*, May 30, 1838, p. 475.

16. *Ibid.*, May 31, 1838, p. 480.

17. Chuprov, *Zheleznodorozhnoe khoziaistvo*, I, 11.

18. *Kratkii istoricheskii ocherk razvitiia i deiatel'nosti Vedomstva Putei Soobshcheniia za sto let ego sushchestvovaniia* (1798–1898) (St. Petersburg, 1898), p. 53.

Volochek System after extensive improvements had been made, no more than 20 versts could be covered in a day.[19] As a result, goods shipped from Astrakhan and the Lower Volga, even under the most favorable conditions, required at least one year to reach St. Petersburg, and more often the journey required one and a half to two years.[20]

Russian waterways had their limitations also because of the boats which moved along them. River and canal barges were practically all very cumbersome and simply and shoddily built, with blunt prows and sterns. They moved slowly through the water and generally did not last more than a few years.[21] The cargo capacity of river barges was reduced by the necessity of carrying bulky equipment such as anchors and sails and most of all by having to carry large crews.

Not only was the usefulness of waterways that did exist impaired by these many limitations, but there were also large parts of Russia that were not served by navigable rivers at all, or if they were, those rivers often did not flow in the right direction to make them economically useful. A good example would be Kursk and Voronezh provinces and part of Tambov Province, which had no water communications with the landings of the Oka and its tributaries which lay to the north and therefore had to rely on "winter roads," with consequent economic loss and impoverishment of the area.[22]

In spite of the interest Nicholas I showed in improving roads and in building *chaussées*, the limitations of Russia's roads in the 1830's were even greater than those of its waterways. The obstacles to the development of a good system of roads in Russia were many. The distances which roads had to cover were greater than in Western Europe, and the population was much more sparse, so that roads were less used. The Russian government was always pressed for money, and roads were expensive to build, especially in the many localities where materials such as stone and sand were scarce. The Russian climate was more

19. Gur'ev, *Ob uchrezhdenii*, p. 48.
20. M. K. Rozhkova (ed.), *Ocherki ekonomicheskoi istorii Rossii pervoi poloviny XIX veka: Sbornik statei* (Moscow, 1959), p. 271.
21. Mel'nikov, "Poezdka," *Krasnyi Arkhiv*, LXXXIX–XC (1938), 315.
22. Rozhkova, p. 270.

severe than that of Western Europe, which made roads difficult to maintain.[23] In some areas—even much later than the 1830's—there were no roads at all, and the only communication with the outside world was by footpath in summer or by sledge in winter, while in the spring and autumn these areas were often completely cut off.[24]

The roads that did exist left much to be desired. Even the *chaussées* had their limitations. In the winter, when covered with snow, they were like any other "winter road." In the spring and autumn, *chaussées* required many repairs and were often barely passable. Thus they showed themselves to best advantage only in the summer, which in Russia was short.[25] They were frequently rough and uneven, and detours often had to be made because bridges were in poor condition or totally lacking.[26]

The main roads other than *chaussées* were kept in no better condition than local roads. They were dirt roads covered usually with a layer of sand which in rainy weather turned into a swamp and which in dry, windy weather sometimes formed drifts many feet high. Bridges, if they existed at all, were badly constructed and often in poor repair. It is reported that often, when coachmen approached a bridge, they would cross themselves before entering upon it.[27] An official Russian publication remarks that before the construction of the Moscow *Chaussée* a trip between the capitals was practically as difficult as a trip into the interior of Africa.[28] Conditions were especially bad at the time of the *rasputitsa*, when roads were for a long time impassable to the extent that even the nearest localities were inaccessible.[29] Roads situated on low ground near a body of water or not protected by drainage ditches were especially difficult. Also, the constant

23. P. I. Rudchenko, *Guzhevye i vodnye puti* (St. Petersburg, 1904), p. 4.
24. *Ibid.*, p. 5.
25. "Donesenie," *Krasnyi Arkhiv*, LXXVI (1936), 142.
26. N. Dubrovin (ed.), *Sbornik istoricheskikh materialov, izvlechennykh iz Arkhiva Sobstvennoi Ego Imperatorskogo Velichestva Kantseliarii* (St. Petersburg, 1876–1917), VIII, 4; Marquis de Custine, *Russia* (2nd ed.; London, 1854), II, 238.
27. Matthesius, *Archiv für Eisenbahnwesen*, No. 5 (1903), pp. 939-940.
28. E. Sokolovskii, *Piatidesiatiletie Instituta i Korpusa Inzhenerov Putei Soobshcheniia* (St. Petersburg, 1859), p. 129.
29. Pel'chinskii, p. 106.

passage of vehicles made deep ruts which were a serious hazard to travel, especially at night.[30]

"Winter roads," which were praised by many as a "natural railway," also had serious limitations. "Winter roads" did not function unless there was sufficient snow. Major George Washington Whistler wrote in December, 1845, that little snow had fallen around St. Petersburg and that this lack of snow was causing distress, since roads were still impassable.[31] When snow did fall, "winter roads" were at their maximum efficiency only at the beginning of the winter, when the covering of snow was not very deep and few sledges had passed. They were much less useful when the snow became deeper, or during the frequent storms which could halt traffic for days, or at the end of the winter, when the thaw set in.[32] In the late 1830's, it took a diligence three days to go from St. Petersburg to Moscow at the beginning of the winter, but five days at the end.[33] Often road conditions were so poor and passage so difficult that peasant carters sold the carts intrusted to them or simply abandoned them, leaving the owners to find them later.[34] Sometimes blizzards were so bad that carts were entirely covered with snow, and carriages passed over them completely unaware.[35] Even when a trip was completed, the bad state of the roads had often caused damage to both vehicles and draft animals.[36]

Even under the best of conditions, shipping goods by road was both slow and expensive. Goods transported along *chaussées* and good "winter roads" could not be carried more than 50 versts per day, or goods on dirt roads more than 30 versts.[37] When there were great distances to be covered, as was usual in Russia, the cost of feeding and maintaining horses and carters

30. Rudchenko, pp. 7-8.
31. New York Public Library, Manuscript Division, Patton Collection, letter of Major George Washington Whistler to General Joseph H. Swift (St. Petersburg, December 19 [N. S.], 1845).
32. Pel'chinskii, p. 107; Pravdin, p. 9, n.*.
33. Pravdin, p. 9, n.*.
34. *Severnaia Pchela*, June 1, 1838, p. 483; Gur'ev, *Ob uchrezhdenii*, p. 16.
35. *Neskol'ko slov o zheleznykh dorogakh v Rossii* (Moscow, 1836), p. 15.
36. Rudchenko, p. 14.
37. Chuprov, *Zheleznodorozhnoe khoziaistvo*, I, 11.

was a large item of expense. It was only because peasant carters were kept in a state of near penury that the price of road transportation was not higher.[38] Furthermore, the capacity of both sledges and carts was limited. The amount which one horse could pull depended upon the strength of the horse and on the condition of the road. A horse could haul more on a "winter road" or *chaussée* than on a dirt road (it was claimed twice as much on a *chaussée* as on a dirt road),[39] but the bad condition of most Russian roads most of the time meant that wagon loads usually were small. Most Russian carts were pulled by one horse and carried a load of not more than 25 poods.[40] As V. P. Gur'ev remarked, it was very inefficient to have 3 million carters going on trips in winter lasting sometimes as much as seventy days, each carter having a sledge carrying only 25 poods.[41]

Transportation by land took too many peasants away from agriculture and was too expensive ever to be the principal means of transporting bulk goods, which were the chief products of Russia. No matter how much Russia's roads might have been improved in the nineteenth century, they would never have been able to deliver bulk commodities quickly and cheaply.[42]

The deficiencies and backwardness of Russia's transportation had especially adverse effects on Russia's economy because of the great distances to be covered between the centers of production and those of consumption. Russia is divided into forest and steppe zones which should form complementary economic units. But for them to do so satisfactorily a better transportation system than that existing before 1835 was required.[43]

Ludwik Tengoborskii, writing in the early 1850's, remarked: "The future fate and progress of our agriculture depend essentially on the extension and perfecting of our means of communication and transport."[44] This view was also expressed by Nebol'sin.[45] What they wrote of Russian agriculture could have

38. Gur'ev, *Ob uchrezhdenii*, p. 16.
39. *Biblioteka dlia Chteniia*, XXIII (1837), Sec. V, 41.
40. Rudchenko, p. 14.
41. Gur'ev, *Ob uchrezhdenii*, p. 15.
42. Nebol'sin, I, 187-188.
43. For remarks on this subject see Matthesius, *Archiv für Eisenbahnwesen*, No. 5 (1903), p. 941.
44. Tengoborskii, I, 279.   45. Nebol'sin, I, 184-185.

been said also of other branches of the Russian economy. Russia's industry and all its foreign and internal trade were hindered by poor communications.[46]

The ultimate effect of poor communications was to raise the price of products for the buyer. But the uncertainties and difficulties of transportation also affected the merchant and the producer adversely. The increase in price over the original value due to transportation costs was especially great for agricultural products, since they either could not endure a long journey well because they were perishable or they had low value in relation to their bulk and therefore incurred disproportionately high freight charges.[47] Tengoborskii estimated in the early 1850's that internal trade added on the average 60 per cent to the original value of agricultural products, the increase varying according to the distance, difficulties, and time interposed betwen production and marketing.[48] Thus the prices the consumer had to pay for agricultural products were often very high in relation to their original value.

The consumers in St. Petersburg were frequently exposed to rises in prices, as well as to possible shortages, caused by a lack of reliability of transportation, for although it seemed that a tremendous amount of goods of all kinds was brought by water into St. Petersburg from the interior, this amount varied sharply from year to year (for example, there was a difference of 35 per cent between the years 1838 and 1839), depending on conditions upon the waterways as well as on supply.[49] Barges carrying provisions to St. Petersburg might be delayed or halted by low water or ice on the Volga or the Vyshnii Volochek System, with the result that the inhabitants of St. Petersburg were threatened with higher prices for food at best or with a shortage of grain and hunger at worst, while barges loaded with the necessary provisions were stranded at a distance of as little as 200 versts from the capital, or perhaps less.[50] Shortages could be at

46. Pel'chinskii, p. 107; S. M. Seredonin, *Istoricheskii obzor deiatel'nosti Komiteta Ministrov* (St. Petersburg, 1902–1905), I, 506.

47. Rudchenko, p. 15.   48. Tengoborskii, II, 153-154.

49. "Donesenie," *Krasnyi Arkhiv*, LXXVI (1936), 142.

50. N. Shcheglov, "O zheleznykh dorogakh i preimushchestvakh ikh

least partially relieved by transporting grain by road from barges already in the Vyshnii Volochek System, but the extra transportation cost incurred by the merchant raised grain prices considerably.[51] When there was a harvest failure in the southern part of Russia, whence most of the capital's grain supply came, the grain-producing areas in the Central Provinces found it difficult to make up the deficiency because of poor communications with St. Petersburg.[52]

Yet the situation of St. Petersburg in respect to its grain supply was fairly good in comparison with some other areas of Russia. In spite of occasional difficulties, the city had the advantage of having relatively good and regular communication by water with the interior; and since there were many merchants engaged in supplying St. Petersburg with grain, prices were held down by competition among the grain dealers.[53] But even so, grain prices were usually high. For instance, in 1843, a year of fairly good harvest, a chetvert (about 6.25 poods) of rye cost on the average 6 rubles 21 kopecks (silver), while in Kursk Province it cost 1 ruble 35 kopecks.[54]

The situation in regard to St. Petersburg's supply of perishable foods also presented a problem. Perishables shipped by road from southern Russia cost 2 to 3 rubles per pood more in St. Petersburg than at their point of origin.[55] In Gogol's *Revizor* Khlestakov, an impecunious young adventurer, tries to impress the inhabitants of a small provincial town with the wonders of the capital. Among these wonders was an *arbuz v 700 rublei*, a watermelon at 700 rubles. To the consumer in St. Petersburg in 1836 this wry jest might have seemed not so far from the truth. Perishables brought long distances by water or road often were damaged or completely ruined. Flour became musty, dropping in value or becoming completely inedible, butter would become rancid, spirits were subject to ullage.[56] As a result St. Petersburg was largely dependent upon its immediate surroundings for such

nad obyknovennymi dorogami i kanalami," *Severnyi Muravei*, No. 1 (1830), p. 5; Gur'ev, *Ob uchrezhdenii*, p. 51.

51. *Severnaia Pchela*, May 30, 1838, p. 475.
52. "Donesenie," *Krasnyi Arkhiv*, LXXVI (1936), 143.
53. Tengoborskii, I, 253.   54. *Ibid.*, p. 255.
55. *Severnaia Pchela*, June 1, 1838, p. 483.
56. V. P. Gur'ev, "Mysli o pervoi kompanii zimnikh dorog v Rossii," *Biblioteka dlia Chteniia*, XXXI (1838), Sec. IV, 3.

provisions as milk, butter, fruit, and vegetables. In the early 1830's, as the population of St. Petersburg expanded outward, reducing the amount of land in the area available for cultivation while at the same time increasing the demand for such provisions, they became steadily higher in price and lower in quality.[57]

Moscow, although located nearer to the grain-producing areas, was less well served than St. Petersburg. Because of the city's lack of good water communications with grain-producing areas and its consequently greater dependence on more expensive road transport, agricultural products often cost more in Moscow than in much more distant St. Petersburg.[58]

Many other areas of Russia were even less fortunate, especially those in "deficit Russia" where there was little or no communication by water with grain-producing areas and few merchants engaged in the grain trade. Not only were prices high,[59] but at times these areas were exposed to famine because the supplies available in "surplus Russia" could not be transported.[60]

The merchant who delivered the goods from producer to consumer was subject to much uncertainty. Faced with the necessity of transporting goods for long distances over a long period of time, and with the possibility of damage to or total loss of his goods during the long transit, the Russian merchant was also threatened with the possibility of losses if there was a sudden drop in price at the place of marketing or if he could not deliver his goods at the stipulated time. Such losses were incurred especially often by Russian merchants delivering goods to St. Petersburg for export.[61] The price levels in the grain market, both for internal consumption and for export, changed often as the demand for grain rose or fell. The grain merchant, buying at least six months in advance of delivery to market, could rarely deliver

57. "Chugunnye dorogi," *Biblioteka dlia Chteniia,* VIII (1835), Sec. III, 117-118.

58. *Severnaia Pchela,* November 20, 1839, p. 1052.

59. For example, Vitebsk in "deficit Russia" and Chernigov in the black-soil area were only a little over 300 versts apart, but since water communications were lacking, road transport had to be relied upon and transportation added over 30 silver kopecks to the cost of every pood of grain consumed in Vitebsk (Tengoborskii, I, 260).

60. Shcheglov, p. 5.

61. *Severnaia Pchela,* May 30, 1838, p. 475.

grain when the demand was greatest because of the slowness and uncertainty of transport.[62] Rye, the most widely cultivated grain and the principal food of the people, was subject to the greatest fluctuations in price.[63]

The length of time needed to transport goods also meant that the Russian merchant's capital was tied up much longer than that of his foreign counterparts, who were increasingly benefited by improved means of transportation in Western Europe, and thus capital, very scarce in the Russia of Nicholas I, could be employed in fewer trading ventures. Also, rates of interest on the capital employed by the merchant in purchasing, transporting, and storing goods over a period often lasting more than a year were 10 to 12 per cent per annum in Russia compared with rates of 4 to 5 per cent per annum abroad.[64]

The producer also suffered, since the merchant, faced with many risks and high transportation costs, was not only forced to charge high prices to consumers to insure a legitimate profit, but was also forced to buy at as low prices as possible.[65] The producer of agricultural products, without a large market in the immediate area in which he produced, was dependent upon the merchant who marketed his products at some distant point, and since the merchant to protect himself would buy at the lowest possible price, the profits of the producer were reduced to a minimum.[66]

Bad transportation not only affected the profits of the producers adversely but also deprived them of markets.[67] Areas in "surplus Russia" were often glutted with products for which there was no market locally, while areas in "deficit Russia" or those affected by local famine suffered from hunger.[68] Grain-producing black-soil areas such as Kursk, Kharkov, and Orel provinces took little or no part in the grain export trade because

62. Nebol'sin, I, 66; Rudchenko, p. 16.
63. Tengoborskii, I, 246.
64. "A. A." [A. V. Abaza], *Mysli moskovskogo zhitelia o vozmozhnosti uchredit' obshchestvo na aktsiiakh dlia sooruzheniia zheleznoi dorogi ot S. Peterburga do Moskvy* (St. Petersburg, 1838), p. 5.
65. Tengoborskii, II, 153.   66. *Ibid.*, I, 247 ff; Nebol'sin, I, 65.
67. Often it was cheaper to transport products by sea from the United States to Riga than to transport them a relatively short distance within Russia (Rudchenko, p. 15).
68. Shcheglov, p. 5.

of poor communications with Russian ports.[69] Whole areas were deprived of a share of trade both with the rest of the country and with foreign countries, quite without reference to what they were able to produce.

Lack of rapid communications also meant that the Russian grain trade could not take advantage of sudden rises in grain prices in Western Europe caused by harvest failure there. When it was known in Western Europe in June that the harvest would fail, supplies at Rybinsk or at points nearer St. Petersburg—that is, those supplies which could arrive in St. Petersburg in three months or less—could be called upon, but supplies from a greater distance would not arrive until the next summer, when the demand for them in Western Europe would be past.[70] The facilities for storing grain in St. Petersburg itself were limited. Furthermore, the grain that did get exported from the port of St. Petersburg was two to three times more expensive than it had been at the place of origin, and therefore grain from countries like European Turkey, Egypt, Hungary, and above all the United States could undersell Russian grain in England, one of Russia's chief markets.[71]

The development of animal husbandry, especially of the cattle trade, was also retarded by bad communications. The provinces where the greatest amount of meat was produced, Bessarabia, the Don Cossack country, Taurida, and Orenburg, were the farthest from districts like St. Petersburg where not enough meat was produced. Every year over 100,000 cattle and sheep were driven from southern Russia to St. Petersburg, mostly in the summer months. During these drives the livestock lost much weight, which, along with the cost of transport, made meat scarce and expensive. Many fewer cattle and sheep arrived in St. Petersburg during the winter months (December to May), making meat during this period four times as expensive as during the summer.[72] Nebol'sin points out that driving cattle from south-

69. Rudchenko, p. 13; Matthesius, *Archiv für Eisenbahnwesen*, No. 5 (1903), p. 944.

70. "Donesenie," *Krasnyi Arkhiv*, LXXVI (1936), 143-144; Nebol'sin, I, 32.

71. Nebol'sin, I, 188.

72. Tengoborskii, I, 295; "Donesenie," *Krasnyi Arkhiv*, LXXVI (1936), 134-135.

ern Russia to Moscow was 33 to 50 per cent cheaper than to St. Petersburg. If cattle could be delivered by railway to St. Petersburg from Moscow, they would be cheaper by at least 30 per cent. Not only would a greater quantity of meat be consumed in St. Petersburg if it were cheaper, but also there would be more Russian cattle products sold in England.[73] Wood was another item made costly by the expense of transport. A sazhen of wood costing 25 to 30 kopecks (silver) in the forest would sell for 3 rubles in St. Petersburg.[74] Forests near rivers were stripped bare, but those farther away from rivers were left untouched.[75]

Russian industry also suffered because of inadequate transportation facilities. According to Tengoborskii's estimate, internal trade added on the average 25 per cent to the original value of manufactured articles.[76]

The metallurgical industry—so important for the growth of Russian industry in general—was particularly adversely affected. Iron was produced in different parts of Russia. Some was produced in the Central Provinces, but that was consumed mostly in the area to manufacture iron products which were then sent throughout the empire. Iron was also imported by water into St. Petersburg and the Baltic Provinces from Finland and even from the Kingdom of Poland. But it was iron from the Urals— from Orenburg, Viatka, and above all Perm Province—upon which the greatest part of Russia relied, both for domestic consumption and for the export trade. At this time the Urals produced the greatest amount of iron and that of the highest quality.[77] The Urals, however, were far removed from the main centers of consumption of iron, and iron is heavy and bulky and therefore difficult to transport. As a result, many areas of Russia suffered from a serious shortage of iron or could obtain it only at very high prices, although the cost of iron in the Ural area itself was lower than in any other European country except Belgium.[78]

Since it generally took "caravans" carrying iron at least several months to reach St. Petersburg, iron merchants there were forced to charge high prices. In no other European country were there

73. Nebol'sin, I, 223.
75. Ibid., I, 163.
77. Nebol'sin, II, 210-211.

74. Tengoborskii, II, 154.
76. Ibid., II, 153-154.
78. Ibid.; Tengoborskii, II, 115.

such varying prices for iron in different parts of the country. For example, a pood of iron costing 74 kopecks (silver) in Perm would cost 1 ruble 13 kopecks in Nizhnii Novgorod and 1 ruble 55 kopecks in St. Petersburg.[79] Because of the high price of iron from the Urals, mechanical establishments in St. Petersburg were forced to use Finnish pig iron, which was poor in quality and could be obtained only in fairly small amounts.[80]

The Western Provinces of Russia, which had poorer communications with the Urals than did St. Petersburg, suffered from even higher prices for iron, the transportation cost well exceeding the original cost of the iron itself.[81]

Iron, because of its high price, became a luxury as an article of daily use for all classes of the population. Most plows in Russia were made of wood; most carts were without iron tires and had wooden axles. Tengoborskii was of the opinion that if iron had been less expensive the domestic market would have consumed more than twice the amount then produced.[82]

Lack of good transport retarded the growth and prosperity of the Russian metallurgical industry in another way. Although it was known by the early 1830's that coal reserves were present in southern Russia in inexhaustible supply, lack of transportation to the potential centers of consumption meant that St. Petersburg was more cheaply supplied with imported English coal, and the rest of Russia simply went without.[83] The iron and copper industries used charcoal for smelting and were located only in wooded areas. In areas where wood was scarce or the forests had to be conserved, the metallurgical industry could not thrive. Without transport it was impossible to substitute coal for charcoal, as had been done in England.[84] The *Gornyi Zhurnal* made the observation in 1832 that after the opening of the Stockton-Darlington Railway (1825) in England coal prices in Stockton dropped from 18 shillings per ton to 7.5 shillings per ton.[85]

Lack of good communications was certainly not the sole

79. Tengoborskii, II, 117-118, 121.
80. *Ibid.*, p. 130.   81. *Ibid.*
82. *Ibid.*, I, 210.   83. *Ibid.*, II, 269.
84. Nebol'sin, II, 206.
85. "O chugunnykh dorogakh i parovykh koliaskakh," *Gornyi Zhurnal* II, kn. IV (1832), 148.

cause of Russia's economic backwardness either in the metallurgical industry or in other branches of the economy, but it was certainly a major cause. If Russia's economy was to expand and to be modernized, means for improving its transportation system would have to be found.

Chapter II. Russian attempts at railway construction before 1835

In the "official" histories of Russian railways written at the turn of the century it is stated that the railway question was raised for the first time in Russia in January, 1835, when the Austrian engineer Franz Anton von Gerstner made his famous proposals to build a network of railways in Russia.[1] This view was also held by scholars in the early Soviet period.[2] But there were natives of mechanical ability who built early private railways in Russia. This activity went generally unnoticed at the time. Perhaps that is one reason why historians also have tended to disregard this early work.

The Russian railways existing prior to 1835 were first discussed by the Soviet scholar V. V. Danilevskii in 1939.[3] Later in the Stalinist era, and especially in the years 1945–1952, a series of Soviet scholars, S. A. Urodkov, F. I. Boiko, and particularly V. S. Virginskii, relying mainly on hitherto unused archival materials in the Central State Historical Archives in Leningrad and other collections, showed that before 1835 native Russian mechanics in the Altai and the Urals built working railways and even two steam locomotives. The thesis these Soviet scholars seem to wish to prove is that Russians, too, were ingenious inventors in the field of railways and produced work which was as good, if not better, than that done at the same time outside Russia.[4] It is continually stressed that these inventors

1. V. M. Verkhovskii, *Kratkii istoricheskii ocherk nachala i rasprostraneniia zheleznykh dorog v Rossii po 1897 g. vkliuchitel'no* (St. Petersburg, 1898), p. 21; N. A. Kislinskii, *Nasha zheleznodorozhnaia politika po dokumentam arkhiva Komiteta Ministrov* (St. Petersburg, 1902), I, 2.

2. See, for example, A. A. Katikman, *"Chugunka" v vozraste 100 let* (Leningrad, 1925), p. 18; K. A. Oppengeim, *Rossiia v dorozhnom otnoshenii* (Moscow, 1920), p. 39.

3. V. V. Danilevskii, "Pervaia chugunnaia doroga, postroennaia na Altae v 1806–1809 gg.," *Trudy Leningradskogo Industrial'nogo Instituta*, I, No. 4 (1939). (Unavailable to me.)

4. See, for example, V. S. Virginskii, *Zhizn' i deiatel'nost' russkikh mekhanikov Cherepanovykh* (Moscow, 1956), p. 138; F. I. Boiko, *Zamechatel'nye russkie mekhaniki Cherepanovy* (Sverdlovsk, 1952), p. 50.

were native Russians of non-aristocratic origin and were the advocates of the new technology. They wanted to improve productivity and labor conditions in Russian industry and therefore had to struggle against reactionary and indifferent factory owners, who were satisfied with servile labor, as well as against Nicholas I, his officials, and the self-seeking, anti-Russian foreigners who had great influence in official circles.

These Soviet scholars, in spite of the political motive of their argument, have rendered a service to scholarship by showing that there were Russians who, before von Gerstner's arrival in Russia, did accomplish something in the field of railways, even though these accomplishments had relatively little significance for subsequent railway development in Russia.

As in England, the beginnings of railway transport in Russia were connected with the mining and metallurgical industries. The first railways built in Russia were factory or mine tramways. The first such tramway of which there is any record was built in 1763–1765 at the Zmeinogorsk Mine of the Kolyvano-Voskresenskie factories in the Altai by the hydro-technician K. D. Frolov (1728–1800). The tramway was used for carrying ore at the mine.[5] The next factory tramway was built in 1788 by A. S. Yartsev, head of the Olonets factories in Petrozavodsk. He built it with the help of the Scottish engineer Charles Gascoyne. The railway was about 500 feet long and was built to carry cannon and other products from one part of the factory to the other.[6] These were the two factory railways of which Professor Virginskii has found any record before that built by P. K. Frolov in the first decade of the nineteenth century.[7]

That railway, one of the two important pre-1835 Russian railway undertakings, was built by the *Oberbergmeister* P. K. Frolov (1775–1839), son of K. D. Frolov. P. K. Frolov had been trained in the Institute of Mining (Gornyi Kadetskii Korpus) and in 1793 entered the service of the Kolyvano-Voskresenskie

5. V. S. Virginskii, "Zheleznodorozhnyi vopros v Rossii do 1835 goda," *Istoricheskie Zapiski*, XXV (1948), 136; V. V. Danilevskii, *Russkaia tekhnika* (2nd ed.; Leningrad, 1948), p. 184.
6. S. Gur'ev, "O perenosnykh zheleznykh dorogakh, ustraivaemykh pri krepostiakh i arsenalakh," *Gornyi Zhurnal*, II, kn. VI (1834), 572.
7. Virginskii, *Istoricheskie Zapiski*, XXV (1948), 137.

factories, where he served, with some interruptions, until 1830.[8] In March, 1806, P. K. Frolov had presented two alternative plans for improving transportation between the Zmeinogorsk Mine, where his father had built a small railway, and the factories nearby. One project called for a canal and the other for a railway. V. S. Chulkov, head of the Kolyvano-Voskresenskie factories, reported to his superiors in St. Petersburg that he had approved both of Frolov's plans as profitable to the treasury and had told him to proceed with one.[9] Frolov decided to build a railway to carry silver ore not worth transporting to more distant points from Zmeinogorsk Mine to a nearby factory.[10]

Construction of the railway started in 1806, but, due to the unevenness of the ground and the complexity of necessary artificial constructions, such as bridges and cuttings, the railway took until 1809 to complete and cost 12,486 rubles.[11] Supplementary work continued until 1810, when reports of the completion of the railway were sent to St. Petersburg.[12]

The total length of the Frolov railway was 1 verst, 366 sazhens. In addition to the main stretch of track, there were two branch lines of 72 sazhens and 25 sazhens.[13] Professor Virginskii points out, with justification, that the artificial constructions on the Frolov railway exceeded those on its English counterparts, which followed more closely the contours of the land.[14] The beginning point of the railway at the Zmeinogorsk Mine was in a cutting 16 feet deep. The ore was loaded into wagons from above by means of chutes. Very little of the railway ran along level ground. It ran for about 450 sazhens through cuttings 1 to 2 sazhens deep and on pillars for 175 sazhens, but the main construction was a bridge with twenty stone pillars and forty-two arches, which was 137 sazhens long and 5 sazhens high.[15] The

8. V. S. Virginskii, *Zamechatel'nye russkie izobretateli Frolovy* (Moscow, 1952), p. 106; Virginskii, *Istoricheskie Zapiski*, XXV (1948), 138.

9. Virginskii, *Frolovy*, p. 117.

10. *Aziatskii Vestnik*, II (1825), 56, n. 1; *Sibirskii Vestnik*, VIII (1819), 113.

11. "O chugunnoi doroge v Kolyvanskikh zavodakh," *Otechestvennye Zapiski*, VII (1821), 175; *Aziatskii Vestnik*, II (1825), 56, n. 1.

12. Virginskii, *Frolovy*, p. 122.

13. *Aziatskii Vestnik*, II (1825), 56, n. 1.

14. Virginskii, *Istoricheskie Zapiski*, XXV (1948), 138.

15. "O chugunnoi doroge," *Otechestvennye Zapiski*, VII (1821), 175-176; *Aziatskii Vestnik*, II (1825), 56, n. 1.

rails, which were produced in the Kolyvano-Voskresenskie factories, were made of cast iron and had a convex surface. The flanges of the concave wheels of the ore wagons rested on the two shelves, thereby avoiding wear on the convex part of the rail. The gauge of the track was 0.5 sazhen (1,067 mm.). The rails were laid on longitudinal crossties held in place at regular intervals by crossbars.[16] There is no doubt that by the standards of its day the railway built by P. K. Frolov was very well engineered.

The Frolov railway was operated only during the summer, but, when it was in operation, it represented a tremendous improvement over the conventional means of ore transport at the Zmeinogorsk Mine. One horse could pull three wagons loaded with 500 poods of ore each, doing the work which twenty-five horses had done. One man and one horse could do the work formerly done by over five hundred ascribed peasants.[17] Peter Frolov could report in November, 1817, that, since the railway had started to operate, its total costs had been 21,289 rubles, and that it had carried over 2.7 million poods of ore. At this rate the savings realized by the operation of the railway would be great enough to pay back the original cost in fifteen years.[18]

16. Virginskii, *Frolovy*, pp. 125-126.
17. *Aziatskii Vestnik*, II (1825), 56, n. 1; "O chugunnoi doroge," *Otechestvennye Zapiski*, VII (1821), 178.
18. Virginskii, *Frolovy*, p. 132. Two further projects of P. K. Frolov's were not realized. As early as 1806–1807 he was proposing railways of even greater length than the one at Zmeinogorsk Mine. In March, 1806, he wrote that he hoped to construct a railway from Zmeinogorsk to the Alei River, nearly 40 versts distant, if he could not build a canal along this route. In March, 1807, Frolov stated that if a canal were built its value could be enhanced by a railway built to connect it with a pine forest 40 versts from the Alei River so that lumber could be delivered to the mines. However, the factory administration began to doubt if it could spend the funds necessary for such improvements and was of the opinion that any railway projects especially should be postponed until the value of the railway already under construction by Frolov had been proven (*ibid.*, pp. 117-120). P. K. Frolov's most ambitious project, however, was that which he proposed in 1812, to link by railway the Volga and the salt-rich Lake Elton in Saratov Province. From the state salt works at Lake Elton, salt was carried to the Volga by ascribed peasants, whose working conditions were very bad (*ibid.*, pp. 134-135). In the years preceding 1812 there had been projects for canals or improved roads between the Volga and Lake Elton, but all had been rejected as impracticable. Among these projects was a survey for a railway drawn up by

49

The other main accomplishment of pre-1835 mechanics in the field of railways was that of E. A. Cherepanov (1774-1842) and especially of his son M. E. Cherepanov (1803-1849), both serf mechanics at the Demidov factories in the Urals at Nizhnii Tagil in Perm Province. M. E. Cherepanov, with the help of his father, built in 1833-1835 the first two steam railway locomotives ever built and operated in Russia.

Steam engines for industrial use and for steamboats had been known in Russia for some time, although they had appeared there later than in Western Europe. The first steam engine in Russia had been built in England and imported by Peter the Great.[19]

In the early 1760's one I. I. Polzunov, who was employed at the Kolyvano-Voskresenskie Mines, where K. D. Frolov was building his railway about the same time, having read an account of the Newcomen steam engine, decided to build a similar one to work the air bellows at the factory for the smelting of silver ore and succeeded in doing so in the years 1764-1765. This was the first steam engine built in Russia. Brandt feels that Polzunov's engine was tantamount to an original invention, since

the French engineer Poidebard, who later decided against the idea, on the ground that similar railways in England had never been built over such long distances (Virginskii, *Istoricheskie Zapiski*, XXV [1948], 139). Frolov, who in 1811 had been sent to St. Petersburg to head a section of the Department of Mines, was sent to Lake Elton to survey possible means of improving the transportation of salt to the Volga, since the war with Napoleon was giving rise to a greater need. Frolov considered the possibility of a canal and of a railway. He decided in favor of the latter and proposed a railway about 140 versts in length, linking Lake Elton with the Nikolaevskaia landing on the Volga. Horse traction was to be used. Frolov's Lake Elton–Volga project was more like a project for a mainline railway than a factory railway. But his plan was rejected by the Department of Mines because it did not want to spend the money necessary for such a large undertaking (Virginskii, *Frolov*, pp. 135-137). P. K. Frolov and Poidebard were not the only men to think of a railway between the Volga and Lake Elton. In October, 1814, one I. Gamaleia, a member of the St. Petersburg Academy of Sciences, wrote a letter from England concerning the general use of steam power as a means of traction in which he suggested that a railway for transporting salt between Lake Elton and the Volga be built and that steam traction be used. Whether Gamaleia knew of Frolov's project is not known (Virginskii, *Zhizn'*, p. 124, n. 303).

19. A. Brandt, *Ocherk istorii parovoi mashiny i primeneniia parovykh dvigatelei v Rossii*, Vol. XXIII of *Sbornik Instituta Inzhenerov Zhelezno-dorozhnogo Transporta* (St. Petersburg, 1892), p. 26.

the book which he had read gave little detailed information on the Newcomen engine.[20]

In 1777 the first Newcomen steam engine imported from Scotland appeared. It was installed in Kronstadt by English craftsmen and was used for pumping water.[21]

The first steam engines to be built in Russia in a shop taking and executing regular orders were built at the state-owned Olonets cannon factory at Petrozavodsk by the Scotsman Charles Gascoyne, who, at the invitation of the Russian government, came to Russia in 1786 with English craftsmen. He became director of the Olonets factories, which continued to produce cannon and other iron products, but now also built steam engines. The first steam engine built by Gascoyne, probably on the Watt system,[22] at the Olonets factories went into operation in 1791 at a mine in Archangel Province.[23]

Another factory, founded by Gascoyne in St. Petersburg, also produced steam engines until it was closed by the Great Flood of 1824.[24] To replace it, the Russian government built the Alexandrovskii factory in the years 1825–1828, which produced metal products as well as steam engines. Later, in 1844, it was leased to the American firm of Harrison, Eastwick, and Winans, who were to build rolling stock for the St. Petersburg–Moscow Railway.[25]

There was also a privately owned factory in Russia which built steam engines for industrial use. The factory of Charles Baird, who had come to Russia with Gascoyne and who has already been mentioned in connection with the building of steamboats, was founded in 1792 but did not start to build steam engines until 1811.[26]

Construction of steam engines by private firms, however, re-

20. *Ibid.*, pp. 27-28.   21. *Ibid.*, pp. 31-33.

22. The Watt steam engine had first been described in a Russian work a few years before by one L. Sabakin, who had just returned from England (*ibid.*, p. 34).

23. S. G. Strumilin, *Istoriia chernoi metallurgii v SSSR* (Moscow, 1954), I, 399-400; Brandt, pp. 35-37.

24. Later this factory functioned on a limited scale and eventually became the famed Putilov Works.

25. V. K. Iatsunskii, "Promyshlennyi perevorot v Rossii," *Voprosy Istorii*, No. 12 (1952), p. 64; Brandt, p. 37.

26. Iatsunskii, p. 64.

mained rare. There was a lack of skilled labor to build, operate, and repair the engines. It was relatively cheaper to use manual labor or water power. Steam engines would be useful mainly in large industrial establishments concentrated under one roof. In the 1830's such establishments were still comparatively rare in Russia. The statistics of the Department of Manufactures and Internal Trade, which were probably incomplete, state that thirteen steam engines were built in 1826 in private factories in Russia, but only eight in 1835.[27] In the first quarter of the nineteenth century, the main initiative came from state-owned factories and from the Russian government, which made efforts to train mechanics and craftsmen skilled in the building and maintenance of steam engines. These men were either sent to England or apprenticed to Baird.[28]

The use of steam engines in industry gradually increased in the first decades of the nineteenth century. The first steam engine used in the Urals was built in 1799. Steam engines were used to replace waterwheels and horses in the Ural mines for lifting ore and pumping out water. Blast furnaces and forges still relied more on water power with steam engines usually held in reserve.[29] In the 1820's steam engines were increasingly used in the growing cotton-spinning industry.[30] By the early 1830's there were about 150 industrial steam engines with an estimated total output of 2,200 horsepower.[31]

The Cherepanovs, before building their two steam locomotives, had built some of these stationary steam engines. In 1820 E. A. Cherepanov, with the help of his young son, built his first

27. M. Zlotnikov, "Ot manufaktury k fabrike," *Voprosy Istorii*, Nos. 11-12 (1946), p. 44.

28. Brandt, p. 39.   29. Strumilin, I, 400-402.

30. V. Pel'chinskii, *O sostoianii promyshlennykh sil Rossii do 1832 g.* (St. Petersburg, 1833), p. 63. The first such machine was used in 1805 at Alexandrovo, near St. Petersburg (Roger Portal, "Das Problem einer industriellen Revolution in Russland im 19. Jahrhundert," *Forschungen zur osteuropäischen Geschichte*, I [1954], 206).

31. Strumilin, I, 403; Pel'chinski, pp. 63-64. The largest steam engine in service in Russia had 60 horsepower and was in use at the St. Petersburg Mint (Brandt, p. 40). Industrial steam engines began to play an important part during the middle of the nineteenth century. For instance, in 1843, although there were only 80 steam engines in the industrial area around Moscow, where there were 1,300 factories, those 80 steam engines supplied a third of the total power (Portal, p. 207).

small steam engine[32] in the machine shop designed to produce various machine tools and other mechanisms for use at the Demidov factories, a shop that he had been instrumental in setting up at the Vyskii Factory in the complex of mines and factories owned by the Demidov family at Nizhnii Tagil in the Urals.[33] In 1821 E. A. Cherepanov was sent to England, where he became convinced of the great usefulness of steam engines in the mining industry and learned about their construction. Upon his return to Russia, he had occasion to inspect factories which built steam engines in St. Petersburg and its environs, including that of Baird.[34] In 1824, E. A. Cherepanov built another small steam engine having 4 horsepower for use in turning a lathe at the Vyskii Factory.[35] Early in 1828, he put into operation a much larger steam engine with more than 30 horsepower, which he also built with the help of his son, and in December, 1830, they completed one with about 40 horsepower for use at the Mednyi (copper) Mine at Nizhnii Tagil.[36] Both engines were used for pumping water from the mines.[37]

Before 1830 no attempt had been made to build a steam locomotive in Russia. However, as the copper-smelting industry developed in the 1820's, a large amount of copper ore had begun to be transported at Nizhnii Tagil from the Mednyi Mine to the Vyskii Factory, a distance of about 3 versts,[38] and as early as January, 1830, it had been suggested to the St. Petersburg office of the Demidov factories that a railway, using steam traction, be built between the Mednyi Mine and the Vyskii Factory.[39]

In the summer of 1833, M. E. Cherepanov was sent to England by his superiors to study various branches of metallurgy and mining, but especially "road steam engines" (*sukhoputnye*

32. V. S. Virginskii, *Russkie izobretateli Cherepanovy: sozdateli pervoi parovoi rel'sovoi dorogi v Rossii* (Moscow, 1953), p. 13.

33. Virginskii, *Zhizn'*, p. 50; Danilevskii, *Russkaia tekhnika*, p. 183.

34. Virginskii, *Zhizn'*, pp. 56-59. Cherepanov was especially influenced by Baird's work with steam engines (R. R. Tonkov, "K istorii parovykh mashin v Rossii," *Gornyi Zhurnal*, II [1902], 184).

35. Virginskii, *Zhizn'*, p. 68; Danilevskii, *Russkaia tekhnika*, p. 182.

36. Virginskii, *Zhizn'*, pp. 84, 87.

37. "Izvestie o sukhoputnom parokhode, ustroennom v ural'skikh zavodakh v 1833 godu," *Gornyi Zhurnal*, II, kn. V (1835), 446.

38. Virginskii, *Cherepanovy*, p. 12.

39. Virginskii, *Zhizn'*, p. 123.

parokhody).[40] In September, 1833, he returned to St. Petersburg. In a letter from the St. Petersburg office of the Demidov factories to its Nizhnii Tagil office, dated September 29, 1833, it was stated that Cherepanov hoped to build "steam carriages" (*parovye telegi*) to transport freight. The Nizhnii Tagil office was instructed to give Cherepanov all necessary assistance. Two locomotives were to be built, one for use in the factory and one to be sent to St. Petersburg.[41]

On his return home M. E. Cherepanov, with his father, began construction almost immediately on the first of the two steam locomotives. In his work he was assisted by a staff of artisans, technicians, and workmen of the Vyskii Factory.[42] In late December, 1833, or early January, 1834, the Demidov factory administration reported that wooden models had been made and metal parts were being cast. By February, 1834, it was reported that the locomotive was finished and ready to be tested.[43]

In building his locomotive Cherepanov had been faced with two problems: (1) the original firebox heated up slowly and did not produce enough steam; (2) a device had to be found which would allow the locomotive to go in reverse as well as forward. Cherepanov found the means to overcome both of these technical difficulties.[44] During one of the trial runs in February, 1834, the locomotive's boiler burst, and Cherepanov was forced to rebuild it in a more durable manner. By late April it was reported that reconstruction of the locomotive was nearing completion. By June, it had been given trial runs again. In August, 1834, it was completely finished.[45]

The first Cherepanov locomotive was not large. Its boiler was 5.5 feet long and 3 feet in diameter, with 80 copper boiler tubes. Its cylinders were 9 inches long and 7 inches in diameter. The locomotive burned charcoal and had a tender for fuel and water as well as a wagon which could carry goods or 40 pas-

40. "Izvestie," *Gornyi Zhurnal*, II, kn. V (1835), 446.
41. For the full text of this letter see, Virginskii, *Zhizn'*, p. 278.
42. Virginskii, *Cherepanovy*, pp. 14-15.
43. Virginskii, *Zhizn'*, p. 136.
44. "Izvestie," *Gornyi Zhurnal*, II, kn. V (1835), 447.
45. Virginskii, *Zhizn'*, pp. 136, 138-139; Boiko, *Cherepanovy*, p. 43.

sengers. It could pull a load of 200 poods (3.6 tons) at a speed of 12 to 15 versts per hour (8 to 10 miles per hour).[46]

When the locomotive had proven itself successful, a short experimental railway 400 sazhens long was built from the Vyskii Factory along Vyskoe Pole.[47] The gauge of the track was 2 arshins, 5 vershoks (1,645 mm.), as compared to George Stephenson's 4 foot 8.5 inch (1,435 mm.) gauge and the 5 foot (1,524 mm.) gauge adopted for the St. Petersburg–Moscow Railway and most other Russian railways.[48] The Cherepanov railway was the first broad-gauge railway in Russia. The rails were of cast iron and were shaped like a mushroom. They were placed in cast-iron rail chairs (*podushki*), fixed to transverse wooden crossties.[49] Rails of this sort had been used as early as the 1810's on English mine railways. An improved version of this type of track was patented by George Stephenson in 1816,[50] and rails of a very similar type were used on the Liverpool-Manchester Railway as well as later on the Tsarskoe Selo Railway. On the St. Petersburg–Moscow Railway and other subsequent Russian railways flat-bottomed rails of the type used on American and most Continental railways were used.

M. E. Cherepanov started to build a second locomotive in October, 1834. In March, 1835, it was announced that the construction of the locomotive was completed and that it had been satisfactorily tested.[51] This second locomotive was more powerful than the first one and could pull a load of up to 1,000 poods (18 tons).[52] Further specifications on this second Cherepanov locomotive are lacking, except that it was stated that it cost 1,456 rubles to build and that 128.5 poods of iron and more than 34 poods of copper were used in its construction.[53]

46. "Izvestie," *Gornyi Zhurnal*, II, kn. V (1835), 447-448; Tonkov, p. 185.
47. Virginskii, *Zhizn'*, p. 139; "Izvestie," *Gornyi Zhurnal*, II, kn. V (1835), 447.
48. Boiko, *Cherepanovy*, p. 42. For the gauges of previous Russian tramways see Virginskii, *Cherepanovy*, p. 18.
49. Virginskii, *Zhizn'*, p. 139; for a diagram see p. 141.
50. Samuel Smiles, *George and Robert Stephenson: The Locomotive*, Vol. V of *Lives of the Engineers* (New York, 1905), pp. 132-133.
51. Virginskii, *Zhizn'*, p. 146; Boiko, *Cherepanovy*, p. 44.
52. *Gornyi Zhurnal*, III, kn. VII (1835), 170.
53. Virginskii, *Zhizn'*, pp. 147, 282.

When the second Cherepanov locomotive had been completed, it was proposed to extend the 400-sazhen experimental railway from the Vyskii Factory to the Mednyi Mine, a distance of about 3 versts, to carry copper ore from the mine to the factory.[54] M. E. Cherepanov started to prepare rails and rail chairs for this railway in the spring of 1835, but the factory administration did not give him permission to start building the railway until July. Construction started soon thereafter, and the railway was completed in 1836.[55] Thus came into being the first operational steam railway in Russia, and at an earlier, if little earlier, date than the Tsarskoe Selo Railway.

As for the further activity of the Cherepanovs in the field of railways, although their factory railway continued to run, they did little if anything more, since the Demidov factory administration laid upon them so many and such varied duties that they did not have time to continue their work with railways.[56] In the opinion of Professor Virginskii, the Demidovs were ignorant of and not interested in the application of such new inventions, and the factory administration thought it more economical to use cheap serf labor than to introduce new techniques.[57]

In the decades following the construction of the Cherepanov locomotives and railway, several short factory and mine railways were built in the Urals and the Altai for transporting ore, but horse traction was used, and the construction of these railways was rather primitive.[58] Horse power continued to be used on factory and mine railways in Russia until the Russian locomotive industry developed later in the century. When steam power was first used on a large scale on factory and mine railways, tender engines from adjoining main-line railways were employed. It was only in the late 1880's that tank engines were developed for use on factory and mine railways.[59]

The question arises how original the steam locomotives of the Cherepanovs were. Soviet scholars, especially Professor Vir-

54. *Gornyi Zhurnal*, III, kn. VII (1835), 170.

55. Virginskii, *Zhizn'*, pp. 147-148; Boiko, *Cherepanovy*, pp. 45-46.

56. Virginskii, *Zhizn'*, pp. 151-152.

57. Virginskii, *Cherepanovy*, pp. 23-24.

58. I. N. Bogachev, *Sekret Bulata* (Sverdlovsk, 1957), pp. 72-74; Virginskii, *Zhizn'*, pp. 156-157.

59. F. I. Boiko, *Parovozy promyshlennogo transporta* (3rd ed.; Moscow, 1957), pp. 12-13.

ginskii, maintain that native Russian inventors and mechanics were men of original genius who owed very little to foreign inventors. Professor Virginskii asserts, "The creation of the Cherepanovs was independent (*samostoiatel'nyi*). They did not have a trace of that worship of everything foreign which was so characteristic of their masters."[60]

It is obvious, however, that M. E. Cherepanov had had much more opportunity to inform himself of previous work done with steam engines and steam locomotives than had Polzunov with steam engines or P. K. Frolov with mine tramways. After M. E. Cherepanov had had experience in building stationary steam engines with his father, he inspected factories producing steam engines both in England and Russia,[61] and he had seen English locomotives. He had access to all the latest Russian and foreign journal articles on the subject,[62] including presumably an article in the *Journal of Mining* (*Gornyi Zhurnal*) describing the latest accomplishments of English locomotive-builders and giving a detailed description of the boilers of Stephenson's *Rocket* and *Novelty*.[63] In short, Polzunov and Frolov can probably lay claim to greater originality than can M. E. Cherepanov, and it would be going too far to maintain that Cherepanov's invention was completely independent of significant foreign or Russian influences.

On the other hand, a great amount of inventiveness and originality cannot be denied Cherepanov. There is some indication that he may actually have started building a steam locomotive before his visit to England in the summer of 1833, since the St. Petersburg office of the Demidov factories in its letter of September 29, 1833, mentioned a " 'steam carriage' already begun by Cherepanov."[64] Further evidence concerning this attempt by Cherepanov seems to be lacking. It is also true that when Cherepanov was in England, he was not permitted to inspect the interiors of locomotives while they were in action and he was not able to bring back diagrams or sketches.[65] He was also handi-

60. Virginskii, *Cherepanovy*, p. 14.   61. Virginskii, *Zhizn'*, p. 278.
62. *Ibid.*, p. 124, n. 302; Boiko, *Cherepanovy*, p. 39.
63. "O chugunnykh dorogakh i parovykh koliaskakh," *Gornyi Zhurnal*, II, kn. IV (1832), 137-153.
64. Virginskii, *Zhizn'*, p. 278; Boiko, *Cherepanovy*, p. 38.
65. "Izvestie," *Gornyi Zhurnal*, II, kn. V (1835), 446; Tonkov, p. 185.

capped while there by language difficulties. Professor Virginskii concludes that although Cherepanov had information about foreign steam locomotives as far as the basic principles of construction were concerned, he had to proceed on his own inventive ability in building his first locomotive.[66]

In this view Professor Virginskii is probably correct. M. E. Cherepanov, like his father, had a reputation among his contemporaries for being an unusually skilled and talented mechanic, especially in matters pertaining to steam engines.[67] The basic components of a steam engine are a firebox, a boiler, and cylinders. The technically most complicated components of a steam locomotive are these, not the connection between the cylinders and driving wheels. If Cherepanov was denied an opportunity to see in detail how the interiors of British locomotives were constructed, he was already familiar enough with the working of steam engines and their parts that, with some experimentation of his own, he should have been able to build a steam locomotive once he had seen superficially the locomotives built by others and studied what had been written concerning the work of others in building them. It is interesting to note that there is at least a superficial resemblance in appearance between Cherepanov's first locomotive and the heavy-duty *Samson*, built by Robert Stephenson and Company in 1830–1831, that is, not long before Cherepanov's arrival in England.[68]

How much of an accomplishment was the first Cherepanov locomotive in comparison with locomotives built during the same period in England? Two pre-Soviet writers state that the Chere-

---

Nine years later, in 1842, Major George Washington Whistler—on his way to Russia to become consulting engineer in the construction of the St. Petersburg–Moscow Railway—in a letter to his brother-in-law remarked about his stay in England: "I have had little satisfaction in many of my visits to public works. There is such a rigid system of police at all these places. You can see nothing as you wish" (New York Public Library, Manuscript Division, Patton Collection, letter of Major George Washington Whistler to Major William G. McNeill [London, July 15 (N.S.), 1842]).

66. Virginskii, *Zhizn'*, p. 120.

67. "Izvestie," *Gornyi Zhurnal*, II, kn. V (1835), 446.

68. Compare a photograph of a model of the first Cherepanov locomotive in Virginskii, *Zhizn'*, p. 143, and a sketch of the *Samson* in James H. G. Warren, *A Century of Locomotive Building by Robert Stephenson and Co., 1823–1923* (Newcastle-on-Tyne, 1923), p. 268.

panov locomotive was small (*nebol'shoi*).[69] But Professor Virginskii points out that the first Cherepanov locomotive had 80 copper boiler tubes compared with the 25 of George Stephenson's *Rocket* and the 89 of his biggest freight locomotive, *Samson*.[70] Professor Boiko goes even further and states that the Cherepanov locomotives were superior.[71]

In the 1830's English locomotive builders, especially George and Robert Stephenson, were considered the best in the world. The locomotive *Samson*, along with a similar locomotive named *Goliath*, represented the maximum development of the freight locomotive with a 0–4–0 wheel arrangement and was a great improvement over the first locomotives built by George Stephenson some fifteen years before. The boiler of the *Samson* was 7 feet in length and 3 feet 6 inches in diameter. Its cylinders were 14 inches in diameter.[72] Thus the *Samson* had somewhat larger measurements than the first Cherepanov locomotive. However, the value of a locomotive is determined not so much by its measurements as by its tractive power and speed. In these respects, the *Samson* was clearly superior to both Cherepanov locomotives. In February, 1831, the *Samson* pulled a train of 30 wagons, weighing 151 tons, at a speed of 20 mph. Even on an incline it could pull 44 tons at 8 mph. Thus it excelled by far the performance of even the second Cherepanov locomotive in respect to tractive effort.[73]

It should be remembered that the *Samson* was the result of the long experience of George Stephenson, who had built many locomotives, while the Cherepanov locomotives were a first attempt. George Stephenson's first locomotive had been put into service in July, 1814, at the Killingworth Colliery in Northumberland. This first Stephenson locomotive had a boiler 8 feet long and 34 inches in diameter with cylinders 8 inches in diameter.[74] Although the speed of this locomotive was only 4 mph less than that of the first Cherepanov locomotive, it could pull a greater load: 8 wagons, with a load weighing 30 tons, i.e., a load 12 tons greater than that pulled by even the second

69. Brandt, p. 61; Tonkov, p. 185.
70. Virginskii, *Zhizn'*, p. 138. According to one authority on Stephenson locomotives, the *Samson* had 140 boiler tubes (Warren, p. 264).
71. Boiko, *Cherepanovy*, p. 50.   72. Warren, p. 264.
73. *Ibid.*, p. 266; Smiles, p. 274.   74. Smiles, p. 98.

Cherepanov locomotive.[75] Furthermore, after a few alterations the tractive power of the first Stephenson locomotive was doubled.[76]

Thus it can be seen that the Stephenson locomotives built in England at the same time that M. E. Cherepanov was building his two locomotives in Russia were superior in performance to Cherepanov's and that even Stephenson's first attempt over fifteen years before was somewhat better in respect to tractive power.

There arises another question: Why did Cherepanov's invention not find a more general application in Russia?

In the first place, the Cherepanovs received no support from "official Russia." No attempts were made to apply their work on a wider scale, though they did receive some attention and praise from representatives of "official Russia." In the autumn of 1834, the civil governor of Perm, Selastennikov, visited the Nizhnii Tagil factories and traveled on the 400-sazhen stretch of track already in operation and declared his satisfaction with this undertaking so advantageous for the Demidov factories.[77] But Selastennikov did nothing further. Count K. F. Toll—who in the late 1830's was to become a determined opponent of railways[78]—in a report of February 17, 1835, on the proposals of the Austrian engineer Franz Anton von Gerstner to build a network of railways in Russia, mentioned that several railways had been constructed at "Siberian" factories and asserted that an exclusive privilege given to von Gerstner to build railways in Russia would hinder the development of such factory railways.[79] On May 27, 1837, Grand Duke Alexander Nikolaevich visited Nizhnii Tagil and inspected the Cherepanov railway, which was already in operation at the time. The Grand Duke merely asked who had built the railway and, on being informed, continued on his inspection tour.[80] "Official Russia," including even Count Toll, was not hostile to the creation of the Cherepanovs or to factory and mine railways in general, merely unconcerned with them. Most

75. Warren, p. 21.   76. Smiles, p. 102.
77. "Izvestie," *Gornyi Zhurnal*, II, kn. V (1835), 448.
78. See chap. v below.
79. "Zapiska glavnoupravliaiushchego putiami soobshcheniia i publichnymi zdaniiami gr. K. F. Tolia, 17 fevralia 1835 g.," *Krasnyi Arkhiv*, LXXVI (1936), 96.
80. Virginskii, *Zhizn'*, p. 153.

members of "official Russia" had little opportunity to take more than cursory notice of the Cherepanov locomotives and railway, which was located far away in the Urals.

In the second place, when, only a year after the Cherepanovs completed their second locomotive, construction on the first non-factory railway in Russia, the Tsarskoe Selo Railway, was started, the Cherepanovs were in no position to compete with foreign firms of wider experience and reputation. Thus it is natural that the builder of this railway, Franz Anton von Gerstner, ordered locomotives from England and Belgium.[81] In addition, it is interesting to note, locomotives could be delivered by sea from England in only a few weeks, whereas to deliver them from the Urals would have taken much longer. Even if von Gerstner had been willing and able to place an order with the Demidov factories for locomotives built by the Cherepanovs, it is doubtful whether the factory administration would have been interested in such an order. By 1835 English locomotive-builders knew that they already had an expanding domestic and foreign market for their products. Russian manufacturers, on the other hand, if they had gone to the trouble and expense of producing locomotives, would not have known whether there would be sufficient demand for locomotives to justify their efforts. Locomotives and rolling stock for the St. Petersburg–Moscow Railway, started in 1844, were built in Russia, but it was the American firm of Harrison, Eastwick, and Winans who were called in to lead the factory producing this equipment. Harrison and Winans already had had extensive experience and had in their service or could train the large number of engineers and technicians necessary to build locomotives and rolling stock on a large scale.[82]

Professor Virginskii and other Soviet scholars have demonstrated that before 1835 there were individual Russians who showed more than a little skill and ingenuity in building mine and factory railways of a pioneering nature. However, for the future of railways in Russia these accomplishments were not important, since their efforts really lay out of the main stream of

81. See p. 113 below.
82. Kislinskii, I, 32-33.

events. Russia, like other countries on the continent of Europe at the time, would rely heavily on foreign technology, especially British, in building its first railways.

Although most of the equipment for Russia's first railway was to come from England, its promotion and the responsibility for its engineering were to be supplied by an Austrian, who had, of course, first of all to obtain the permission and co-operation of the Russian government. This story is the subject of the next chapter.

Chapter III. The beginnings of the discussion of the railway question in Russia (January, 1835– March, 1836)

At the outset the Russian government had no clear idea of what its attitude or its role should be in relation to railways. Neither Tsar Nicholas I nor his advisers realized what was involved. They had little idea of how much government participation was desirable at the beginning (if they decided to allow railway construction, a question in itself for a long time during these early years), and even less how much would be finally necessary. They could not have guessed how important railways would seem to the Russian government of the 1860's.

In the 1830's railways seemed just another innovation in transportation such as steamboats or diligences, especially since railways posed many of the same questions of what the government should allow, such as what the length of an exclusive privilege should be, whether there should be freedom to fix rates, or relief from taxation, and so on. It was assumed at the beginning that it was best for a private company to take the financial risk involved in the new enterprise. With steamboats and diligences the government had participated directly only after it became clear that there was profit in these undertakings. In the pages that follow it will be seen, however, that because of the expense of complicated machinery, auxiliary buildings, and, above all, the roadbed, the need for some financial assistance for railways from the government was recognized from the beginning. The government attempted to meet the need by offering to cede land, to give extended freedom from taxation, and, though grudgingly, to grant exemption from the heavy import duties on iron. Later, when the size of the undertaking for a railway of some length began to be realized, nervousness about the safety of so much capital became apparent. But it was only after some years more that the permanence and monopolistic nature of railways was fully realized. Since in Russia the government felt primarily responsible for transportation, when the exact nature and the importance of railways were seen, government participation was inevitable.

In this feeling of its way the Russian government was following a pattern usual elsewhere. In most European countries railways were at first built by private capital, then, because of financial difficulties or the government's desire for more construction, help would be given by the government; then finally some government construction and operation would follow. Only in England was there enough capital to build the necessary railways without government help. Even there, where government interference was avoided if possible, more and more regulation was found necessary by the 1840's. In general, when railways were new, the necessities of each situation rather than planning determined the course of action, although after these first years Austria, France, and Prussia came to make comprehensive plans as Belgium had done from the outset.

From this account of the Russian government's first attempts to determine its responsibilities, a picture can be drawn of the exercise of power by an absolute ruler somewhat different from that which is generally thought of in connection with Nicholas I. The Tsar, who could, on occasion, be so arbitrary, shows himself during these negotiations heedful of advice that often ran contrary to his wishes. His government over several years was more exacting in dealing with railway projects than he obviously preferred that it should be. Yet even the Tsar and those of his government who were most in favor of railways felt that they would have to proceed cautiously in allowing any railway construction, especially that of major railways.

Although Nicholas I was politically one of the most conservative of monarchs, political considerations were never to be a major factor in the government discussions on the railway question. While the possibility that railways might cause political and social upheavals in Russia was raised by the Russian press and public opinion and occasionally by some government officials, the Tsar and most of his high officials (even those opposed to railways on other grounds) had very little fear that railways might set undesirable political and social forces in motion, or at least they felt that these forces could be effectively controlled. In this respect they were like Prince Metternich in Austria, who after 1835 saw the potential advantages of railway construction, while staunchly upholding the existing order. Nicholas I was interested in the introduction of technological innovations from abroad, not to change the existing order but rather to strengthen it. Political conservativism does not necessarily preclude a genuine desire for economic progress.

The main problem in deciding whether to allow railway construction in Russia was always financial. The Russian government, perhaps more than governments in economically more developed countries, from the beginning paid the greatest attention to the question of the potential financial success of railways. Because of the large amounts of capital necessary to build railways over long distances and because of the scarcity of this capital in Russia, the lack of profitableness or outright failure of any railway enterprise would have far-reaching consequences affecting the immediate interests of the public and the state, as well as the long-range economic development of the nation. For this reason the Tsar and his paternalistic government were much less likely than governments in some other countries to follow a permissive policy in this matter.

Really purposive discussion of railways for Russia began with the proposals, on January 6, 1835, of the Austrian engineer Franz Anton von Gerstner to provide Russia with a system of railways, but from 1803 on the Russian public had been informed by the Russian press of railway developments abroad and in Russia, and in the early 1830's individual Russians began making suggestions for the construction of railways along definite routes. There were also the beginnings of an opposition by those who did not want railways.[1] However, in Russia the railway question

1. The press notices in the period 1803–1825 had been few and isolated and consisted mainly of reports of the attempts to build railways and steam locomotives in England and France (I. B. Rozenfel'd, "Ocherki istorii zheleznodorozhnogo khoziaistva v Rossii," *Zhurnal Putei Soobshcheniia*, II [1917], 8; V. S. Virginskii, *Zhizn' i deiatel'nost' russkikh mekhanikov Cherepanovykh* [Moscow, 1956], p. 124, n. 303), although the Frolov railway was also briefly mentioned (*Sibirskii Vestnik*, VIII [1819], 113; "O chugunnoi doroge v Kolyvanskikh zavodakh," *Otechestvennye Zapiski*, VII [1821], 173-179). After 1825 the opening of the Stockton-Darlington Railway in England caused the Russian press to take greater and more frequent interest in railway developments abroad ("Chugunnye dorogi i parovye pushni," *Syn Otechestva*, CI [1825], 309-312; cf. *Moskovskii Tele-*

before 1835 did not reach the extent and intensity that it had reached in economically and technologically more advanced countries such as England, or that it would reach in Russia after 1835.

The subject of railways had more than once been brought directly to the attention of the Tsars before von Gerstner's arrival. In September, 1804, an Englishman sent Tsar Alexander I a description and a model of a railway used in England, explaining that such railways were found to be very useful, especially in

graf, XII [1826], Sec. I, 28-29). The Stephenson locomotive trials of the late 1820's and the opening of the Liverpool-Manchester Railway in 1830 were also commented upon favorably ("O parovykh povozkakh," Syn Otechestva, CXXXI [1830], 378-380; "O chugunnykh dorogakh i parovykh koliaskakh," Gornyi Zhurnal, II, kn. IV [1832], 137-153).

The introduction of railways into Russia was definitely and specifically advocated in the Russian press for the first time in 1830, when a professor of physics at the University of St. Petersburg, N. Shcheglov, wrote an article in his journal, Severnyi Muravei, stating that experience abroad had shown that railways were a form of transportation superior to both roads and waterways. He suggested that a railway be built, using horse traction, from Tver to Novgorod or even St. Petersburg to avoid the low water and rapids on the Vyshnii Volochek System (N. P. Shcheglov, "O zheleznykh dorogakh i preimushchestvakh ikh nad obyknovennymi dorogami i kanalami," Severnyi Muravei, Nos. 1-2 [1830], pp. 4-5, 14-15). This article was assertive enough and attracted enough favorable attention to call forth the opposition of Major General M. Destrem, a Frenchman who had entered Russian service in 1810 and who since 1828 had been head of the Commission of Projects and Estimates of the Main Administration of Transport (E. Sokolovskii, Piatidesiatiletie Instituta i Korpusa Inzhenerov Putei Soobshcheniia [St. Petersburg, 1859], pp. 93-96). General Destrem's main contention was that a network of canals would benefit Russia more than railways would. His main arguments were: (1) railways in Russia would be more expensive to build and maintain than canals; (2) the majority of goods usually transported in Russia were of a nature that could be better carried by canals than by railways; (3) it would be very expensive to operate railways during the severe Russian winter (M. Destrem, "Obshchie suzhdeniia ob otnositel'nykh vygodakh kanalov i dorog s koleiami i prilozhenie vyvodov k opredeleniiu udobneishego dlia Rossii sposoba perevozki tiazhestei," Zhurnal Putei Soobshcheniia, kn. XXI [1831], 1-90).

In the years 1834–1835 there continued to be articles on railways published in the Russian press. The Zhurnal Obshchepoleznykh Svedenii published two short notices on railways in England and France: "O vygodakh, dostavliaemykh kanalami, rekami i zheleznymi dorogami dlia perevozki i splava tiazhestei," Zhurnal Obshchepoleznykh Svedenii, I [1834], 52–54; "Chugunnye dorogi," Zhurnal Obshchepoleznykh Svedenii, I [1834], 307-309. But it was the Biblioteka dlia Chteniia which devoted the most attention to railways. There was an article describing the rapid growth of

industrial enterprises, and could often take the place of canals. The description and model were stored with the Office of Road Construction (Ekspeditsiia Ustroeniia Dorog). In 1816 the Bavarian engineer Josef von Baader showed a model railway to Alexander I and to Kaiser Franz I of Austria. On this railway a dog could pull a load of 350 pounds. However, neither ruler seems to have taken any real interest.[2] On the other hand, Nicholas I had a passion for technology[3] and would have a natural interest in railways. One of his biographers states that he was interested in railways from his first knowledge of them.[4] In 1816, while still Grand Duke, he visited the north of England and saw one of John Blenkinsop's locomotives run on a railway from Middleton to Leeds. A model of this locomotive was sent to him.[5] Eight years later an Englishman reported that the Tsar of Russia had a model of a Blenkinsop locomotive—perhaps the one given to Nicholas I—and at that time had a "professional agent" investigating the railways of the north of England.[6] Baron Krüdener, the Russian envoy in Washington, is said to have gone up to Baltimore in 1830 and to have had a ride in the sailing car de-

railways in America, in which it was implied that conditions in America were similar to those in Russia and that Russia should also reap the benefits of railway construction ("Chugunnye dorogi v Amerike," *Biblioteka dlia Chteniia,* VI [1834], Sec. VII, 23-28). Another article published early in 1835 tried to refute the arguments already raised by the public that Russia, being an agricultural state, could not benefit from railways and that "winter roads" would suffice ("Chugunnye dorogi," *Biblioteka dlia Chteniia,* VIII [1835], Sec. III, 106-120).

2. *Kratkii istoricheskii ocherk razvitiia i deiatel'nosti Vedomstva Putei Soobshcheniia za sto let ego sushchestvovaniia* (*1798–1898*) (St. Petersburg, 1898), pp. 23-24; "Chugunnye dorogi i parovye pushni," *Syn Otechestva,* CI (1825), 311.

3. Monas remarks this (Sidney Monas, *The Third Section: Police and Society under Nicholas I* [Cambridge, Mass., 1961], p. 85), and Riasanovsky comments that Nicholas' interest in "engineering, architecture, building of every kind" ranked in importance from childhood with his consuming interest in things military and was developed further in the course of his training as a military engineer (Nicholas V. Riasanovsky, *Nicholas I and Official Nationality in Russia, 1825–1855* [Berkeley, 1959], p. 198).

4. M. A. Polievktov, *Nikolai I: biografiia i obzor tsarstvovaniia* (Moscow, 1918), p. 279.

5. Robert Young, *Timothy Hackworth and the Locomotive* (London, 1923), p. 276; James H. G. Warren, *A Century of Locomotive Building by Robert Stephenson and Co., 1823–1923* (Newcastle-on-Tyne, 1923), p. 16.

6. Joseph Sandars, *A Letter on the Subject of the Projected Railroad between Liverpool and Manchester* (5th ed.; Liverpool, 1824), p. 24.

vised to run on the tracks of the Baltimore and Ohio (which began by using horse traction) and to have asked for a model to send to the Tsar.[7] In 1831 a Mr. William Read of the Peterhof Paper Mill wrote to *Mechanics' Magazine* that he had finished a model locomotive of silver, the better to explain the operation of the Liverpool-Manchester Railway,[8] but whether this model was meant for the Tsar's benefit is not clear.

S. I. Mal'tsov, later famed as an enlightened landowner and industrialist, but in the early 1830's still a young guards officer, recounts in his memoirs that he had ridden on the Liverpool-Manchester Railway, which convinced him that railways might be successfully operated in Russia, and that he raised the subject with Nicholas I, who reminded him that it might be impossible to operate railways during the severe Russian winter and that in England they were dangerous and ran over people.[9] Soviet scholars, such as Professor Virginskii, who try to show Nicholas I to be the "captive" of such "reactionary" opponents of railways as Count Kankrin, state that the Tsar suggested that Mal'tsov be sent to an insane asylum for suggesting the construction of railways over long distances,[10] but they quote Nicholas I out of context. In the winter of 1835–1836, at a ball given by Count Kankrin, Nicholas I asked Mal'tsov where he would build the railways which he had suggested. Mal'tsov answered in a jocular manner, "One from Moscow to China and another to India." The Tsar laughed and said to Count Kankrin, "Send him to an insane asylum."[11] Plainly it was not intended that Mal'tsov become another Chaadaev, for surely we must dismiss the last-quoted remark as humorously intended, and common sense suggests that Nicholas I's earlier discouraging remarks to Mal'tsov were merely

7. Edward Hungerford, *The Story of the Baltimore & Ohio Railroad, 1827–1927* (New York, 1928), I, 80-81.

8. *Mechanics' Magazine*, December 17, 1831, p. 208.

9. S. I. Mal'tsov, "Iz vospominanii S. I. Mal'tsova," *Zapiski Moskovskogo Otdeleniia Imperatorskogo Russkogo Tekhnicheskogo Obshchestva*, IV (1886), 39. Mal'tsov, writing over fifty years later, seems confused on small details and is not disinclined to stress the importance of his own part in influencing the Tsar (as well as in the early development of Russian railways in general). It is possible that Mal'tsov exaggerated the Tsar's doubts to enhance the impression of his own persuasiveness.

10. See, for example, V. S. Virginskii, *Vozniknovenie zheleznykh dorog v Rossii do nachala 40-ykh godov XIX veka* (Moscow, 1949), pp. 252-253.

11. Mal'tsov, p. 40.

the sort of thing that a serious-minded man might say in reply to a young man's enthusiastic proposal at a time when railways were almost untried and their supposed dangers loomed large.

Since the evidence is fragmentary, the Tsar's early feeling about railways cannot be defined with certainty, but surely it should not be said that his disposition toward railways was "reactionary."

Michael Speransky, in July, 1835, stated that the Russian government had been interested in railways for some time previously, ever since experience had shown their usefulness, and was aware that railways could be especially useful in a large country like Russia. But, at the same time, it was felt that such an undertaking should be started not by the government directly but by private enterprise.[12]

In the years 1834–1835, two projects for short railways had been submitted by Russian citizens to the government, one meant to be partially and the other wholly private. Neither project received approval. In April, 1834, the collegiate councilor A. Bestuzhev submitted a memorandum to the Main Administration of Transport and Buildings (Glavnoe Upravlenie Putiami Soobshcheniia i Publichnymi Zdaniiami) suggesting the construction of a railway between the Volga and the Don. Bestuzhev proposed that the government should contribute 2 million rubles. He thought landowners and factory owners, moved by patriotism, would probably contribute considerable additional sums to the undertaking. Bestuzhev himself would give a considerable sum. The necessary materials for construction could be obtained from the state factories in Perm Province and from the Shepelov works near Murom, while state and appanage peasants of Penza Province could be hired for the necessary labor. Since the proposals of Bestuzhev were without either preliminary surveys or accurate

12. "Proekt otveta predsedatelia osobogo komiteta M. Speranskogo Fr. fon Gerstneru, iiul' 1835 g.," *Krasnyi Arkhiv*, LXXVI (1936), 101. As early as 1831 there had been some discussion in Russian government circles about the possibility of building a railway about 240 versts in length between the Niemen River and the Baltic port of Windau. Concrete action was not taken on the matter, probably because a water system, including a long and expensive canal, was already under construction along much the same route (Destrem, pp. 77-78).

estimates of cost, even of the most indefinite nature, the government did not deem it necessary even to consider the project.[13]

Early in 1835, the governor of Tambov Province, N. M. Gamaleia submitted a proposal to the Main Administration of Transport and Buildings to build a railway in his province since the rich agricultural area south of the Oka River was without adequate water communications with the outside world, although the government and the merchants of the area had made attempts to improve them. To assure regular delivery of supplies of grain to St. Petersburg and also to Moscow at low prices without losses to merchants or further cost to the government Gamaleia proposed to form a stock company to build a railway using steam traction which would run from Morshansk to the mouth of the Tsna, a distance of 100 versts (as compared with a distance by water of 208 versts). He claimed that a few "capitalists," probably local merchants, had already expressed interest in buying shares.

Gamaleia thought that there would be heavy traffic because shippers would be attracted by the lower freight rates and by the speed of the railway. Goods could be shipped at the rate of 10 kopecks per pood, and the trip would take four days instead of the three weeks or more needed for the journey by water. Gamaleia estimated that 10 million poods of freight shipped by the railway would thus bring a revenue of 1 million rubles a year. Of this sum only 20 per cent would be needed for the expenses of maintenance and operation. Because building materials such as iron and lumber were inexpensive in the area, the roadbed would cost 4.8 million rubles, and total construction costs would be only 5 million rubles. Gamaleia estimated that the stockholders would receive a yearly return of 16 per cent on their investment, a return which might increase to 30 per cent or more as the prosperity of the railway increased.[14]

Although no direct support was requested from the government, Count K. F. Toll, head of the Main Administration of

13. I. P. Borichevskii, "Predlozheniia chastnykh lits ob ustroistve zheleznykh dorog postupivshie v G.U.P.S. i P. Z. do 1860 goda," *Zhurnal Putei Soobshcheniia*, XXXIX, kn. I (1863), 127-128.

14. N. S. Mordvinov, "Zapiska o chugunnoi doroge," *Arkhiv grafov Mordvinovykh*, ed. V. A. Bil'basov (St. Petersburg, 1901–1903), X, 472-476.

Transport and Buildings, turned the proposal down.[15] It was not until later that Toll became an implacable foe of railways; it is, however, possible that he had been already influenced by the article by General Destrem, written in support of canals as opposed to railways.[16] On the other hand, it should not be forgotten that the government had spent considerable sums on improving navigation on the river Tsna, and Toll may have considered a railway along the same route superfluous. Furthermore, even a cursory examination of Gamaleia's project would indicate that he was too optimistic in his estimates. His reckoning of freight shipments of 10 million poods per year assumed that nearly all the goods shipped from Morshansk, consisting mostly of bulky raw materials, would be shipped by railway. Surely only a part of the goods shipped from a locality having both water and rail connections would be shipped by the latter. Certainly, too, steam locomotives, rolling stock, and other equipment would have cost more than 200,000 rubles. The estimate that the expenses of operation and maintenance would take only 20 per cent of revenues and that the stockholders would receive a yearly 16 per cent profit was quite unrealistic. In any event, Gamaleia's project, like that of Bestuzhev, whatever its merits, was rejected by the Russian government.

Bestuzhev and Gamaleia were local officials who, like Prince D. V. Golitsyn with his projects for roads and later for railways, wished to improve communications in a given locality by new methods of transportation and who, like Prince Golitsyn, found the indifference or hostility of the central government insuperable. These were unusually forward-looking men. In the early 1830's, most local officials, if not actually hostile to railways, were ignorant of or indifferent to them, as had been Selastennikov, the governor of Perm Province, who had inspected the Cherepanov railway in the autumn of 1834. Interest in railways was to become more general only after the arrival in Russia of the foreign engineer, Franz Anton von Gerstner.

Before his arrival in Russia von Gerstner[17] had established

15. A. Sushkov, "Vospominaniia o grafe K. F. Tole," *Chteniia v Imperatorskom Obshchestve Istorii i Drevnostei Rossiiskikh pri Moskovskom Universitete,* LV (1865), 212.

16. See p. 65, n. 1, above.

17. Franz Anton von Gerstner was born in 1796 in Prague and was the

a reputation as a railway engineer by building the first section of the Linz-Budweis Railway, linking the Moldau and Danube rivers in Austria. This was the first public railway on the European continent to be authorized and completed. It was, however, a pupil of von Gerstner, not he, who completed it.

Costs were unexpectedly high. This was due partly to factors beyond von Gerstner's control: the newness of the enterprise, which did not allow him to make estimates of costs based on experience and which led to costly technical mistakes; the sharp rise in wages and in the cost of materials in the years 1826–1827; the hostility of local landowners and peasants, whose opposition often contributed to the raising of costs.[18] But the high cost was also due to von Gerstner's insistence on the best construction.

After about one-half of the proposed distance had been completed, the stockholders and even some of von Gerstner's engineer colleagues turned against him, maintaining that the rest of the railway should be built more inexpensively. Von Gerstner refused to allow the railway to be built with heavier gradients and sharper curves, since this would prevent eventual use of steam traction, for which he hoped in spite of the fact that only horse traction had been authorized.[19] Also, as von Gerstner later pointed out, inferior construction, although it represented a saving in

son of the famed Franz Josef von Gerstner, professor of mechanics and mathematics and director of the Polytechnisches Institut there. Franz Anton, after studies in Prague, became in 1818 professor of practical geometry at the Polytechnikum in Vienna, where he soon established an excellent professional reputation. In 1822 he was sent to England to study railways, returning to Austria convinced of their future. On September 7, 1824, von Gerstner received a privilege from Kaiser Franz I to build a railway using horse power between Budweis in Bohemia and Mauthausen in Upper Austria (R. Huyer, "Die Budweis-Linzer Pferdeeisenbahn," *Mittheilungen des Vereins für Geschichte der Deutschen in Böhmen*, XXXI [1893], 88-92; *Geschichte der Eisenbahnen der Österreichisch-ungarischen Monarchie* [Vienna, 1898], I, 91-92). Later the terminus of the railway was changed to Linz.

18. Huyer, *Mittheilungen*, XXXII (1894), 86-87.

19. During the winter of 1826–1827, von Gerstner at his own expense went to England and was much impressed by advances made in steam traction by George Stephenson and the success of its application on the Stockton–Darlington Railway. From then on, von Gerstner worked for the introduction of steam traction on his railway (*Geschichte der Eisenbahnen der Österreichisch-ungarischen Monarchie*, I, 97).

initial outlay, would reduce the capacity of the railway and increase the cost for motive power, both of which would reduce profits.[20]

However, the advocates of less expensive methods of construction prevailed, and von Gerstner was forced to resign as *Bauführer*. He also voluntarily renounced all claim to the 100,000 florins in stock due him upon completion of the railway. He had previously said that he would refuse compensation if the cost exceeded a certain amount, doing so, as he said, because of the importance of the undertaking for the public welfare and because of his own personal honor.[21] Even if von Gerstner had been allowed to complete the Linz-Budweis Railway as he had wished, he probably would not have been able to introduce steam traction, since that would have encountered the certain opposition of Kaiser Franz I, who was opposed to steam railways, "lest revolution come into the country."[22] In any case, in the early 1830's von Gerstner was looking for another location in which to realize his dream of steam railways.

In Russia, as in Austria, he was to insist on high quality in the construction of railways. He was to continue, too, to disregard his own time and money as well as the expense to stockholders in achieving high quality.

S. I. Mal'tsov claimed that he met von Gerstner in Vienna and persuaded him to come to Russia.[23] However, it is likely that von Gerstner was invited to come to Russia by Major General K. V. Chevkin, chief of the Corps of Mining Engineers (Korpus Gornykh Inzhenerov) and later a strong partisan of railways. It is said that Chevkin was friendly with him because their wives had gone to school together in Vienna.[24] Be that as it may, in 1834 von Gerstner was invited, not to make proposals concerning

20. Franz Anton von Gerstner, *O vygodakh postroeniia zheleznoi dorogi iz Sanktpeterburga v Tsarskoe Selo i Pavlovsk* (St. Petersburg, 1836), p. 49.

21. *Geschichte der Eisenbahnen der Österreichisch-ungarischen Monarchie*, I, 96.

22. Jerome Blum, "Transportation and Industry in Austria, 1815–1848," *Journal of Modern History*, XV (1943), 26.

23. Mal'tsov, p. 39.

24. P. E. Gronskii, "Ocherk vozniknoveniia i razvitiia zheleznykh dorog v Rossii," *Zapiski Moskovskogo Otdeleniia Imperatorskogo Russkogo Tekhnicheskogo Obshchestva*, IV (1886), 11.

the construction of railways, but to inspect the Russian mining and metallurgical industry.[25]

Von Gerstner arrived in Russia in August, 1834, and traveled from St. Petersburg to Moscow and thence to Kazan and the Urals to inspect iron and copper mines and metallurgical factories. On his trip he assembled data on Russian agriculture, industry, and trade. Von Gerstner was impressed by the great natural wealth of the country and thought that the productive forces of Russia should be developed by a system of railways.[26] In September, with the help of the Austrian ambassador to St. Petersburg, Count Karl Ficquelmont, von Gerstner quickly gained access to Nicholas I, who told him of his desire to see a railway built between St. Petersburg and Moscow, if possible by a stock company.[27]

Von Gerstner thereupon prepared a memorandum containing a proposal to provide Russia with an extensive system of railways. This was the first concrete proposal ever made to provide Russia with such a system. The memorandum was sent in a letter to Nicholas I on January 6, 1835. In his letter von Gerstner expatiated upon his past career and qualifications as a railway builder. He cited the advantages which railway construction had brought to England, France, Germany, and especially to America. As a specific example of such advantages, he wrote of the Liverpool-Manchester Railway, which had aided British trade and industry and which had provided a rapid and inexpensive means of transport for travelers. He also mentioned that the Liverpool-Manchester Railway had been beneficial to the state for the transportation of troops to suppress disorders in Ireland—a point which

25. N. A. Kislinskii, *Nasha zheleznodorozhnaia politika po dokumentam arkhiva Komiteta Ministrov* (St. Petersburg, 1902), I, 3; A. I. Shtukenberg, "Iz istorii zheleznodorozhnogo dela v Rossii. Nikolaevskaia doroga mezhdu Peterburgom i Moskvoiu," *Russkaia Starina*, XLVI (1885), 310. Word of von Gerstner's activities had spread to Russia. See, for example, "Chugunnye dorogi i parovye pushni," *Syn Otechestva*, CI (1825), 309; Destrem, pp. 13, 33-35.

26. Österreichisches Haus-, Hof-, und Staatsarchiv, Vienna, letter of Count Karl Ludwig Ficquelmont to Prince Klemens Metternich, 1836, No. 21 (May 5/17); von Gerstner, *O vygodakh*, p. 6.

27. Baron M. A. Korf, "Imperator Nikolai I v soveshchatel'nykh sobraniiakh," *Sbornik Imperatorskogo Russkogo Istoricheskogo Obshchestva*, XCVIII (1896), 125; Christopher Kreeft (trans.), *First Russian Railroad from St. Petersburg to Zarscoe Selo and Pawlowsk* (London, 1837), p. 5.

he no doubt thought would not be lost on Nicholas I—and for transporting the post at one-third of the former cost.

Von Gerstner tried to forestall arguments that might be used against him by stating that the operation of American railways and the Linz-Budweis Railway showed that railways could be operated in areas having severe winters. He also maintained that the expensive earthworks necessary on the Linz-Budweis Railway because of the mountainous terrain would not be necessary on the flat plains of Russia.

Von Gerstner then stated that in no other country on earth would railways be as useful as in Russia, with its tremendous distances. This would be especially so from the standpoint of external and internal security, since any railway which he built between any two provincial cities, could, upon twenty-four-hour advance notice, carry at least 5,000 foot and 500 horse, together with all artillery, baggage, and horses, at a rate of at least 200 versts per day.[28]

Von Gerstner spoke of a "whole system (*set*) of railways," but he talked in concrete terms of a railway between St. Petersburg and Moscow, with an eventual extension to Nizhnii Novgorod, or, even better, to Kazan, which could be joined with the Caspian Sea by an improved steamboat service. There was also mention of a railway from Moscow to Odessa or Taganrog. But von Gerstner's primary aim was the construction of a railway between the capitals. Von Gerstner stated that such a railway would allow travel between these two cities within twenty to twenty-four hours, while troops and provisions could be transported within two to three days. The railway would also help agriculture in the area and would allow the cheap and efficient provisioning of St. Petersburg. If a railway were built from Moscow to Kazan, goods for export could be transported by steamboat and railway from the Caspian Sea to St. Petersburg in ten to fifteen days and help to secure a favorable balance of trade.[29]

Von Gerstner stated that before he could begin to build any

28. "Zapiska glavnoupravliaiuschego putiami soobshcheniia i publichny-mi zdaniiami gr. K. F. Tolia, 17 fevralia 1835 g." *Krasnyi Arkhiv*, LXXVI (1936), 90-92.

29. *Ibid.*, pp. 91-92; V. M. Verkhovskii, *Kratkii istoricheskii ocherk nachala i rasprostraneniia zheleznykh dorog v Rossii po 1897 g. vkliuchitel'no* (St. Petersburg, 1898), p. 21.

main-line railway it would be necessary for him (at his own expense), employing skilled engineers as he had in Austria, to survey the proposed route in order to make accurate estimates of construction costs. He also wished to build a small experimental railway. If this railway was an unqualified success, von Gerstner said, he would start building the railway between St. Petersburg and Moscow. In any event, he would not set up a stock company for the construction of a St. Petersburg–Moscow Railway for a period of at least two years from the date of the granting of his privilege, and then only if it had been proven that railway construction in Russia was feasible.[30]

In return for the promise to build railways under the abovementioned conditions, von Gerstner asked for concessions from the Russian government which seemed large, especially when one considers that these concessions were for the whole of Russia, not just for one railway.

Von Gerstner asked for the following terms:

A privilege, exclusive for the first twenty years, to build both main-line and branch railways in Russia, the Grand Duchy of Finland, and the Kingdom of Poland. Any railway built without von Gerstner's permission during the first twenty years would become his property. He would have the right to build railways wherever he wished, without advance permission by the government.

To carry out any railway project, von Gerstner asked for the right to form a stock company, the statutes of which would be reviewed and approved in advance by the government.

Von Gerstner's railways were to have all the privileges of construction projects undertaken by the state, both in respect to the railway itself and to the necessary auxiliary establishments; all state lands necessary would be ceded by the state to von Gerstner without compensation, and the peasants living on such lands would be compensated by the state. Lands owned by private individuals would be ceded by mutual agreement. If no agreement was reached, the land could be taken upon proper legal evaluation according to the law of eminent domain. Both state and private lands were to be ceded under the same conditions for building inns to a distance of one verst to either side

30. "Zapiska Tolia,"*Krasnyi Arkhiv*, LXXVI (1936), 93.

of the railway and for factories and other industrial establishments to a distance of three versts to either side of the railway throughout its entire length. Von Gerstner would have the exclusive right to build such factories, which would also be exempted from all taxation for a period of ten years.

Rails for the railways to be built by von Gerstner were to be manufactured in Russia, but, if he so wished, he was to have the right to import rails from abroad duty free.[31]

Von Gerstner was to have the right to determine the type of motive power to be used on any railway built by him. He was also to have the right to set rates for the transportation of passengers and freight. (Military personnel and supplies and the government post were to be transported at a 50 per cent discount.)

Railways built by von Gerstner, the land under them, and the appurtenances belonging to them, as well as all revenues gained, were to be exempt from all taxation for a period of fifty years.

At the end of fifty years the stock company formed by von Gerstner was still to own all movable and immovable properties of the railways constructed, but would have the right to sell them either to the government or to private persons. At this time the government would be obliged to renew the privilege, if it had been proven that the railways constructed served the public interest.

In return for these concessions, von Gerstner promised to have 100 versts of railway open to traffic within four years, using English rails, or within six years, using Russian rails. If he failed to do this, the privilege was to become invalid.[32] Although he asked for a considerable number of concessions from the Russian

31. This last-mentioned concession would be a large one, since in the 1830's all import of iron and cast iron by sea was forbidden and the customs duties for imports by land were prohibitively high (Ludwik Tengoborskii, *Commentaries on the Productive Forces of Russia* [London, 1855], II, 109; G. P. Nebol'sin, *Statisticheskoe obozrenie vneshnei torgovli v Rossii* [St. Petersburg, 1850], II, 210). By the customs tariff of 1822 the duty was 250 per cent of the cost of iron and 600 per cent of the cost of pig iron (P. I. Liashchenko, *History of the National Economy of Russia to the 1917 Revolution* [New York, 1949], p. 338).

32. Borichevskii, pp. 128-130; "Zapiska Tolia," *Krasnyi Arkhiv*, LXXVI (1936), 92.

government, he did not ask for any form of guarantee of a minimum dividend to the stockholders such as was asked for later railways. In fact, he specifically stated that the government would not have to spend any money on his projects.[33]

Von Gerstner admitted in his letter to Nicholas I of January 6, 1835, that he had requested many concessions, but stated that Franz I had granted similar concessions in September, 1824, in connection with the proposed railway between Budweis and Mauthausen.[34] Actually only a few of the concessions granted by Kaiser Franz I were as wide in scope as those requested from Nicholas I.[35] In asking for so many and such wide concessions, perhaps von Gerstner was using the negotiating technique of asking initially for as much as possible, with the hope of receiving reasonable terms later. In subsequent negotiations he scaled down his original requests in the hope of reaching a concrete agreement.

Nevertheless, Nicholas I was interested in von Gerstner's proposals. P. P. Mel'nikov has said that he, better than any of those surrounding him, understood the importance of railways, especially for Russia, in which such great distances had to be covered.[36] His interest in railways was surely in keeping with his previous interest in Russia's waterways and roads, especially in newer techniques of road building. Nicholas I seldom, however, gave his approval of a proposition without assigning a committee to study it. In this case he first handed von Gerstner's proposals over to the Main Administration of Transport and Buildings.

The head, Count K. F. Toll, received von Gerstner's letter, together with the project and supplementary materials, on January 14, 1835. He then set up a commission of four members of the Main Administration of Transport and Buildings: Lieutenant General K. I. Potier, who was then director of the Institute of Transport Engineers; Major General A. D. Gottmann; Colonel Z. von Laurenberg; and Major P. P. Mel'nikov. This commission

33. P. P. Migulin, *Russkii gosudarstvennyi kredit* (*1769–1899*) (Kharkov, 1899–1904), I, 253; "Zapiska Tolia," *Krasnyi Arkhiv*, LXXVI (1936), 92.

34. "Zapiska Tolia," *Krasnyi Arkhiv*, LXXVI (1936), 92.

35. For details of the privilege of September 7, 1824, see *Geschichte der Eisenbahnen der Österreichisch-ungarischen Monarchie*, I, 92-94.

36. P. P. Mel'nikov, "Svedeniia o russkikh zheleznykh dorogakh," ed. M. Krutikov, *Krasnyi Arkhiv*, XCIX (1940), 150.

studied von Gerstner's materials and by January 29 was ready to submit its report, which dealt with von Gerstner's proposals from the standpoint of (1) their technological feasibility and (2) their effect on the interests of the state.

Concerning the first question, the commission found that the example of von Gerstner's Linz-Budweis Railway showed that railways could operate in snow and severe cold and that the level terrain of Russia would facilitate railway building. The commission decided that either steam or horse traction could be used but suggested that the former be used for passenger traffic and the latter for freight traffic. Count Toll in his memorandum added that von Gerstner, because of his knowledge of and earlier successes in building railways in Austria, would be competent to build them in Russia.[37]

The question whether the terms of the privilege requested by von Gerstner were in the interest of the state was more complicated. The commission during the course of its discussions held many conversations with von Gerstner, who agreed to alter some of its terms. But there remained several points which the commission was reluctant to approve.

Instead of giving von Gerstner a privilege to construct railways throughout Russia, the commission recommended that a privilege be granted only for a specific railway route. Other entrepreneurs should be forbidden to construct a parallel railway but might build railways elsewhere in Russia. Count Toll proposed that von Gerstner be allowed to build a railway only if he convinced the government of its usefulness first and stated the route of the railway and the kind of railway to be built.

As for the question of duty-free import of rails from England, both the commission and Count Toll were of the opinion that rails could be produced in Russia and that therefore it was not necessary to import them from England.

Although the commission found it fitting that the state should cede land without compensation for the railway and all necessary auxiliary establishments, it objected to a similar cession of land for inns. Count Toll asserted that if von Gerstner received this right he might be able to compel the cession of land wherever

37. "Zapiska Tolia," *Krasnyi Arkhiv*, LXXVI (1936), 93-94, 97; Mel'-nikov, "Svedeniia," *Krasnyi Arkhiv*, XCIX (1940), 145.

he wished without regard to the public interest or to the fact that the land in question might be occupied by important government establishments. He felt also that, though railways might be in general useful to the state, the right to obtain land gratis for the building of inns should not be granted, since this right was not essential for the construction of railways. Count Toll remarked that von Gerstner compared the terms of his privilege with those granted to Charles Baird for steamboats, but Count Toll felt that Baird's privilege was to be distinguished from that requested by von Gerstner in that Baird had asked for no condition which might infringe on public or private property rights. The Count was also of the opinion that von Gerstner should not be given the right to have his privilege renewed after fifty years.[38]

The papers submitted originally by von Gerstner, together with the full report of the commission and Count Toll's additional remarks, were given on February 3 to Nicholas I, who stated that he was in general agreement with the report of the commission but felt that von Gerstner should be allowed to import rails for the first 500 versts of railway. He also made a few notes on the text of the requested privilege and then gave Count Toll further instructions for negotiations with von Gerstner on setting up an amended text of the privilege.

Count Toll then conferred with von Gerstner, who agreed to the deletion of some of the terms of the original privilege and the addition of some others. This revised draft was submitted on February 12 to the Tsar, who gave his approval with the proviso that the privilege was not to apply to the Grand Duchy of Finland.

On February 17, 1835, Nicholas I received officially the final draft of the request for an exclusive privilege to build railways in Russia signed by von Gerstner, together with a lengthy and detailed memorandum describing the negotiations between von Gerstner and the Main Administration of Transport and Buildings in the preceding month.[39]

38. "Zapiska Tolia," *Krasnyi Arkhiv*, LXXVI (1936), 94-97.
39. *Ibid.*, pp. 97-98; Mel'nikov, "Svedeniia," *Krasnyi Arkhiv*, XCIX (1940), 145. The terms of the privilege requested by von Gerstner were altered in the following respects: Von Gerstner was to receive a thirty-year exclusive privilege to build railways throughout Russia, except in the Grand Duchy of Finland (factory railways were also exempted from the

In view of the importance of the matter of railways for the state, the Tsar decided to have a committee formed at a high level to discuss the matter further. This committee was made up of some of the members of the State Council: Count Toll; Count N. N. Novosil'tsev, chairman of the State Council; Count A. I. Chernyshev, the minister of war; Count E. F. Kankrin, the minister of finance; Count D. N. Bludov, minister of the interior; and Count M. M. Speransky. Nicholas I asked that the head of the Third Section, Count A. K. Benckendorff, and Prince P. M. Volkonskii, minister of the imperial court and appanages, be added to this committee. These were two men for whom Nicholas I felt personal friendship. Count Benckendorff was one of the Tsar's closest associates. Prince Volkonskii, a personal friend of Alexander I, continued under Nicholas I to be on familiar terms with the imperial family. Nicholas I also decided that the deliberations of the committee should take place in his presence.

In discussing matters which he considered especially important, Nicholas I preferred unofficial committees to the State Council, since such committees consisted only of members whom he had chosen and the matter at hand could be discussed informally without set rules of procedure. Any decision reached could be carried out in the form of a direct imperial command. The Tsar was frequently present at the meetings of such committees and often took a leading role in them.[40]

This committee was formed on February 17, 1835. Von Gerstner's project and the memorandum prepared by Count Toll were submitted to each member. The committee met—for the first and

---

restrictions of the terms of the privilege). Von Gerstner might build railways anywhere that he wished, but, before undertaking construction of any railway, he would have to submit plans to the government for approval in advance. The government also reserved the right of controlling passenger and freight rates. In each of the provinces in which von Gerstner had proposed to build railways, at least 50 versts would have to be built within ten years, or the privilege would become invalid for that province. Auxiliary buildings necessary for the railway could be constructed on state lands ceded without compensation, but only on a strip of land extending for 100 sazhens on either side of the railway. However, von Gerstner could receive state lands to build factories to a distance of 2 versts on either side of the railway. (The question of building inns seems to have been omitted entirely.) (Virginskii, *Vozniknovenie*, pp. 136-137.)

40. Verkhovskii, p. 24; Korf, p. 125; for a more complete discussion of this aspect of the Tsar's methods see Riasanovsky, pp. 188-192.

last time—on February 28, 1835.[41] Nicholas I opened the meeting by stating all the advantages which he felt large-scale railway construction would bring to Russia and stressed especially the speedy movement of troops. He then presented two questions for discussion by the committee: (1) the usefulness of the railways in general and (2) whether to accept von Gerstner's proposals for building railways in Russia.[42]

As to the first question, most members of the committee agreed that railways would be useful. Count Kankrin objected that railways would harm the peasant carting industry and perhaps waterways, but the other members of the committee said that peasant carters would have the opportunity to find new means of livelihood, and railways would create new occupations and new markets for products, which would benefit the population.

Concerning the second question, there was more discussion by members of the committee. The questions of the feasibility of railways in general and of the terms of von Gerstner's exclusive privilege were considered more or less to have been settled already. But another issue not specifically discussed previously was raised, that of the financial feasibility of von Gerstner's proposals, that is, whether the necessary capital could be raised and whether there would be enough revenue to cover costs of operation and maintenance and to pay a dividend to the stockholders.

Count Kankrin and Prince Volkonskii said that the capital would have to come from abroad and therefore all profits would accrue to foreigners, and the government would receive no direct benefit for fifty years, until it could levy taxes on the railways. But the other members of the committee, especially Speransky, contended that, even if the capital were supplied by foreigners and profits were paid them, the increased economic activity and employment within Russia resulting from the construction and operation of the railway would benefit Russians more than foreigners. Several members of the committee remarked that because of the undeveloped condition of Russia's internal trade and the cheapness of water transportation there was no certainty that a railway would produce enough revenue to cover operation and maintenance costs and reward the stockholders.

41. Korf, p. 123.   42. *Ibid.*, pp. 125-126.

Nicholas I, in answer to a suggestion of Count Toll that the profitableness of privately-built railways was primarily the concern of the company stockholders, laid down a principle which was to continue to determine the attitude of the Russian government toward private railway ventures. He stated that such a gigantic undertaking as railway construction, affecting the whole empire and bound up with the general interest of the state, went far beyond the interests of the private investor. Therefore the state should not allow any railway venture without being assured in advance that it would be profitable and would not ruin the stockholders. Both the dignity of the state and its material interests demanded this. If stockholders were ruined they would have the right to complain that they had been misled by the privilege granted by the government and by Nicholas I's personal support of the venture, and the Treasury would have to take over the burden of operating and maintaining these railways.[43]

By enunciating this policy Nicholas I gave the opponents of railways, such as Count Kankrin, and also the partisans of railways, such as Count Speransky, cause to judge von Gerstner's proposals, as well as those put forth by others later in the 1830's, very critically from the financial standpoint. It was this question of the financial feasibility of railways built either by private companies or by the state that was to be the main issue in the railway question until the authorization of the St. Petersburg–Moscow Railway in January, 1842.

Count Toll seems to have acted in a relatively objective manner during this period. Thirty years afterward Mel'nikov remarked that Count Toll became a determined opponent of railways only later.[44] He had been a little more severe when considering von Gerstner's original proposals than the commission under him but, at this time, could be considered by Baron M. A. Korf, who was present at the meeting of February 28, 1835, to be an advocate of railways.[45] It is also interesting to note that Nicholas I appointed Count Toll to the special committee, while Count Kankrin was not included. There is no doubt about the

43. *Ibid.*, pp. 126-127.
44. Mel'nikov, "Svedeniia," *Krasnyi Arkhiv*, XCIX (1940), 150.
45. Korf, p. 125.

position of Count Kankrin, the minister of finance. From the very beginning he was against granting a privilege to von Gerstner.

The meeting of the committee closed with the decision to form a special committee of four members: Count Toll as chairman, Count Speransky, Count Novosil'tsev, and Baron Korf. This special committee would conduct further negotiations with von Gerstner. Also Count Toll was to send one of his officers to inspect the Linz-Budweis Railway. Count Kankrin was also to send his agents to find out what benefits this railwway had brought to trade and commerce in Austria.[46]

The special committee was to exist for nearly a year, carrying on negotiations with von Gerstner. It was disbanded on February 11, 1836, when its functions were transferred to the Main Administration of Transport and Buildings. The discussion of the special committee at first centered on the possibility of von Gerstner's building main-line railways, more particularly the railway between St. Petersburg and Moscow with an extension to Nizhnii Novgorod. However, the question of a railway between St. Petersburg and Tsarskoe Selo, first proposed by von Gerstner in March, 1835, gradually became more important, especially from December, 1835, on.

The activity of the special committee, which in the opinion of one contemporary was set up through the influence of one of the Tsar's favorites, Prince P. G. Oldenburg, who was friendly to von Gerstner,[47] was, if so, nonetheless marked by a great deal of caution. Michael Speransky, an aging bureaucrat, was an intelligent and enlightened man concerned with the progress and welfare of the empire, but also a cautious man. Although he, like Nicholas I, understood the importance of railways, he was well aware of the largeness of the undertaking.[48] Speransky was of the opinion that the government should encourage new enterprises, but only ones likely to be successful. One or two conspicuous failures would irreparably destroy the confidence of the public in similar undertakings[49] Count Toll, although at this time not definitely opposed to railways, as he became later,[50]

46. *Ibid.*, p. 128.   47. Gronskii, p. 11.
48. Mel'nikov, "Svedeniia," *Krasnyi Arkhiv*, XCIX (1940), 150.
49. Virginskii, *Vozniknovenie*, p. 142.
50. See chap. v below.

had nevertheless adopted a conservative and critical attitude toward the proposals of von Gerstner.

Count Kankrin, who had already voiced objections to railways in the committee meeting of February 28, once out of the presence of Nicholas I, went further; he submitted memoranda to the special committee giving more detailed objections to the introduction of railways into Russia. At least one pre-Soviet authority has expressed the opinion that these admonitions were partially instrumental in producing a fundamental change in the attitude of the committee. Whereas before there had been a spirit of optimism, now there was a feeling of doubt.[51]

Von Gerstner, perhaps aware of the fact that he was going to encounter stronger opposition to his plans, on March 9, 1835—that is, ten days before the first report of the special committee —made a petition to the government to found a stock company with a capital of 3 million rubles, to build a railway from St. Petersburg to Tsarskoe Selo, Pavlovsk, and Kolpino as an experiment to show the advantages of railways to the state, the possible stockholders, and the general public. Von Gerstner estimated yearly revenues of 600,000 rubles and operation and maintenance costs of 300,000 rubles, thereby giving a yearly profit of 10 per cent on the original capital. This company would be obligated to prepare plans for the railway between St. Petersburg and Moscow. Von Gerstner, with the help of engineers chosen by him, would carry out the preliminary surveys and actual work on construction of the experimental railway, assuming personal responsibility for the quality of construction. But he would make no purchases and conclude no contracts without authorization of the company.[52]

Von Gerstner, who in his original letter to Nicholas I of January 6, 1835, had made brief mention of such an "experimental" railway, had built a similar railway in the Vienna Prater before embarking on the construction of the Linz-Budweis Railway. But the proposal of March 9 was the first of a definite route for such a railway. The special committee's answer to von Gerstner was that, limited in scope as his project was, it would probably not attract enough capital, since in the opinion of the com-

51. Kislinskii, I, 11.   52. Verkhovskii, p. 27.

mittee there was little prospect that the enterprise would be profitable.[53]

Von Gerstner was not daunted, since in March, 1835, the railway between the capitals was still his primary concern. In the first three weeks of March, the special committee entered into written and verbal negotiations with him on this matter and on March 19, 1835, submitted a memorandum to the Tsar, in which it was stated that the estimates given by von Gerstner were without concrete proof and therefore unsatisfactory. Nicholas I told the special committee to report its findings to von Gerstner so that he could give more definite proof.[54] This the committee did and also asked where von Gerstner would collect the necessary capital.

Von Gerstner submitted a memorandum to the special committee in which he stated that the railway between the capitals would be about 600 versts in length (that is, over 70 versts shorter than the Moscow *Chaussée*) and would have branch lines with a total length of about 100 versts.[55] He stated that the subgrade would cost 40 million rubles; bridges, 5 million rubles; rails and other metal products, 23 million rubles; rolling stock (600 carriages, 30 locomotives or 200 horses) and auxiliary buildings, 7 million rubles. Total: 75 million rubles. Yearly revenues would be 6 million rubles from passengers (120,000 passengers at 50 rubles per passenger) and 9 million rubles from freight (12 million poods at 75 kopecks per pood). Total: 15 million rubles. Of this sum one-half, that is, 7.5 million rubles, would be used for operation and maintenance. The rest would be a profit of 7.5 million rubles, giving a profit of 10 per cent on the original capital.[56] He still gave no definite proof for his figures. As for what means he had at his disposal, von Gerstner merely answered that

53. Virginskii, *Vozniknovenie*, p. 162.
54. V. V. Salov, "Nachalo zheleznodorozhnogo dela v Rossii, 1836-1855," *Vestnik Evropy,* CXCVI (1899), 232; Verkhovskii, pp. 26-27.
55. Virginskii, *Vozniknovenie,* p. 140; von Gerstner wanted to make the route longer, so that it might go through all the larger settlements, such as Novgorod and Torzhok, to give the railway more economic value, but Nicholas I wanted the railway built in a straight line, so that the journey could be made within one day, presumably to make military transport more rapid (Oscar Matthesius, *Russische Eisenbahnpolitik im XIX. Jahrhundert, 1836-1881* [Inaugural dissertation, Berlin, 1903], p. 24, n. 1).
56. Borichevskii, p. 131.

he would set up a company, once the privilege had been granted to him.[57]

Von Gerstner's estimates were given to the Commission of Projects and Estimates of the Main Administration of Transport and Buildings for further consideration. On April 24, Lieutenant General M. Destrem, who was head of the commission, reported that, although the commission had found the estimates of revenue reliable, it had come to the conclusion, using data based upon the costs of construction of the Liverpool-Manchester Railway and the Moscow *Chaussée*, that von Gerstner had greatly underestimated the costs of construction and maintenance and that the profits to the stockholders would therefore be less than he had estimated.[58]

The special committee informed von Gerstner that his estimates were not sufficiently supported and that it was also questionable whether he could find the necessary capital. The committee added that the government felt itself obliged to support only well-considered and solid enterprises, since otherwise the steadily growing number of potential investors in Russia might lose confidence in such enterprises.[59]

On April 20, 1835, von Gerstner had written a memorandum, *Mémoire sur l'avantage de l'introduction des chemins de fer en Russie,* in which he argued the advantages of railways and pointed out particularly the advantages which the Russian government would have had in recent wars waged against the Turks, Persians, and Poles if Russia had had a railway system. Von Gerstner also emphasized his qualifications and experience as academician and railway builder. In conclusion, he said that he was willing to content himself with the construction of a railway between St. Petersburg and Tsarskoe Selo if he did not receive permission to build the railway between the capitals.[60]

This memorandum, together with a report of the activities of the special committee since March, was given by Count Toll to Nicholas I on June 8, 1835. The Tsar studied these papers and

57. Salov, p. 232.
58. Mel'nikov, "Svedeniia," *Krasnyi Arkhiv,* XCIX (1940), 146-147; Virginskii, *Vozniknovenie,* p. 141.
59. Verkhovskii, p. 28.
60. Mel'nikov, "Svedeniia," *Krasnyi Arkhiv,* XCIX (1940), 147; Virginskii, *Vozniknovenie,* p. 131.

handed them back to Count Toll with a notation that he had read these papers with great interest and was still convinced, as before, of the advantages of railways. But he was not sure that von Gerstner could obtain enough capital to undertake such a huge enterprise as the St. Petersburg–Moscow Railway and wished that he could have more proof from von Gerstner either by letter or in a personal audience. The railway to Tsarskoe Selo would be authorized, however, if plans were presented.

On June 19 von Gerstner's papers and Nicholas' notation were given by Count Toll to Speransky, who, because of Toll's coming absence from the capital because of ill health, was to assume further responsibility for negotiations between the special committee and von Gerstner. Count Novosil'tsev was to be chairman of the committee during Toll's absence.[61]

On July 2, 1835, the special committee sent a memorandum to Nicholas I containing its general observations on the formation of stock companies for railway construction in Russia. It was suggested that von Gerstner be informed that he might build railways only upon formation of a company with proof of sufficient capital or credit. The government would support such a company in a manner consistent with the laws and interests of the state. As for the railway to Tsarskoe Selo, von Gerstner might build it without special permission if it were built by a company formed for building the railway between St. Petersburg and Moscow. But if a separate company were formed for this purpose, because of the risk of lack of profits, it should have to have special authorization, which should be granted only upon petition by reliable investors. These considerations were approved by Nicholas and reported to von Gerstner by Count Novosil'tsev on July 6.[62]

In the spring of 1835 the main concern had been whether von Gerstner's estimates were accurate; now in the summer of 1835 it was whether he could attract enough capital and credit to form a stock company to build a railway. Both the Tsar and the special committee were thinking increasingly in terms of a railway to Tsarskoe Selo, but the primary issue was still the railway between the capitals.

61. Verkhovskii, pp. 28-29; Salov, p. 233.
62. "Proekt otveta," *Krasnyi Arkhiv*, LXXVI (1936), 101; Salov, p. 234.

In July, 1835, the main interest of von Gerstner, too, was still the railway between the capitals. He stated that he would find the necessary capital for the longer railway and added that, while he had been on a trip to Moscow, Prince D. V. Golitsyn, Count S. G. Stroganov, Johann Plitt, consul of the Free City of Frankfurt am Main, and Count Benckendorff had indicated their readiness to participate in the financing of the construction of the railway to Tsarskoe Selo as an experiment before construction of the railway between St. Petersburg and Moscow.[63]

Von Gerstner wished to make surveys of the routes over which he hoped to build railways to obtain a more accurate estimate of construction costs as he had already suggested in his letter to Nicholas I on January 6, 1835.[64] Accordingly, in August, 1835, he requested and received permission to make surveys along the Moscow *Chaussée*. During the autumn, von Gerstner at his own expense made surveys of more than 800 versts and had other engineers survey an additional 100 versts.[65]

At first von Gerstner had wanted a privilege before setting up a stock company to build a railway, but he was now willing to reverse the order. He therefore sought permission to have prospectuses printed at his own expense to be distributed without charge both in Russia and abroad to invite investment in a stock company to build a railway between St. Petersburg and Moscow. In the prospectus it would be stated that von Gerstner had the exclusive right to form such a company upon condition that within a year of the date of publication of the prospectus 100 million rubles was subscribed and 5 million rubles was actually on hand. The rights that would be granted to the company by the government would be stated in the prospectus. Von Gerstner also requested that the government agree that when 50 million rubles had been subscribed the subscribers would be allowed to select a committee which together with von Gerstner would negotiate further with the government. As for the terms of the privilege that were to be advertised, von Gerstner was willing to make substantial concessions.[66]

63. Mel'nikov, "Svedeniia," *Krasnyi Arkhiv*, XCIX (1940), 147.
64. See p. 76 above.
65. Von Gerstner, *O vygodakh*, p. 6; Shtukenberg, p. 310.
66. (1) The privilege could be granted not in his name alone but in the names of the founders of the company which he set up. (2) An ex-

The special committee, in answer to his new proposals, replied, with imperial approval, that the government was still convinced of the potential benefits of railways in Russia and was always prepared to help and protect such an undertaking. If a company with sufficient capital and credit requested permission to construct a railway along a definite route, the government would give it all aid consonant with the interests of the state and the laws of the empire. The special committee therefore granted von Gerstner permission to print and distribute prospectuses if he would accept more exacting conditions for setting up the stock company and make concessions in the terms of the privilege he had originally proposed and if he submitted the draft of the prospectus for approval before having it printed.[67] The changes

clusive privilege to build railways in all of Russia was no longer requested, but only for a railway linking St. Petersburg, Moscow, and Nizhnii Novgorod and for the environs of the capitals; it was to be provided that no other such privilege would be granted elsewhere for three years. (3) Von Gerstner now proposed to use rails manufactured in Russia, if Russian ironmasters could deliver them within a year at a price no more than 15 per cent higher than that of English rails delivered at St. Petersburg (Mel'nikov, "Svedeniia," *Krasnyi Arkhiv*, XCIX [1940], 147-148).

67. In respect to setting up the stock company, the special committee stated that the capital actually on hand after one year had to be 20 million rubles, instead of 5 million. When 50 million rubles had been subscribed, the government would enter into negotiations concerning further terms of the privilege only if among the subscribers there were men known in the business world or those who enjoyed public confidence. Von Gerstner would have to select one or more well-known bankers in Russia and one or more abroad who would agree to receive subscriptions.

Upon formation of the company the terms of the privilege would be these: (1) Von Gerstner's company would be granted an exclusive fifty-year privilege, not to build railways throughout Russia, but to build only a railway between St. Petersburg and Moscow with an extension to Nizhnii Novgorod if the company wished. The special committee refused von Gerstner's request that the privilege be extended another fifty years and stated that at the end of fifty years the railway would become the property of the government. (2) The railway was to have every advantage of a project undertaken by the state itself. State lands were to be ceded without charge, both to the railway itself and for necessary auxiliary structures to a distance of 100 sazhens to either side of the railway. (No provision was now made for the cession of land to build inns or factories at a distance greater than 100 sazhens). Privately owned lands could be taken upon proper legal evaluation according to the law of eminent domain, if no voluntary agreement had been reached between the company and the owners. This provision was to apply only while the railway was being built. Afterward additional private lands could be acquired only by volun-

in the terms suggested for the privilege were in keeping with recommendations that Count Toll had made during the February deliberations. These terms offered by the special committee were presented to Nicholas I on December 3, 1835, and were confirmed by him.[68]

Even though von Gerstner seemed now to have a privilege for building the St. Petersburg–Moscow Railway within his grasp, his dream was not to be realized. He was not able to interest Russian and foreign investors in his project. The special committee had felt that von Gerstner would not be able to attract foreign capital unless Russian bankers enjoying a European reputation supported the enterprise. Apparently they did not. Von Gerstner might have raised the necessary capital if the government had given some form of direct financial aid by taking some of the shares of stock itself or by guaranteeing a minimum yearly profit to the stockholders. The special committee had stated that, since von Gerstner's personal credit was unreliable, the government might take part in the enterprise, but they were reluctant to recommend this because of the indefiniteness of von Gerstner's estimates of the probable construction cost and the revenues.[69]

---

tary agreement. Appanage lands were to be ceded by the same procedures as private lands. If the railway ran through localities having important buildings, either state-owned or private, the general rules for the acquisition of land were not to apply, but special permission would have to be obtained in each case. (3) The railway would be exempt for fifty years from all taxes and levies. (4) The committee retreated from the stand of the commission of the Main Administration of Transport and Buildings by allowing von Gerstner to fix passenger and freight rates, stating that the public was not compelled to use the railway but could use the *chaussée* as an alternate form of transportation. (5) The company could import duty-free all necessary machines, locomotives, and other rolling stock. However, the special committee did not allow von Gerstner to import rails from England without customs duties. It was stated that the government would supply the Russian rail manufacturers with whom von Gerstner entered into agreement with the necessary tools and equipment without charge (*ibid.*, pp. 148-149).

68. Contrary to the stipulation of the special committee, Nicholas I allowed von Gerstner to import rails duty-free for the first 500 versts of his railway (*ibid.*, p. 150).

69. *Ibid.*, p. 150; Virginskii, *Vozniknovenie*, pp. 143-144. Von Gerstner's cause had probably not been helped when in June Lieutenant Colonel N. O. Kraft, who had been sent to Austria in March by Count Toll, returned to Russia and gave an unfavorable report on von Gerstner's performance

At the same time that von Gerstner was trying to attract capital for the railway between Moscow and St. Petersburg, he was beginning to direct his efforts more and more toward building the "experimental" railway between St. Petersburg and Tsarskoe Selo and Pavlovsk. From December, 1835, to March 21, 1836, when it was authorized, this project gained in importance. Even as late as February, 1836, however, von Gerstner asked for permission to conduct further surveys along the route between the capitals. The special committee refused his request, stating that such a request should not be granted until the Tsarskoe Selo Railway had been completed and had shown the practicableness of such enterprises.[70]

In late November, 1835—before it had become obvious that he would not be able to assemble the necessary capital for a main-line railway—von Gerstner had repeated his proposal of March 9, 1835, to build a short railway. Whereas then he had proposed to build a railway St. Petersburg–Tsarskoe Selo–Pavlovsk–Kolpino, he now proposed to build two such railways: St. Petersburg–Tsarskoe Selo–Pavlovsk and St. Petersburg–Peterhof–Oranienbaum. The former was to be completed in 1836 and the latter in 1837, if he was allowed to import English rails duty-free.[71]

This request was submitted to Nicholas I, who on December 17, 1835, stated that if von Gerstner and a stock company formed by him were able to assemble the necessary capital and submitted the exact route of the proposed railways to government approval, the government was willing to authorize the project and give aid to it.[72]

In a letter to von Gerstner of December 21, 1835, Count Novosil'tsev outlined more explicitly the government's policy toward these two small railways. Von Gerstner might invite participation of investors both in Russia and abroad. His company

---

in building the Linz-Budweis Railway, stating that von Gerstner had greatly underestimated construction costs and that the railway had yielded a small profit to the stockholders only after several years of deficit operation (Verkhovskii, p. 32; Mel'nikov, "Svedeniia," *Krasnyi Arkhiv*, XCIX [1940], 146).

70. Salov, p. 235.
71. Mel'nikov, "Svedeniia," *Krasnyi Arkhiv*, XCIX (1940), 154.
72. Salov, p. 235.

would have a ten-year exclusive privilege to build railways from St. Petersburg to Tsarskoe Selo–Pavlovsk and St. Petersburg to Peterhof–Oranienbaum. The privilege for the actual construction of the railways would be given only when the amount of the capital had been subscribed and one-fifth was actually on hand. Each investor had to deposit one-fifth of the amount pledged in a banking house designated by von Gerstner. The capital had to be assembled within a year from the date of publication of a prospectus, and the two railways had to be built within two years from the date of the granting of the privilege or it would be invalid.[73] The conditions stipulated in Count Novosil'tsev's letter for the setting up of the stock company and for the terms of the privilege itself (cession of state and private lands, freedom from taxation, fixing of passenger and freight rates, the exclusive use of Russian rails, etc.) were similar to those stipulated on December 3, 1835, for the building of the St. Petersburg–Moscow Railway except for the length of the privilege and the lack of any reversion to the government. The government's policy toward von Gerstner's two small railways was the result of opinions formed and decisions made during the course of the year 1835 in connection with the discussion concerning the construction of main-line railways.

In January, 1836, von Gerstner turned to the Russian public to attract capital for his smaller enterprise. Just as in October, 1824, he had written a pamphlet, *Über die Vortheile einer Eisenbahn zwischen der Moldau und der Donau*, to attract capital for that project, so in January, 1836, he composed a similar pamphlet entitled *O vygodakh postroeniia zheleznoi dorogi iz Sanktpeterburga v Tsarskoe Selo i Pavlovsk* (*On the Advantages of Building a Railway from St. Petersburg to Tsarskoe Selo and Pavlovsk*). Twelve thousand copies of this pamphlet, printed in Russian, French, and German, were to be distributed without charge throughout the empire.[74]

Before he wrote his pamphlet, von Gerstner made very careful surveys of the route between St. Petersburg and Tsarskoe Selo–Pavlovsk, which had a total length of 25 versts 250 sazhens. The

73. Von Gerstner, *O vygodakh*, pp. 3-5.
74. *Ibid.*, p. 62; review of von Gerstner, *O vygodakh*, in *Teleskop*, XXXIII (1836), 284.

proposed route of the railway began on a large square then near the center of the city near the junction of the Fontanka and Vedenskii canals. Thence the railway was to go along the Vedenskii Canal at street level to the Obvodnyi Canal, which would be crossed by a substantial bridge. Then there was to be a short curve, the only one on the entire length of the railway. Then the route of the railway would, with very easy gradients, follow a straight line for 24 versts (crossing the Moscow *Chaussée* about halfway at 12.5 versts distance) to the Apollon Church in Pavlovsk Park.[75] The railway was to touch only the outskirts of the town of Tsarskoe Selo, since the main part of the town lay on the slope of a hill, and von Gerstner wanted to avoid all heavy gradients or cuttings which might fill with snow. A connecting omnibus service, or perhaps later a branch line, along the main boulevard of the town or skirting the town limits in a circular route would link the town with the railway and allow passengers to alight where they wished. The whole railway was to be single-tracked and built on an embankment averaging in height 9-10 feet and wide enough to allow a second track to be built later.[76]

Von Gerstner proposed to complete the railway between St. Petersburg and Tsarskoe Selo by October 1, 1836, and to open the extension to Pavlovsk in the spring of 1837. He wished to show during the course of the winter of 1836–1837 that the railway could operate successfully.[77]

Perhaps because the special committee had previously expressed doubts that a railway to Tsarskoe Selo could be profitable (because of a lack of passengers) von Gerstner showed in his pamphlet that there was already considerable traffic by *chaussée* between St. Petersburg and Tsarskoe Selo. He was not relying, however, merely on siphoning off part of this travel to his railway. By building the railway he hoped to create traffic, just as railways were built in America in the hope of encouraging the growth of settlement and commerce. Von Gerstner stated that the climate of St. Petersburg in summer was both unhealthy and

75. Von Gerstner was proposing to build the Tsarskoe Selo Railway in much the same manner in which he had built his part of the Linz–Budweis Railway, that is, substantially in a straight line with as light gradients as the terrain allowed.

76. Von Gerstner, *O vygodakh*, pp. 19-20.

77. *Ibid.*, p. 28.

unpleasant and therefore the population ought to live outside the city. He was of the opinion that more people would build villas in Tsarskoe Selo and Pavlovsk, both of which had a beautiful and healthful location, but for the fact that a dusty journey of two and a half to three hours was necessary to reach them. If a railway offering rapid and inexpensive travel were built, residents of St. Petersburg who had daily business in the city could afford to live in Tsarskoe Selo and commute instead of staying in Tsarskoe Selo only on weekends. Von Gerstner envisioned that if the railway were built the wealthier segments of the population would build villas both in Tsarskoe Selo–Pavlovsk and along the railway. The population of St. Petersburg would also make day excursions to walk in the parks and gardens of Tsarskoe Selo and Pavlovsk both in summer and winter. In Tsarskoe Selo an inn would be built to entertain these people. In Pavlovsk Park a new "Tivoli" would be built as a meeting point for the populace of the capital for dining, dancing, and games on the model of London's Vauxhall Gardens or Vienna's Prater.[78]

Von Gerstner estimated that construction costs would total 3 million rubles, the largest items of expense being rails and rail chairs, rolling stock, auxiliary buildings, embankments, and bridges.[79]

He stated that revenues would come largely from passengers. Basing his estimates on the experience of foreign railways, he noted that when a railway had been built the number of passengers increased yearly, soon exceeding the original estimates. He stated that the yearly number of passengers on a railway was roughly equal to the total population of the area served by it. The area to be served by the Tsarskoe Selo Railway had a total population of about 465,000. Von Gerstner said that he would conservatively estimate the number of passengers at 300,000, but practically all would travel in both directions, making a total of 600,000 tickets sold yearly. If the average fare was 1 ruble 48 kopecks (passengers were to be carried in carriages of three classes, with fares for the trip from St. Petersburg to Tsarskoe Selo ranging from 2 rubles 50 kopecks to 80 kopecks), there would be a yearly passenger revenue of 890,143 rubles. In regard

78. *Ibid.*, pp. 37-39.
79. *Ibid.*, pp. 22-27.

to freight traffic, he estimated that it might be considerable, since there would be traffic to supply the needs of the imperial court and to provision five army regiments stationed in Tsarskoe Selo and Pavlovsk. At a rate of 6 kopecks per pood for ordinary goods, the total yearly revenue from the transportation of freight would be approximately 79,857 rubles. Von Gerstner estimated the total revenue from passenger and freight traffic, plus revenue from the inn at Pavlovsk, at 1 million rubles yearly.[80]

Von Gerstner's estimates of expenses for operation and maintenance of the Tsarskoe Selo Railway were based on those of the Liverpool-Manchester Railway and the Lyons–St. Etienne Railway. Although he admitted that these railways did not have the expense of snow clearance, they did have expenses which the Tsarskoe Railway would not such as the higher cost of land.

If the ratio of passengers and freight revenues to expenses was proportionately the same as on the Liverpool–Manchester Railway, there would be a profit of 521,446 rubles, or 17.5 per cent on the original capital. Even if the Tsarskoe Selo Railway was only as profitable as the Lyons–St. Etienne Railway, there would still be a profit of 406,084 rubles, or 13.3 per cent on the original capital. If the capital of the Tsarskoe Selo Railway was raised to 3.5 million rubles or if there was far less than the anticipated number of passengers, the railway would still give the profit of 5 per cent usual in the empire.[81]

In O vygodakh von Gerstner stated that the building of the Tsarskoe Selo Railway was only the beginning and that it was to be the first railway only because plans had already been drawn up for it and construction could therefore begin immediately, with completion by October 1, 1836. At this time a similar stock company would be established to build the other experimental railway from the terminus of the Tsarskoe Selo Railway in St. Petersburg to Peterhof and Oranienbaum, with completion scheduled for July 1, 1838. Von Gerstner hoped that by that time the

80. Ibid., pp. 42-44.
81. Ibid., pp. 54-57. A. I. Chuprov, writing at a much later period, declared that these estimates of von Gerstner were much more thorough and sound than many estimates made later by other railway entrepreneurs (A. I. Chuprov, "Pervaia zheleznaia doroga v Rossii," in Iz proshlogo russkikh zheleznykh dorog [Moscow, 1909], p. 6).

success of these undertakings would have increased the public's confidence in railways to the extent that it would participate in the building of a railway between St. Petersburg and Moscow, to be completed within six years, and of an extension to Nizhnii Novgorod later. Then another railway would be built between Moscow and Odessa or Taganrog.[82]

Von Gerstner concluded his pamphlet by looking forward to the day when, as in America, the barriers of time and space would be overcome by railways linking all parts of the empire. Then it would be possible to travel from St. Petersburg to Nizhnii Novgorod or Odessa in three days, and goods could be shipped along the same route in ten to fourteen days.[83]

Von Gerstner still had to find the necessary financial backing for his project. He had tried to raise the necessary capital for his St. Petersburg–Moscow Railway project by public subscription but had failed to interest either Russian or foreign investors. He realized that it was quite possible that sufficient capital could not be raised even for the much less expensive Tsarskoe Selo Railway project. Three million rubles was still a large amount of capital to raise in the Russia of the 1830's. Capital was scarce and dispersed, and public distrust of railways was still great. Therefore von Gerstner sought backers who were wealthy enough to subscribe in a short time the necessary capital in a closed subscription, so that the requirements of the government would be satisfied. These backers should be influential enough to induce others to take shares of stock in the company when it was later distributed publicly on a broader basis.

Von Gerstner managed to gain the support of Count A. A. Bobrinskii, an enlightened landowner who had large landholdings in Tula and Kiev provinces and who was a millionaire owning over twelve thousand serfs. On his estates in Kiev Province he had introduced sugar refining factories and was in general interested in the latest advances in science and technology. Also willing to participate in von Gerstner's enterprise were Benedict Kramer, a commercial councilor, merchant of the First Guild, and director of the Russian American Company, and Johann Plitt, consul of the Free City of Frankfurt am Main, whom von

82. Von Gerstner, O vygodakh, pp. 6-7.
83. Ibid., pp. 65-66.

Gerstner had interested in the railway while in Moscow during the preceding summer.

These men were well chosen, since they were wealthy enough by themselves to be able to raise the capital necessary to start with and had good reputations and, between them, close connections with the Russian nobility, the merchant class, and financial circles in Germany. They, together with von Gerstner, were to be the founders of the company formed to build the railway from St. Petersburg to Tsarskoe Selo and Pavlovsk; their participation would instil public confidence in the enterprise.[84]

On February 3, 1836, a letter signed by these four founders, along with a copy of *O vygodakh,* was given to the special committee for consideration. The letter stated that the four founders were convinced of the usefulness of the Tsarskoe Selo Railway for the inhabitants of St. Petersburg and for showing the potential advantages of railways for Russia. The letter further stated that they and a few other people had already subscribed the three million rubles of capital and that one-fifth of this sum was already on hand. Therefore a privilege was requested, as well as permission to announce their intention to complete the railway between St. Petersburg and Tsarskoe Selo by October 1, 1836, in the St. Petersburg newspapers and to distribute *O vygodakh.*[85]

The special committee, under Count Novosil'tsev, after examining these materials, stated on February 7 that the major obstacle to the granting of a privilege had been removed by the subscription of the necessary capital and that there were no further obstacles to the plan. The special committee therefore decided to give the proposals directly to the Tsar for approval without submitting them first to the State Council, with the recommendation that a ten-year exclusive privilege be granted

84. "Pis'mo Fr. fon Gerstnera predsedateliu osobogo komiteta M. Speranskomu," *Krasnyi Arkhiv,* LXXVI (1936), 101-102. Von Gerstner also tried to gain the support and favor of high government officials in the State Council, including Speransky, by reserving a few shares of stock for them.

85. "Zaiavlenie predsedateliu Gos. soveta gr. N. Novosil'tsevu gr. A. Bobrinskogo, Benedikta Kramera, Frantsa fon Gerstnera i Ivana-Konrada Plitta na privilegii dlia obrazovaniia kompanii Tsarskosel'skoi zhel. dorogi, 3 fevralia 1836 g.," *Krasnyi Arkhiv,* LXXVI (1936), 103-104.

on the bases agreed upon and outlined to von Gerstner in Novo-silʼtsevʼs letter of December 21, 1835. The special committee also asked for imperial permission to disband and to hand over all its papers to the Main Administration of Transport and Buildings, which would continue negotiations with von Gerstner.

On February 11, 1836, Nicholas I agreed to the privilege for the Tsarskoe Selo Railway and to the disbanding of the special committee, but in characteristic fashion he wanted details altered and ordered changes in the proposed route of the railway. If it were to begin within the limits of St. Petersburg, it would have to start at the Obukhov Bridge, 170 sazhens from the starting point proposed by von Gerstner, and proceed along the Obuk-hovskii Prospekt, which was the beginning of the Moscow *Chaussée*, since on the route originally proposed a new gate[86] would have to be built at the city limits. Nicholas proposed as an alternative that the railway should start at the Ligovka on the cityʼs edge over two versts further from the center of the city than the originally proposed starting point. Nicholas also did not want the railway to cross Volkovo Pole, on which was located an artillery proving ground. He wanted to know, too, if his brother the Grand Duke Mikhail Pavlovich would allow the rail-way to go through Pavlovsk Park.[87] Count Toll, in his capacity as head of the Main Administration of Transport and Buildings, reported to the four founders on February 12 that their request for a privilege would be granted with these changes suggested by the Tsar.

On February 17 the founders went to Count Toll, saying that these proposed changes would cause great difficulties and losses to their company. To reroute the railway along the heavily trav-eled Obukhovskii Prospekt would be dangerous for the public and would necessitate the destruction of many buildings. To locate the terminus of the railway outside the city would dis-courage many people from traveling on the railway. Since the railway was the first in Russia, it should be given every advantage. Therefore the company wished to build a new gate at its own

86. A gate (*zastava*) was a wooden barrier at the city limits, at which the documents of travelers entering St. Petersburg were checked. See John S. Maxwell, *The Czar, His Court, and People* (New York, 1848), p. 181.

87. Verkhovskii, pp. 34-36; Melʼnikov, "Svedeniia," *Krasnyi Arkhiv,* XCIX (1940), 157.

expense at the Obvodnyi Canal or the Ligovka and would inspect passengers entering the city either there or at the terminus, allowing nobody to alight between these points. As for the artillery proving ground, the company proposed to drain a marshy area near Volkovo Pole at its own expense and have the artillery proving ground transferred there.

On February 18, the Grand Duke Mikhail Pavlovich inspected the proposed 600-sazhen route through Pavlovsk Park and approved it. He also wrote a letter to Count Toll, stating that the railway was a worthy enterprise and should be encouraged. He wished to contribute to the success of the venture and therefore was allowing the company to build its "Tivoli" in Pavlovsk Park if plans were submitted to him in advance and the land underneath the buildings was not considered the property of the company.

On February 21, Nicholas agreed to these proposals of the company and allowed it to retain the route originally proposed. Passengers should not be allowed to alight within the limits of St. Petersburg until checked by the company at the terminus of the railway under the supervision of the military governor general of St. Petersburg. Nicholas I added two new conditions: (1) the company would be obliged to build a bridge over the Second Obvodnyi Canal, if it were ever built, and (2) for the protection of the public, locomotives would have to carry bells or other warning devices to be used in Pavlovsk Park at all times and everywhere along the railway at night.

All these questions having been settled, Count Toll on March 15 presented the regulations (*polozhenie*) of the company for imperial approval along with a request by the founders that if the original capital of 3 million rubles should prove insufficient to complete the railway, they should be allowed to issue additional stock up to the value of 500,000 rubles.[88] These regulations "concerning the founding of a stock company for the construction of a railway from St. Petersburg to Tsarskoe Selo, with an extension to Pavlovsk" were approved by Nicholas I on March 21, 1836.[89]

88. Verkhovskii, pp. 36-37; Mel'nikov, "Svedeniia," *Krasnyi Arkhiv,* XCIX (1940), 157-158.
89. For the full text, see *Polnoe Sobranie Zakonov Rossiiskoi Imperii,* 2nd

ser., XI, No. 9009 (March 21, 1836), reprinted in von Gerstner, *O vygo-dakh*, pp. 69-72. A summary follows.

The company had an exclusive ten-year privilege to build and operate a railway from St. Petersburg to Tsarskoe Selo with an extension to Pavlovsk. After the expiration of the privilege, the railway was to remain the property of the company. (Giatsintov asserted that the Russian government was giving von Gerstner a free hand because it considered his enterprise more substantial than most [P. N. Giatsintov, "Pravitel'stvo i chastnaia zheleznodorozhnaia promyshlennost' v Rossii v tsarstvovaniia Imperatorov Nikolaia I i Aleksandra II," *Russkoe Ekonomicheskoe Obozrenie*, No. 8 (1902), p. 5]. But the more usual view is that the Russian government did not yet understand the economic and cultural significance of railways and therefore had not yet formulated any real policy toward private railway companies. See, for example, Kislinskii, I, 12-13; I. B. Rozenfel'd, *Pervaia zheleznaia doroga v Rossii [Petrozavodsk*, 1925], p. 53.)

The railway was to run as a single-track railway (with provision to be made for the eventual addition of a second track) along the route originally proposed by von Gerstner with additional permission to build a branch line around the town of Tsarskoe Selo for the convenience of passengers.

If the proposed Second Obvodnyi Canal were built, the company would be obliged to build a bridge over it at its own expense. The artillery proving ground on Volkovo Pole was to be moved by the company to another place proposed by the company at the company's expense.

If the original capital of 3 million paper rubles was not sufficient to build the railway and to put it into operation, the company might issue additional stock to the amount of 500,000 rubles.

The company in building the railway would have all the rights and privileges of works undertaken by the state. Uninhabited state lands necessary for the railway were to be ceded without charge, as were inhabited state lands, with the government compensating any peasants living on it with other land. But the company would have to pay for any buildings belonging to these peasants which it demolished. As for privately owned lands, the company was to attempt to enter into an agreement with the owner. If they could not agree, the law of eminent domain was to apply, with the company paying the price determined by a legally conducted evaluation. The company would be allowed to enter such land before the price had been finally determined. Land obtained from private owners after the completion of the railway would have to be obtained exclusively by free agreement between the company and owners. The rules for the alienation of appanage land were to be the same as those for private land.

The company could obtain state and private lands under the same conditions for auxiliary buildings necessary for the railway—but for no other purpose—to a distance of 100 sazhens to either side of the railway.

The amount of iron necessary for rails would have to be obtained from Russian ironmasters, if they were able to deliver the stipulated amount in acceptable quality and form by the date specified by the company at a price no more than 15 per cent greater than foreign iron delivered at St. Petersburg. If the Russian ironmasters failed to meet these conditions, the company might import foreign iron duty-free but in no greater amount than was necessary to build the railway. This iron was to be used for no other

101

A ukase of the Senate, incorporating the regulations of March 21, 1836, and an order from Nicholas I of February 21 concerning warning devices for locomotives and the regulations for the inspection of passengers entering St. Petersburg, was published on April 15, 1836.[90]

The *Ustav* (statute) of the Obshchestvo Tsarskosel'skoi Zheleznoi Dorogi (Tsarskoe Selo Railway Company), the headquarters of which were in St. Petersburg, was given imperial confirmation on July 6, 1837, and published by a ukase of the Senate on August 12, 1837.[91]

Thus the Tsarskoe Selo Railway, the first railway in Russia except for factory and mine railways, came into being as a corporate entity in the spring of 1836. Between the time of von Gerstner's first proposals of January 6, 1835, and the regulations of March 21, 1836, fourteen and one-half months had elapsed, a comparatively short time in which to reach a decision to build railways. In the final analysis, it was undoubtedly the insistent wishes of Nicholas I himself which led to the authorization of the Tsarskoe Selo Railway, since he hoped that the experiment would justify his favorite project of a railway between the cap-

purpose, and if it were not used it would have to be shipped abroad again at the company's expense. The company was allowed to import duty-free all locomotives, rolling stock, and other machines necessary for the railway.

The company was exempted for the duration of the privilege from all taxes levied by the state.

The company was allowed to build and operate in the town of Tsarskoe Selo an inn for travelers in the manner it deemed most advantageous. Under the same conditions several buildings for the shelter and entertainment of the public might be built in Pavlovsk Park, as long as plans for the type of buildings to be built and of their location were submitted in advance to the Grand Duke Mikhail Pavlovich and as long as the land under them was not considered the property of the company.

The four founders of the company were allowed to form their own agreements with those who were to carry out the actual construction of the railway and might hire engineers, craftsmen, and workers. The founders might dispose of their capital as they saw fit and might fix the number and value of the shares of stock.

Since travel on the *chaussée* remained free as before, the company might fix its own passenger and freight rates.

If the railway were not completed within two years from the date of the granting of the privilege, the privilege would be void.

90. Mel'nikov, "Svedeniia," *Krasnyi Arkhiv*, XCIX (1940), 158-159.

91. For the full text, see *PSZ*, 2nd ser., XII, No. 10419 (July 6, 1837).

itals.[92] It is to be presumed he felt that even if this enterprise failed, it would not be a national disaster, but if it succeeded, further railway construction might be undertaken in the future.

Public opinion did not, of course, have to be considered by the government in Russia as in Western Europe, but it was not negligible. The question whether railways could operate in the Russian winter seems to have remained in many minds despite the answer in the affirmative by the commission of the Main Administration of Transport and Buildings and the committee of February 28, 1835. Ficquelmont, writing in May, 1836, stated that this question was still very much an issue and that the Tsar had let the Tsarskoe Selo Railway be authorized so that von Gerstner could prove thereby that railways could operate in winter.[93] Von Gerstner himself had stated that he wished to complete the Tsarskoe Selo Railway by the winter of 1836 to prove this point.[94] So great were the doubts on all scores that, according to P. P. Mel'nikov, von Gerstner would not have been able to assemble the necessary amount of capital to build even the Tsarskoe Selo Railway had it not been for the help of Count Bobrinskii.[95]

Even though it had not yet by any means been decided that other railways would be built in Russia, the railway question had been brought fully to the attention of the Russian government for the first time through the proposals of von Gerstner, and it had been forced to make some sort of decision on this matter which had such great import for the future of the country. Having carried on extensive negotiations with von Gerstner for over a year, by March, 1836, the Russian government had come to some definite conclusions as to how it should treat proposals for railways in Russia.

As a result of the negotiations, the government showed itself willing to grant an exclusive privilege for a definite number of years to a railway undertaking if it had reliable backers and if

92. Mel'nikov, "Svedeniia," *Krasnyi Arkhiv*, XCIX (1940), 159; Österreichisches Haus-, Hof-, und Staatsarchiv, Ficquelmont to Metternich, 1836, No. 21 (May 5/17).

93. Österreichisches Haus-, Hof-, und Staatsarchiv. Ficquelmont to Metternich, 1836, No. 21 (May 5/17).

94. Von Gerstner, *O vygodakh*, p. 18.

95. Mel'nikov, "Svedeniia," *Krasnyi Arkhiv*, XCIX (1940), 154.

it had a percentage of the necessary capital on hand within a specified time. This exclusive privilege would not be given except for a definite route approved in advance by the government. The term of the privilege would vary acording to the length and relative importance of the railway and the amount of expense involved in construction. The privilege would not be renewed or extended upon its expiration.

The Russian government also showed itself willing to grant concessions such as cession of state land and freedom from taxation. These concessions would deprive the Treasury of potential revenues, but at least would not involve expenditure of funds already on hand.

Once the Russian government had decided in connection with von Gerstner's projects for the Tsarskoe Selo Railway and for a St. Petersburg–Moscow Railway to grant an exclusive privilege and the concessions mentioned above, it was willing to offer approximately the same advantages to promoters of later railway projects, such as those planning to build the Warsaw-Vienna Railway in 1839 and the Leipzig bankers Dufour and Harkort, who proposed to build the St. Petersburg–Moscow Railway in 1841.[96]

The policy of the Russian government toward railways at this time was connected with its policy toward stock companies in general. By 1835 enough stock companies had been formed or were in the process of formation in Russia to prompt the government to draft a general law to regulate them. This law on stock companies was promulgated on December 6, 1836. The terms of this law were in many respects very similar to those of the law of March 21, 1836, bringing the Tsarskoe Selo Railway into existence. For instance, it was stated that an exclusive privilege would be granted for a term of years for an enterprise requiring large preliminary expenses and special technology (railways were cited specifically as an example of such an enterprise) but that this privilege would not be prolonged or renewed. If an enterprise was important enough to the public interest and especially deserving of aid, the government would grant concessions, such as freedom from taxation. However, it was specifically stated that

96. See pp. 195, 208-209 below.

the government would not undertake in any way to guarantee the success of an enterprise.[97]

Such a policy on the part of the Russian government should have allowed stock companies of modest size to come into existence or even a project requiring as much capital as the Tsarskoe Selo Railway. But railways extending hundreds of versts in length would require much larger amounts of capital, which could not be raised either within Russia or abroad at that time by private initiative alone. The failure of von Gerstner to find sufficient capital for his St. Petersburg–Moscow Railway project had shown that the Russian government would have to give some form of direct aid to a private company or build railways itself. Even in the richer countries of Western Europe, except in England, the raising of capital through public subscription of stock or through banks eventually proved inadequate, and some form of direct financial support or construction directly by the state became unavoidable.

Russia had no bankers who could perform the function that such bankers as the Rothschilds did abroad. When the special committee expressed the opinion that von Gerstner would not be able to attract foreign capital unless Russian bankers enjoying a European reputation supported the undertaking, they were understating the problem. It is more likely that only the cooperation of foreign bankers of the stature of the Rothschilds could have made it possible to raise the capital needed, if indeed it could have been raised at all at this time. Private banking houses in St. Petersburg were not joint-stock banks and were small and would hardly have had the necessary standing for so large an enterprise. Count Kankrin abhorred the whole notion of private banks and had effectively prevented their development. Most banking activity in Russia at this time was carried on by the state banking system.

Von Gerstner had been unusually fortunate in being able to raise enough capital for the Tsarskoe Selo Railway through finding men who performed the function of investment bankers by subscribing the necessary capital in a closed subscription and later distributing the shares publicly on a broader basis, part of

97. For the full text, see *PSZ*, 2nd ser., XI, No. 9763 (December 6, 1836).

them to German banks, which in turn distributed the shares to German investors. Much the same method had been used in gathering capital for the Paris–St. Germain Railway, which corresponded in many ways to the Tsarskoe Selo (it was a suburban railway, often called a "toy" by its detractors, and was meant by its promotors first to accustom the people of Paris to railways and second as a segment of a longer railway, Paris–Rouen–Le Havre), and even in France difficulty was experienced in finding the necessary amount.

A St. Petersburg–Moscow Railway was a very different undertaking because of its length. It would have been the largest and most expensive single construction project ever undertaken in Russia, with perhaps the exception of the building of St. Petersburg by Peter the Great. The fact that costly methods of construction were planned and that foreign equipment and personnel would have had to be relied upon intensified the problem. If the assistance of the great banking houses was necessary to gather capital to construct railways of lesser length in such countries as France and Austria, it would certainly have been necessary in Russia for this railway.

But at this stage international bankers could hardly have been expected to be interested in building railways in Russia. Profits would have seemed more certain nearer home in one of the many more densely populated areas where railways were still not built; bankers would hardly have preferred to hold shares in a Russian railway company. As for the people among whom they might have attempted to distribute shares, many considered Russia a distant and semibarbarous land. Dislike and distrust of the Russian political and social system, the instability and fluctuation of Russia's currency, fear that the Russian government might reduce profits by excessive regulation and interference would all have tended to discourage the foreign investor.

It was also unlikely that any large number of investors could be found among the Russian public. That there were well-to-do Russian citizens interested in railways was attested by the fact that half the original capital for the Tsarskoe Selo Railway was to be subscribed by Russians, but finding capital for the much longer St. Petersburg–Moscow Railway would have required the participation of many investors, large and small, and this was another matter.

No class of the population could be depended upon to invest large amounts of capital in a railway. The landowning nobility was the richest class in Russia and therefore invested proportionately more in commercial enterprises than the upper class in countries where industry and trade were better developed, but capital was not plentiful even among members of this class. There were a few Russian landowners who engaged in large-scale capitalistic farming, but most were men of very modest means with little land and few serfs. Even the larger landowners were often in financial straits and were falling increasingly into debt, generally to meet expenses of conspicuous and unproductive consumption, not for the improvement of their estates.

The Russian merchant class was small and weak. There were substantial and progressive merchants, but they were the exception rather than the rule. Most merchants conducted their activities on a limited and local scale and made very small profits. Even larger merchants, who engaged in trade over long distances, often made little profit because of the difficulties of transportation.

Industrial capital also was largely lacking in Russia. Much of Russia's need for manufactured goods continued to be supplied by the so-called cottage industry. Furthermore, one-man businesses and family partnerships had given way in only a few cases to joint-stock companies with sizable capital. The main assets of most factories were land and serf labor.

Furthermore, the little capital that was available in Russia was not likely to be invested in railway enterprises to any significant extent. The public was generally distrustful in money matters and would have been especially doubtful of anything as new and untried as railways. It might have been possible to raise capital for little local lines such as were built in the United States and England, but in sparsely settled Russia few such lines would have been profitable.

Plainly von Gerstner was a little impractical in hoping to raise funds for a railway between St. Petersburg and Moscow at this early date. He was able, however, to go forward with the building of the Tsarskoe Selo Railway.

Chapter IV. The construction and operation of the Tsarskoe Selo Railway; further proposals by Franz Anton von Gerstner to build railways in Russia

Part 1. The Construction of the Tsarskoe Selo Railway (March, 1836–April, 1838)

Almost as soon as the Tsarskoe Selo Railway had been authorized by the regulations (*polozhenie*) of March 21, 1836, construction was begun, since von Gerstner had promised that the railway would be completed by October 1, 1836. Von Gerstner would have to go abroad to order the equipment necessary for the railway, but meanwhile construction of the earthworks, buildings, and bridges was to be started as soon as possible. Getting equipment from abroad in time was to be the main problem, because neither the terrain nor the gathering of a labor supply seemed likely to present any great difficulties. The stock of the company still had to be distributed and on as broad a basis as possible, pursuant to the wishes of Count Kankrin.

Of these three problems—constructing a solid roadbed, getting equipment, and distributing the stock—the last was most easily attended to. The stock originally consisted of 15,000 shares with a value of 200 rubles each. It was subscribed almost immediately after the publication of von Gerstner's *O vygodakh* on March 20, 1836.[1] Many of the stockholders in Russia were of the nobility, but more than a few large stockholders were merchants. Many were naturalized Germans. By January, 1837, there were 700 stockholders, of whom 641 were resident in Russia (predominantly in St. Petersburg and Moscow provinces), while 59 were resident abroad.[2] The foreign stockholders, although rela-

1. Franz Anton von Gerstner, *Pervyi otchet ob uspekhakh zheleznoi dorogi iz Sanktpeterburga v Tsarskoe Selo i Pavlovsk* (St. Petersburg, July 26, 1836), p. 3; Christopher Kreeft (trans.), *First Russian Railroad from St. Petersburg to Zarscoe-Selo and Pawlowsk* (London, 1837), p. 6.

2. Franz Anton von Gerstner, *Third Report on the Railroad from St. Petersburg to Zarscoe-Selo and Pawlowsk* (St. Petersburg, January 29,

tively few in number, held large blocks of stock, nearly 50 per cent of the capital. The stock had been distributed abroad by banking houses, mainly in Germany—especially Dresden—and in Austria. Russia's first railway was built, then, with the help of a great deal of foreign capital.[3]

Von Gerstner's relationship to the Tsarskoe Selo Railway was approximately the same as that which he had had to the Linz-Budweis Railway, except that he was not only managing engineer but also one of the directors. He was to have complete supervision over construction of the railway and choice of engineers and other construction personnel. No other engineers were to be consulted, except for making tests of the quality of construction eight days before the scheduled opening of the railway. He was not to make any purchases and was not to conclude contracts nor make any payments unless authorized by the directors of the company upon his report of the necessary conditions. He was to be responsible personally for any losses caused by faulty work until the inspection eight days before the scheduled opening of the railway. Also, all properties of the company lost or destroyed during construction were to be replaced at von Gerstner's own expense.[4]

In return, von Gerstner asked that 17.5 per cent of the total capital spent be at his personal disposal. As he stated, this percentage was only about one-half of the percentage normally spent by the state for the administration of similar works. Of this 17.5 per cent of the total capital, 4 per cent was to be for preliminary works, including von Gerstner's planned trip to England and for the distribution of *O vygodakh*. Ten per cent was to be used for paying the salaries of engineers and other supervisory personnel and for the costs of their equipment and other expenses. Also this sum was to pay for periodic reports (*otchety*) to the stockholders and the general public informing them of the

1837), p. 14; V. S. Virginskii, *Vozniknovenie zheleznykh dorog v Rossii do nachala 40-ykh godov XIX veka* (Moscow, 1949), p. 165.

3. Franz Anton von Gerstner, *Bericht über den Stand der Unternehmung der Eisenbahn von St. Petersburg nach Zarskoe-Selo und Pawlowsk* (Leipzig, 1838), p. v; *Zheleznaia doroga ot S. Peterburga do Tsarskogo Sela i Pavlovska* (St. Petersburg, 1837), p. 19.

4. Franz Anton von Gerstner, *O vygodakh postroeniia zheleznoi dorogi iz Sanktpeterburga v Tsarskoe Selo i Pavlovsk* (St. Petersburg, 1836) p. 60.

progress of work on the railway. The remaining 3.5 per cent was to be used to help von Gerstner or his engineers pay for any damages for which they might be held responsible.[5]

Von Gerstner lost no time in going abroad to take care of the problem of equipment. A week after the authorization he left for Western Europe to place orders for rails, locomotives, other rolling stock, and miscellaneous equipment which it had not proved possible to procure in Russia, and to engage foreign engineers. He left Austrian engineers to carry out preliminary works in Russia in the meanwhile.[6] Before returning to Russia on June 17, 1836, von Gerstner traveled through a number of countries, but especially England and Belgium, where he inspected several railways. Most of his orders for equipment, a total of eighteen contracts, were placed in these two countries. He chose the very best manufacturers he could find, many of whom he had known for several years. All promised to make deliveries in time to allow the opening of the railway by October 1, 1836.[7]

At first von Gerstner had hoped that he might be able to obtain rails in Russia. Since 1822 the Russian iron industry, although remaining far behind the English, had made advances.[8] In January, 1835, von Gerstner had stated that Charles Baird had told him that rails could be produced in Russia within six months, perhaps in the Urals. In November, 1835, the special committee had come to the conclusion that it would not be difficult to manufacture rails in Russia, since there were rolling machines in the Urals, especially at the Demidov factories, which had produced rails for the Cherepanov railway. The special committee hoped that the Uralian ironmasters would take the initiative and offer to produce rails for the Tsarskoe Selo Railway.[9]

Accordingly, on February 3, 1836—that is, before the granting of the privilege for the Tsarskoe Selo Railway—von Gerstner

5. *Ibid.*, p. 62.
6. *Ibid.*, p. 28.
7. Von Gerstner, *Pervyi otchet*, pp. 4, 11.
8. Between 1822 and 1831, the output of cast iron had risen by 26 per cent and that of iron by 9 per cent, and the number of factories producing iron and cast iron had risen from 111 to 198 (V. Pel'chinskii, *O sostoianii promyshlennykh sil Rossii do 1832 g.* [St. Petersburg, 1833], pp. 55, 58-59).
9. Virginskii, *Vozniknovenie*, pp. 145-146, 148-149.

placed an advertisement in the St. Petersburg papers for 110,000 poods of iron rails and 40,000 poods of cast-iron rail chairs, half of this order to be delivered at St. Petersburg by the end of May and the other half by the middle of August.[10]

Actually such expectations were unrealistic. In Russia in the 1830's iron cost four times as much to produce as cast iron. In England it was only twice as expensive, since the so-called puddling process was being increasingly used, while it was introduced into Russia only in 1836. Furthermore, the cost of working iron in Russia raised the price of the finished product considerably.[11] As a result, it was estimated that both iron rails and cast-iron rail chairs would cost twice as much if made in Russia as if made in England,[12] whereas the company was obligated to pay only 15 per cent more. Even if rails could have been produced in Russia at an acceptable price, it was not certain whether the Ural factories could have produced enough rails and of the requisite quality. But it was certain that they could not have delivered to St. Petersburg by August, 1836, because of the slowness of water transportation between the Urals and St. Petersburg.

In any case, no ironmaster came forward with an offer to supply rails and rail chairs for the Tsarskoe Selo Railway, and von Gerstner was obviously compelled to order them abroad.[13] The founders of the company had accordingly applied to the Russian government for permission to be released from their obligation to use Russian iron, giving as the reason that iron could not be delivered from the Urals within the stipulated time. The Committee of Ministers, not wishing to delay completion of the railway, allowed the free import of iron but expressed the opinion that in the future the company should place its orders far enough in advance to allow Russian ironmasters to make delivery. The decision to allow the free import of iron was confirmed by imperial decree on April 14, 1836, and again on May 20, 1837.[14]

10. *Ibid.*, p. 164.

11. S. G. Strumilin, *Istoriia chernoi metallurgii v SSSR* (Moscow, 1954), I, 424-425; Pel'chinskii, p. 57.

12. N. Atreshkov (Otreshkov-Tarasenko), *Ob ustroenii zheleznykh dorog v Rossii* (St. Petersburg, 1835), p. 48.

13. Von Gerstner, *Pervyi otchet*, p. 13.

14. N. A. Kislinskii, *Nasha zheleznodorozhnaia politika po dokumentam arkhiva Komiteta Ministrov* (St. Petersburg, 1902), I, 13.

Von Gerstner consequently ordered iron rails and cast-iron rail chairs at three factories in England: the Butterley Factories in Derbyshire, the Bedlington Ironworks near Newcastle-on-Tyne, and Guest, Lewis, and Company at Merthyr-Tydvil in South Wales. The rails were to be of the bullheaded type, shaped like a mushroom in cross-section, such as were used on the Liverpool-Manchester Railway and on the railway built by the Cherepanovs in the Urals. It was also necessary to order "pins" to attach the chairs to the crossties and wooden blocks, or "keys," to hold the rails in place in the chairs. All three factories promised to have the orders placed with them ready no later than September.[15] The orders were slightly larger than had been originally estimated because von Gerstner in his characteristic fashion ordered rails weighing 65 pounds per yard (very heavy by the then existing standards) instead of 60 pounds per yard and also ordered heavier rail chairs. He also ordered a greater quantity of rails than planned to provide for side tracks and double track within St. Petersburg. The total amounts ordered were 1,928 tons of rails and 650 tons of rail chairs.[16]

The locomotives and other rolling stock ordered in England and Belgium had to be built to von Gerstner's own specifications, since he had chosen a gauge of 6 feet (1,829 mm.) for his railway, instead of the 4 feet 8.5 inches (1,435 mm.) most usual in England and Belgium, and which is now accepted as standard gauge. He chose the 6-foot gauge on the advice of English engineers because he felt that standard gauge was too narrow for the faster and more powerful locomotives then being built. Also a broader gauge would allow heavier loads to be carried at higher speeds in a more stable manner.[17] Von Gerstner wished to adopt this gauge for all future railways he might build in Russia and

15. Von Gerstner, *Pervyi otchet*, p. 7; *Gornyi Zhurnal*, II, kn. VI (1842), 11.

16. Franz Anton von Gerstner, *Vtoroi otchet ob uspekhakh zheleznoi dorogi iz Sanktpeterburga v Tsarskoe Selo i Pavlovsk* (St. Petersburg, October 7, 1836), p. 11; *Zheleznaia doroga ot S. Peterburga do Tsarskogo Sela i Pavlovska*, p. 15.

17. Von Gerstner, *Pervyi otchet*, pp. 4-6; Kreeft, pp. 9-10. Von Gerstner was not the only builder who preferred the broad gauge. The English engineer Isambard Kingdom Brunel adopted a gauge of 7 feet for his Great Western Railway. Many railways in the American South were originally built to a gauge of 5 feet or even 5 feet 6 inches.

hoped that it would be adopted widely outside Russia.[18] As it turned out, the Tsarskoe Selo Railway was the only Russian railway ever to be built with this gauge, nearly all subsequent railways being built with a gauge of 5 feet (1,524 mm.).[19] The Tsarskoe Selo Railway was converted to that gauge early in the twentieth century, when it became part of a railway from St. Petersburg to Vitebsk.[20]

Von Gerstner had originally felt that he should order five locomotives—four for ordinary traffic and a fifth to handle the extra traffic on Sundays and holidays.[21] However, in England he decided to order seven locomotives, having also in mind the railways which he hoped to build between St. Petersburg and Peterhof-Oranienbaum and between Moscow and Kolomna. He ordered two locomotives from Robert Stephenson and Company at Newcastle-on-Tyne and another two from Timothy Hackworth and Company of New Shildon. Each of these companies was to send the first locomotive to Russia in the late summer of 1836 and the second locomotive in the spring of 1837. Another two locomotives were ordered from Charles Tayleur, Jr., and Company (Vulcan Locomotive Works) at Newton-le-Willows, both to be delivered in the spring of 1837. The seventh locomotive was ordered in Belgium at the factory of John Cockerill at Seraing-sur-Meuse. Each of these locomotives was to be larger and more powerful than those customarily built, having at least 40 horsepower instead of the 30 to 35 horsepower usual for the newest locomotives in England, and a speed of at least 40 versts per hour.[22]

Von Gerstner had also originally hoped to be able to have much of the rolling stock built in Russia. On February 3, 1836, at the same time that he advertised for rails, he had advertised

18. Franz Anton von Gerstner, *Berichte aus den Vereinigten Staaten von Nordamerika über Eisenbahnen, Dampfschiffahrten, Banken und andere öffentliche Unternehmungen* (Leipzig, 1839), pp. 64, 67.

19. The railway built from Warsaw to the Austrian and Prussian borders was built with a gauge of 4 feet 8.5 inches to connect with the Austrian and Prussian railway systems. (See p. 198 below.)

20. A. I. Sokolov, *Nakanune 100-letiia: Pervaia russkaia zheleznaia doroga v proshlom* (Leningrad, 1925), p. 33.

21. Von Gerstner, *O vygodakh*, p. 26.

22. Von Gerstner, *Pervyi otchet*, pp. 7-8; Kreeft, p. 12.

in the St. Petersburg newspapers for 100 carriage underframes, half of which were to be delivered in St. Petersburg by the end of May and the other half by August.[23] However, as in the case of the advertisement for rails, no Russian manufacturer seems to have come forward to make an offer, so von Gerstner ordered most of his rolling stock from England, Ireland, and Belgium, though some of the carriage bodies were to be made in Russia.

While in Belgium, von Gerstner ordered sixteen carriage underframes from Cockerill and engaged a noted Brussels carriage-maker to build the bodies. These carriages were to be of four types, of which he ordered four each: "berlins," "diligences," "char-à-bancs," and "wagons." The berlins were to seat twenty-four persons in armchairs in three compartments of eight chairs each.[24] They were very luxuriously appointed and were meant for carrying important people such as the imperial family or high nobility and officials.[25] The diligences were slightly less luxuriously appointed, corresponding to second-class carriages. The char-à-bancs were open carriages with wooden benches, corresponding to third class, while the wagons were also open but without benches. These wagons—eventually used for a fourth class—were meant for the common people and could each transport forty persons.

In Dublin, von Gerstner ordered twenty carriage underframes with patent-buffers from the firm of John and Robert Mallet. The bodies for these carriage underframes were to be built in St. Petersburg on the model of the carriage bodies made in Brussels.

In England, von Gerstner ordered ten freight wagons, one for carrying private carriages, three for sheep, cattle, and horses, two for timber, and four for general merchandise.[26] While in England he also ordered miscellaneous equipment, including six turntables, four switches for side tracks along the railway, two sets of scales for weighing carriages, and a crane. In London and Vienna

23. Virginiskii, *Vozniknovenie,* p. 164.

24. Similar carriages in Europe seated only eighteen passengers, but because of the broad gauge of the carriages ordered for the Tsarskoe Selo Railway, two extra persons could be seated in each of the three compartments.

25. *Severnaia Pchela,* October 7, 1836, p. 913.

26. Von Gerstner, *Pervyi otchet,* pp. 8-9; cf. E. I. Mokrshitskii, *Istoriia vagonnogo parka zheleznykh dorog SSSR* (Moscow, 1946), pp. 109-110.

he ordered warning devices, to be placed on the locomotives as Nicholas I had ordered. They were organ-like instruments consisting of eleven pipes and a trombone. In London he also ordered four-faced illuminated tower clocks for the stations in St. Petersburg, Tsarskoe Selo, and Pavlovsk. These clocks were for the use of the railway and the public and were to be visible for several versts. He ordered wall clocks as well for the waiting rooms at the four passenger stations. In addition, he placed orders for various pieces of equipment for the inn at Pavlovsk, including armchairs, washroom facilities, and three fountains, one for the grand ballroom and two for the gardens outside.[27]

Von Gerstner had also gone to Western Europe to engage skilled engineers and craftsmen to act as his assistants.[28] As early as February 28, 1835, Nicholas I had given him permission to hire engineers wherever he wished, except in France.[29] He hired seventeen engineers, who were to serve as superintendents, and thirty inspectors. Ten Englishmen and two Belgians were engaged to serve as engine-drivers and to erect machinery, including locomotives, make repairs, and instruct Russian craftsmen. While the railway was being built, one could hear English, German, Russian, Flemish, and even Italian being spoken.[30]

With the necessary equipment ordered and necessary foreign personnel obtained, von Gerstner returned to Russia and found that during his sojourn abroad, work was started as had been planned on the earthworks, bridges, and buildings necessary for the railway. As early as March 14, 1836, invitations for contracts for building earthworks and bridges and for the procurement of items which could be produced in Russia, such as wooden cross-ties, were published in the St. Petersburg newspapers.

A labor force also had had to be obtained. Construction was to be carried on in sections assigned to contractors or to co-operative groups of thirty to forty men each (*arteli*). Weekly payments were to be made to the contractor or leader in the presence of the workers on the basis of work done during the preceding week,

27. Von Gerstner, *Pervyi otchet*, pp. 10-11.
28. Von Gerstner, *O vygodakh*, pp. 28, 63.
29. Baron M. A. Korf, "Imperator Nikolai v soveshchatel'nykh sobraniiakh," *Sbornik Imperatorskogo Russkogo Istoricheskogo Obshchestva*, XCVIII (1896), 127-128.
30. Von Gerstner, *Third Report*, p. 18.

with extra bonuses for work especially well done.[31] The private contractors hired some workers from the St. Petersburg area, but most were proprietary serfs hired for the summer from land-owners often hundreds of versts away. This meant that additional workers could not be hired quickly and that many would have to leave early in the autumn to return home for the winter.[32] By the summer of 1836, there were 2,500 workers employed, of whom 1,800 were working on the embankments. In addition, 1,400 soldiers were hired, but because they were unused to such work and for other reasons, only 200 remained at the end of the summer.[33]

The acquisition and clearing of most of the land had proved a fairly simple matter. Practically all the land along the proposed route was state or appanage land, consisting mostly of forest, communal pasture, or agricultural land. Along the whole route not one building would have to be demolished. Only within the limits of St. Petersburg would private land have to be bought. Half of the square between the Fontanka and the Vedenskii Canal, site of the proposed St. Petersburg terminal, was in private hands, as were seven gardens over a stretch of 550 sazhens between the Obvodnyi Canal and the Ligovka.[34]

The clearing of state land proceeded rapidly. Forests to either side were cleared to a width of 60 sazhens, as was done when building *chaussées*. The state peasants living along the projected route of the railway, realizing that they would receive adequate compensation for losses incurred, ceded their land willingly, harvested their crops prematurely, and even helped to clear the forests.[35]

In March, 1836, drainage of the swampy areas along the proposed route had begun. It had been suggested that such swampy places should be avoided by building the railway in a more circuitous route, but von Gerstner insisted that the railway be built in a straight line as planned. By July all the swampy areas had been drained.[36]

31. Von Gerstner, *Vtoroi otchet*, p. 10.
32. Von Gerstner, *Bericht über den Stand*, p. xiii.
33. Von Gerstner, *Vtoroi otchet*, p. 7.
34. Von Gerstner, *O vygodakh*, pp. 20, 22.
35. Von Gerstner, *Third Report*, pp. 16, 19.
36. Von Gerstner, *Pervyi otchet*, p. 11.

The most important construction work was the building of embankments, which were to run nearly the entire length of the railway. Although these were to average 9 to 10 feet in height, in some places they were to be 20 feet high. These embankments were built to facilitate the clearing of snow and so that there would be no gradient of more than 1:504, with the average of 1:1028. The embankments were to be 2.5 sazhens wide to allow the eventual construction of a second track. On either side drainage ditches were to be dug. Von Gerstner estimated that a total of 71,000 cubic sazhens of earth would have to be moved.[37]

Work on the embankments outside St. Petersburg began on May 9 and proceeded rapidly in the early part of the summer, so that by late July, 10 versts had been completed.[38] However, work began to go more slowly because of rain in July and August, so that by the end of September only 7 additional versts had been built. Also there were delays in starting the embankments over the former artillery proving ground at Volkovo Pole while the artillery proving ground was being transferred to its new location.[39] Departure of many of the workers early in the autumn also slowed the work so that, in spite of hopes that the embankments could be completed in 1836, by the end of that year only about six-sevenths of the necessary embankments outside St. Petersburg had been finished. It was hoped that the work could be brought to a successful conclusion in the spring of 1837 within four to six weeks.[40] Work on the embankments was started again in April, 1837, after the spring thaw,[41] but because of delays imputable to some of the contractors, the earthworks were not completed until the end of September, 1837.[42]

There was also delay in building the railway over the distance of 2 versts 160 sazhens between the Fontanka and the Ligovka within the limits of St. Petersburg. Von Gerstner stated that he would have started building first within the limits of St. Petersburg if he could have obtained land from the seven private

37. Von Gerstner, *O vygodakh*, p. 22.
38. Von Gerstner, *Pervyi otchet*, p. 12.
39. Von Gerstner, *Vtoroi otchet*, p. 6; Severnaia Pchela, October 7, 1836, p. 914.
40. Von Gerstner, *Third Report*, pp. 8-9.
41. *Railway Magazine and Annals of Science*, No. 16 (June, 1837), p. 413.
42. Von Gerstner, *Bericht über den Stand*, p. xiii.

owners of gardens between the Obvodnyi Canal and the Ligovka and from the owner of the land on the Fontanka. During his trip to Western Europe the directors of the company had entered into negotiations with these owners, but the latter had demanded exorbitant prices for their land.[43] Upon his return to Russia von Gerstner invoked the right of eminent domain to take possession of the private land lying between the Obvodnyi Canal and the Ligovka (but not the land on the Fontanka). On September 24, 1836, the military governor general of St. Petersburg granted the company permission to start building in this area,[44] and work began in April of 1837.[45]

Von Gerstner had estimated originally that twenty-four bridges would be necessary, one within St. Petersburg and twenty-three outside the city. The bridge over the Obvodnyi Canal was to be the largest, being 9 sazhens in length and wide enough for two tracks. It was to have seven wooden arches resting on stone piers. Outside the city the other twenty-three bridges would each be only 1 to 2 sazhens in length and would be built entirely of wood, since otherwise too much time and expense would be involved.[46] However, when the construction of the railway was undertaken, it was found that seventeen additional bridges would be necessary for crossing streams and country roads. Furthermore, it was discovered that the bridge over the Obvodnyi Canal would be 12 sazhens instead of 9 sazhens long.

Work started on nearly all bridges during von Gerstner's absence in Western Europe. Piles were sunk for the bridge over the Obvodnyi Canal and the stonework was begun. But von Gerstner, upon his return to Russia, found the work for this important bridge faulty. The work continued under his own supervision, additional piles being sunk to make the bridge more solid. Stonework could not be recommenced until August 23, but it was hoped that the bridge would be completed in October.[47] However, as with the work on the embankments, there continued

43. Von Gerstner, *Vtoroi otchet*, p. 7.
44. *Severnaia Pchela*, September 29, 1836, p. 885; von Gerstner, *Bericht über den Stand*, pp. xii-xiii.
45. *Railway Magazine and Annals of Science*, No. 16 (June, 1837), p. 413.
46. Von Gerstner, *O vygodakh*, p. 23.
47. Von Gerstner, *Vtoroi otchet*, p. 7.

to be delays, and by the end of 1836 the bridge was still not finished.

Work on the other bridges was accomplished comparatively rapidly. By the end of the year, thirty-four bridges, all built of wood and none more than 3.5 sazhens long, were completed, and construction on the remaining bridges had been started,[48] with final work done in 1837 after the spring thaw.[49]

Work was also started in 1836 on the necessary auxiliary buildings for the railway. In addition to the stations at St. Petersburg, Moscow *Chaussée*, Tsarskoe Selo, and Pavlovsk, offices and living quarters for supervisory personnel and sheds and repair shops for locomotives and carriages had to be built both in St. Petersburg and Tsarskoe Selo. In addition, along the railway at intervals of 2 versts, barracks (*kazarmy*) were to be built, each housing ten to fifteen workers for clearing snow.[50]

The construction of the station at the St. Petersburg terminus was not started until the summer of 1837, and even then it was only a "temporary" building; but both von Gerstner and the other directors of the company felt that no expense should be spared in preparing amusement facilities and accomodations as luxurious and capacious as possible at Pavlovsk and Tsarskoe Selo in order to induce the public to ride on the railway in large numbers.[51]

The combined passenger station and inn at Tsarskoe Selo was built to von Gerstner's plans. It had a frontage of 300 feet and a tower 77 feet high and was connected to the railway by a covered gallery. One half of the building consisted of waiting rooms for travelers, and offices and living quarters for officials. The other half of the building was occupied by the inn.[52] At the time of the official opening of the Tsarskoe Selo Railway on October 30, 1837, the building was so nearly completed that a banquet could be held in it.

For the building at Pavlovsk, plans were submitted by thirteen architects, including two from Germany. Grand Duke Mikhail

48. Von Gerstner, *Third Report*, p. 9.
49. *Railway Magazine and Annals of Science*, No. 16 (June, 1837), p. 413.
50. Von Gerstner, *O vygodakh*, pp. 25-26.
51. *Zheleznaia doroga ot S. Peterburga do Tsarskogo Sela i Pavlovska*, p. 15.
52. Von Gerstner, *Third Report*, p. 10; von Gerstner, *Bericht über den Stand*, p. vii.

Pavlovich preferred the plans submitted by a Berlin architect but agreed to allow the contract to be awarded to the St. Petersburg architect Stackenschneider, who had submitted a lower bid.[53] The building was built of wood on a stone foundation and was semicircular. It was connected to the railway by a covered gallery 33 sazhens long. For nearly the whole length of the building there was another gallery, under which guests could stroll in bad weather or dine in good. Inside was a large hall 120 by 50 feet for balls, concerts, and banquets. In the center of this room there was a fountain built in London with two hundred jets powered by a steam engine of eight horsepower. In addition, there were five smaller halls, as well as forty rooms in the wings for hotel guests and twelve rooms for hotel personnel.[54] By March, 1838, the building at Pavlovsk was largely completed.[55]

Starting in late July, 1836, and in increasing measure throughout August and September and until the close of navigation, the equipment ordered in England and Belgium began to arrive in St. Petersburg. Most of the rails, rail chairs, pins, and keys arrived in August and September, but small amounts continued to arrive in October and even November. By the close of navigation all rail chairs, pins, and keys had arrived. However, about 200 tons of rails had not arrived, either because they had been prepared too late for shipment or because they had been lost in shipwrecks. As a result, 1.5 versts of embankment could not have been laid with rails until the following spring, even if they had been entirely completed.[56]

The laying of the rails began on August 27, 1836, at various places along the railway where the embankments were already completed. By the end of the year, rails had been laid down between Pavlovsk and Kuzmino, a distance of 7.5 versts, and for short distances in three other places.[57] The track was solidly constructed. Not only were the heaviest rails and rail chairs then available used, but also the pine crossties, placed at intervals of

53. Von Gerstner, *Pervyi otchet*, p. 12.
54. Von Gerstner, *Vtoroi otchet*, p. 8; von Gerstner, *Bericht über den Stand*, p. vii.
55. Von Gerstner, *Third Report*, p. 9; von Gerstner, *Bericht über den Stand*, p. viii.
56. Von Gerstner, *Third Report*, p. 11, 13.
57. Von Gerstner, *Vtoroi otchet*, p. 7; Kreeft, p. 15.

3 feet, were treated with tar to preserve them, just as today railway crossties are treated with creosote. To prevent the dislocation of the track during freezes and thaws, bundles of faggots were laid under the track. A layer of rubble was also to be placed under the crossties, and a 4-inch layer of gravel ballast covered with sand was to be placed between the rails. However, it was decided to postpone the laying of the ballast to the spring of 1837, when the embankments would have settled.[58] At that time it was laid to a depth of 14 inches instead of the 4 inches originally planned. The laying of the rails was not completed until the end of October, 1837.[59]

At first, as stipulated in the privilege of March 21, 1836, the railway was to be single-tracked, with embankments built to receive a second track later. Two or more tracks were to be laid at side tracks and at the stations in Tsarskoe Selo and Pavlovsk. Also within the limits of St. Petersburg the railway was to have two or three tracks.[60]

Von Gerstner wanted a double line within St. Petersburg because he planned to have the railway which he hoped to build to Peterhof and Oranienbaum use the trackage of the Tsarskoe Selo Railway within the city. He built the embankments sufficiently wide to make provision for a second track on the rest of the Tsarskoe Selo Railway not only because he hoped that traffic to Tsarskoe Selo and Pavlovsk would increase but also because he hoped that the Tsarskoe Selo Railway would become the first section of the railway between St. Petersburg and Moscow. But a second track was not added to the Tsarskoe Selo Railway until the 1870's.[61]

With this much construction completed, although major engineering works remained unfinished and much of the equipment ordered abroad, including all three locomotives expected by that time, had not yet arrived, von Gerstner was ready to start trial runs over a part of the railway by late September, 1836, so that

58. Von Gerstner, *O vygodakh*, pp. 23-24; von Gerstner, *Vtoroi otchet*, p. 7.
59. Von Gerstner, *Berichte aus den Vereinigten Staaten*, p. 61.
60. Kreeft, p. 17.
61. P. E. Gronskii, "Ocherk vozniknoveniia i razvitiia zheleznykh dorog v Rossii," *Zapiski Moskovskogo Otdeleniia Imperatorskogo Russkogo Tekhnicheskogo Obshchestva*, IV (1886), 12.

he could state that at least a small part of the railway was open to traffic before October 1, 1836. Since the steam locomotives had not yet arrived, horse power was to be used. For the trials von Gerstner chose the stretch of track between Pavlovsk and Tsarskoe Selo, where rails were already laid and where the trials would attract the most attention.

On Sunday, September 27, the first trials were made using horses to pull two char-à-bancs and two wagons recently arrived from Belgium. Two trains of two carriages each were run, each train carrying sixty to seventy passengers, who were onlookers invited to ride without charge. The trials, which were well attended by the public, were successfully conducted without mishap. The horses pulling the carriages managed to cover the distance of 3 versts between Tsarskoe Selo and Pavlovsk in fifteen minutes.[62] On the following Sundays, October 4 and 11, similar trials were held and were attended with great success.[63]

The three locomotives ordered abroad, the delivery of which had been promised for 1836, arrived in October of that year.[64] The Hackworth locomotive had a 2–2–2 wheel arrangement, with driving wheels 5 feet in diameter. The locomotive also had a tender with a capacious tank.[65] The first Stephenson locomotive was on the model of George Stephenson's *Patentee*, which had first appeared in 1833 and was widely used both in England and abroad. It also had a 2–2–2 wheel arrangement, but with driving wheels 6 feet in diameter.[66] The Cockerill locomotive was presumably of similarly large dimensions, although specific information is lacking.[67]

62. *Severnaia Pchela*, September 29, 1836, p. 885; von Gerstner, *Vtoroi otchet*, p. 20.

63. *Severnaia Pchela*, October 7, 1836, p. 913; von Gerstner, *Bericht über den Stand*, p. xv.

64. Von Gerstner, *Third Report*, p. 12.

65. Robert Young, *Timothy Hackworth and the Locomotive* (London, 1923), pp. 274, 276.

66. James H. G. Warren, *A Century of Locomotive Building by Robert Stephenson and Co., 1823–1923* (Newcastle-on-Tyne, 1923), pp. 322, 340; V. S. Virginskii, *Dzhordzh Stefenson, vydaiushchiisia angliiskii inzhener-izobretatel'* (Moscow, 1956), pp. 28-30.

67. Theodore B. Hodges, "The Iron King of Liège: John Cockerill" (unpublished Ph.D. dissertation, Columbia University, 1960), I, 232; cf. Natalis Briavoinne, "Sur les inventions et perfectionnements dans l'industrie depuis la fin du XVIII-e siècle jusqu'à nos jours," in *Mémoires couronnés*

The Hackworth and Stephenson locomotives were reputed to have attained speeds of 72 mph and 65.5 mph, respectively, during tests at the factory in England.[68] However, since neither factory had tracks with a gauge of 6 feet, the locomotives had been tested by suspending them in mid-air and counting the number of revolutions per minute without allowance for friction of the rails. Their true maximum speed was probably about 40 mph, similar, that is, to that of the best English locomotives.[69]

Since most of the other rolling stock and miscellaneous equipment ordered abroad arrived in the early autumn of 1836,[70] by November, 1836, von Gerstner was ready to start trials using steam locomotives. He was anxious to show that locomotives altered to suit the 6-foot gauge could operate successfully.[71]

On November 3, 1836, the Hackworth locomotive, attended by Timothy Hackworth's seventeen-year-old son John and a small staff, was tested on the railway between Pavlovsk and Tsarskoe Selo in clear but very cold weather. The trial took place in the presence of Nicholas I and the imperial family and a large number of people of all classes of society. At noon, in front of the Tsarskoe Selo Station, there was a service of consecration lasting forty-five minutes. A Te Deum was sung for God's blessing upon the railway and upon the Tsar and his family, that they might be conveyed safely by the railway. The locomotive and five carriages were blessed with holy water. After the service, the five carriages were quickly filled by some of the crowd of onlookers, and the train proceeded to Pavlovsk at a speed of only

par l'Académie Royale des Sciences et Belles-lettres de Bruxelles, XIII (1838), 64.

68. Mechanics' Magazine, September 17, 1836, p. 432, and October 1, 1836, p. 464.

69. Severnaia Pchela, October 7, 1836, pp. 913-914; Neskol'ko slov o zheleznykh dorogakh v Rossii (Moscow, 1836), p. 21, n. 1.

70. On August 23, two char-à-bancs and two wagons built in Belgium had arrived and were the ones used in the first trials of the railway in September and October. On September 19 the twenty carriage frames arrived from Dublin. On September 30, two berlins and two diligences arrived from Belgium. On October 21 materials for the eight other carriages arrived from the Cockerill factory at Seraing-sur-Meuse. On October 16, twelve freight wagons arrived from England, as well as the turntables and the crane (von Gerstner, Vtoroi otchet, pp. 4-5; von Gerstner, Third Report, p. 12).

71. Von Gerstner, Vtoroi otchet, p. 13.

about 20 versts per hour, since the crowd was pressing close to the railway and there was the danger of accidents. The train then returned to Tsarskoe Selo and continued 2 versts down the line toward Kuzmino. During the rest of the day several more trips were made, since many people wished to ride on the new conveyance.

The trials were a great success, both from the technical standpoint and from that of public relations. The crowd was pleased and also the imperial family, all of whom expressed approval. Grand Duke Mikhail Pavlovich actually rode on the train, and Nicholas I himself said of the locomotive, "It is the finest that I ever saw."[72]

Similar trials continued on Sundays throughout November, 1836. These trials were successful and without mishap, except that one of the cylinders on the Hackworth locomotive cracked. However, a replacement was made in a Moscow ordnance factory from a pattern made by one of the Hackworth engineers.[73]

One problem was fuel. It had been originally planned to use birch wood, to prove that imported English coke would not be necessary, even if coal-fired locomotives would give a better performance. But the sparks from the birch wood set the clothes of the passengers on fire. Ordinary coal was tried, but it also produced sparks and objectionable smoke. Imported English coke was therefore used, which increased operating expenses considerably.[74]

By November 28 the ground had frozen to a depth of fourteen inches and had then thawed, and it was snowing heavily when a trial using the Stephenson locomotive, the largest and most powerful ordered, was made on the stretch of railway between Pavlovsk and Kuzmino. The next day the locomotive pulled eight carriages with 256 passengers over the 7.5-verst distance in seventeen minutes, giving a perfectly satisfactory performance in spite of the snowy weather.[75]

On January 2, 1837, all three locomotives were used between Pavlovsk and Kuzmino, each pulling fifteen carriages. To facili-

72. *Severnaia Pchela*, November 15, 1836, p. 1045; Young, p. 276. Also *Railway Magazine and Annals of Science*, No. 12 (February, 1837), p. 136.
73. Von Gerstner, *Bericht über den Stand*, p. xv; Young, p. 276.
74. *Severnaia Pchela*, December 1, 1836, p. 1097.
75. *Ibid.*; von Gerstner, *Third Report*, p. 7.

tate snow removal, the locomotives were equipped with snow-plows in front and with brushes between the wheels.[76] The weather was very cold, ranging from —10° R. to —18° R. (9.5° F. to —8.5° F.) The following day, a train of twenty-three vehicles, carrying not only passengers but also livestock, assorted goods, and road vehicles mounted on flatcars, was run successfully in the presence of a large crowd which had come out from St. Petersburg by sledge. On January 4 there was a blizzard, but nevertheless trips were made without incident.

On Sunday, January 24, in unusually pleasant weather, all three locomotives were again tested, each pulling a train of eight carriages without mishap. A total of ten trips was made, and 1,833 passengers were carried. Although there had been much snow-fall, the wind had swept the snow from the embankments, except at Tsarskoe Selo, where the track was level with the ground, and in Pavlovsk, where the forests had been cleared only to a width of 4 sazhens. Through January 28, the total cost of snow removal had been 300 rubles.[77]

These trials of January, 1837, showed that railways could be operated in even the worst weather conditions, and after January 24 all trials were suspended for the rest of the winter. They were conducted on Sundays throughout the summer of 1837, but more to maintain the interest of the public in the railway than to test locomotives.[78]

In the spring and summer of 1837, when communication by sea with Western Europe had been reopened and work on the railway could recommence, the remaining equipment ordered from abroad arrived, and work started again on the embankments, bridges, and the laying of rails. The second Stephenson locomotive arrived early in September, as did the two locomotives ordered from Charles Tayleur, Jr., and Company (Vulcan Locomotive Works). The Vulcan locomotives had a 2–2–2 wheel arrangement and driving wheels 5 feet 6 inches in diameter.[79]

76. Von Gerstner, *Pervyi otchet*, p. 8; Kreeft, p. 18.

77. *Severnaia Pchela*, January 8, 1837, pp. 17-18, and January 26, 1837, p. 89; von Gerstner, *Third Report*, pp. 15-16.

78. I. B. Rozenfel'd, *Pervaia zheleznaia doroga v Rossii* (Petrozavodsk, 1925), p. 97.

79. *The Vulcan Locomotive Works, 1830–1930* (London, 1931), p. 48; *Zheleznaia doroga ot S. Peterburga do Tsarskogo Sela i Pavlovska*, p. 17.

The Tsarskoe Selo Railway now had a total of six locomotives: two Stephenson, two Vulcan, one Hackworth, and one Cockerill. By March, 1838, the Tsarskoe Selo Railway also possessed forty-four carriages, seating a total of 1,878 passengers, and nineteen freight wagons.[80]

Before the railway could be opened to traffic, a site for a terminal in St. Petersburg had to be chosen. The original plan to use the square at the junction of the Fontanka and the Vedenskii Canal had to be abandoned temporarily because early in 1837 part of the wooden wall of the canal had collapsed, and to repair it would have cost the company too much. Also, one owner of land on the Fontanka kept demanding too high a price for his land, and in this one case the directors of the company seemed very reluctant to invoke the right of eminent domain.

Therefore, early in August, 1837, Nicholas I proposed to give the company a site for a St. Petersburg terminal on Semenovskii Square, 1,450 feet farther out from the center of the city than the site originally chosen. On this square a parade ground and a wooden church of the Semenovskii Guard was located. The Tsar planned to have the wooden church torn down and to erect a stone church nearby within five years. This would allow the company use of the whole square. The company accepted this offer, and work on a temporary wooden station building was started on August 9 and finished on September 25. Living quarters for supervisory personnel and a locomotive shed and repair shop were also built.[81]

From September 25, locomotive trials were conducted from the newly completed St. Petersburg terminal over a stretch of track 5 versts in length extending out beyond the city limits. The locomotives recently arrived from England were used, since the locomotives which had arrived during the previous autumn were still at Tsarskoe Selo and could not conveniently be brought to St. Petersburg because the rails were not yet laid. During these trials a locomotive attached to a train of twelve carriages pulled them to the end of the track. Since there was no turntable at this place, another locomotive was attached to the rear of the train to pull it back to the St. Petersburg terminus. Although no public

80. Von Gerstner, *Bericht über den Stand,* p. vii.
81. *Ibid.,* pp. xii-xiii; *Severnaia Pchela,* September 30, 1837, p. 875.

notice of these trials was given, many thousands of the inhabitants of St. Petersburg gathered every day either to take a ride or just to look.[82] These trials took place mainly in the period between September 25 and 30, but continued intermittently throughout October until all the rails between St. Petersburg and Kuzmino had been laid and the Tsarskoe Selo Railway was ready for its formal opening.

The formal opening of the Tsarskoe Selo Railway took place on October 30, 1837. At the temporary St. Petersburg terminal, members of the State Council, the Committee of Ministers, and many other high Russian officials, both civil and military, were assembled. There were in addition representatives of the diplomatic corps and of the Russian academic and business worlds, invited by the company. There was also a large crowd of curious onlookers.

The train which was to go to Tsarskoe Selo consisted of eight carriages and was pulled by one of the Stephenson locomotives, with von Gerstner himself driving the locomotive. The train started at 12:30 P.M. and made the trip to Tsarskoe Selo in thirty-five minutes. In the station building at Tsarskoe Selo there was a luncheon for honored guests, at which the president of the State Council proposed a toast to the Tsar and to the directors of the company. The return trip to St. Petersburg required twenty-seven minutes, and speeds up to 60 versts per hour were attained. Upon the arrival of the train in St. Petersburg, the passengers were so pleased that they cheered von Gerstner.[83]

To commemorate the occasion a medal was struck with a facsimile of one of the Stephenson locomotives. Nicholas I, however, ordered the medal withdrawn from circulation.[84]

After the formal opening of the railway, service between St. Petersburg and Tsarskoe Selo (but not to Pavlovsk) was insti-

82. *Severnaia Pchela*, September 30, 1837, p. 875.

83. *Ibid.*, November 2, 1837, p. 991; von Gerstner, *Bericht über den Stand*, pp. xvii-xviii.

84. The Tsar may have ordered the medal withdrawn because of one of its inscriptions, which expressed Pan Slav sentiments: "Stroitel' pervoi zheleznoi dorogi byl Frants Gerstner, redom chekh edinoplemennyi Rossiianam" (The builder of the first railway was Franz Gerstner, by birth a Czech, kinsman of the Russians). See facsimile of the medal in Warren, p. 94. Nicholas disapproved of Pan Slavism since he did not want to encourage Slavs in other countries to think of revolt against their rulers.

tuted. Normal traffic could not of course be expected at first. For the first few days until November 2 there were daily trips to Tsarskoe Selo with the trains consisting of carriages of three classes. However, after November 2, it was decided to run only first- and second-class carriages. The reason for this measure, according to von Gerstner, was that too much confusion was created by running trains with three classes of carriages. One of the main problems of operating the railway since September 25 had been the handling of huge crowds, especially of the common people, who wished to ride on the trains. By using only first- and second-class carriages, many of the more disorderly elements of the capital would be excluded merely because they would not be able to afford the higher fares.[85] After November 2 trains were run only on Sundays until December 25. From then until the end of the year there were daily trips again.[86]

During the rest of the winter of 1837–1838 steam-powered trains were run only irregularly, mainly on Sundays and holidays. In the month of January, 1838, steam-powered passenger trains were run on a total of twelve days.[87] On January 30, daily service was started between St. Petersburg and Tsarskoe Selo, but as an economy measure horse power was used, with the trip taking eighty-seven minutes.

From April 4, 1838, steam power was used exclusively, and regularly scheduled trips between St. Petersburg and Tsarskoe Selo were inaugurated.[88] It is on this date that the full operation of the Tsarskoe Selo Railway may be said to have begun.

Normal conditions must have been impatiently awaited by more than a few persons, for more depended on the financial success of this railway than the satisfaction of its stockholders. If Russia was to proceed with railway building, this venture must not be a failure. Eagerness to see what profits would prove to be would be all the more understandable because the expense of construction had been greater than anticipated and revenues, to justify the cost, would have to be correspondingly higher.

85. Another concession to Russian social conditions was differentiating the tickets for each class by color, since most Russians were illiterate. Also, seats were not reserved, so that greater numbers could be handled more quickly.

86. Von Gerstner, *Bericht über den Stand*, pp. xviii, xxvii, 18.

87. *Ibid.*, p. xxi; *Severnaia Pchela*, January 15, 1838, p. 48.

88. *Severnaia Pchela*, May 30, 1838, p. 473.

The amount of capital for the railway's construction had had in fact to be increased three times. In the privilege of March 21, 1836, the capital of the Tsarskoe Selo Railway had been set at 3,000,000 rubles, with permission to issue additonal shares worth 500,000 rubles. By September, 1836, a total of 1,632,622 rubles had been spent (of which 913,599 rubles had been spent abroad).[89] By the end of December of that year, 2,462,167 rubles had been spent (of which 1,105,920 rubles had been spent abroad).[90] Consequently, in late September, 1836, the directors of the company announced that the permitted 500,000 rubles of additional stock were being issued. The reasons given were that the price of iron in England had risen and von Gerstner had ordered heavier rails and rail chairs than had been originally planned; therefore the iron needed would cost 325,000 rubles more than had been anticipated. Also the buildings at Pavlovsk were costing more than had been expected.[91]

But by August, 1837, it was obvious that even the 3,500,000 rubles would not be adequate to build the railway. Through July 31, 1837, total expenses had been 3,431,600 rubles, that is, nearly the total amount of the capital, and the railway was still far from completed.[92]

Von Gerstner decided the government must be asked for a loan. In January, 1828, he had been faced with a similar situation in building the Linz-Budweis Railway. To raise the necessary additional capital, he had persuaded the Austrian government to guarantee a loan by promising to ship salt, a government monopoly in Austria at that time, by the railway for the following six years.[93] Although the Russian government had stated that it would not give any kind of financial help to such enterprises as the Tsarskoe Selo Railway, early in July, 1837, the company applied to the Russian government for a loan of 1,500,000 rubles, stating that such a measure was necessary because the railway was being built more solidly than had been originally planned.

89. Von Gerstner, *Vtoroi otchet*, p. 9.
90. Von Gerstner, *Third Report*, p. 13.
91. Von Gerstner, *Vtoroi otchet*, pp. 11, 19-20.
92. *Zheleznaia doroga ot S. Peterburga do Tsarskogo Sela i Pavlovska,* p. 14.
93. See R. Huyer, "Die Budweis-Linzer Pferdeeisenbahn," *Mittheilungen des Vereins für Geschichte der Deutschen in Böhmen,* XXXII (1894), 87-88.

The stockholders, at their first full meeting of August 16, 1837, confirmed this action of the directors by the overwhelming vote of 175 to 11.[94]

This petition was discussed in the Committee of Ministers on August 3. In the meeting it was pointed out that the loan was a risk, since the company had as yet little property to attach. Count Kankrin, never missing an opportunity to criticize railways, stated that the profitableness of all railways had yet to be proven. But the Committee of Ministers was of the opinion that the Russian government would have to grant the loan, since it represented too great a risk for private banking houses to assume. If the government refused to grant the loan, it would expose itself to criticism from partisans of railways both in Russia and abroad that merely for financial reasons it was unwilling to support useful and beneficial undertakings on which considerable sums of money had already been spent. The government also felt that public confidence in the Tsarskoe Selo Railway should not be shaken. Therefore, although with misgivings, it felt compelled to grant the loan.[95]

On August 31, Nicholas I provisionally allowed the loan and set up a commission to evaluate the attachable properties of the railway and estimate the additional amount of money necessary for its completion. By a ukase of November 7, 1837, the loan was allowed, and a sum of 1,500,000 rubles was transferred to the company from the State Loan Bank. The loan was to be repaid at 6 per cent yearly interest, with extinction in thirty-seven years. As collateral, the government might attach all present and future properties of the railway. Also the state could administer the railway if the company failed to meet its yearly payments. Representatives of the Ministry of Finance and of the Main Administration of Transport and Buildings were to see that the loan

94. Von Gerstner, *Bericht über den Stand*, p. viii; *Zheleznaia doroga ot S. Peterburga do Tsarskogo Sela i Pavlovska*, pp. 14, 20.

95. V. M. Verkhovskii, *Kratkii istoricheskii ocherk nachala i rasprostraneniia zheleznykh dorog v Rossii po 1897 g. vkliuchitel'no* (St. Petersburg, 1898), p. 43; Kislinskii, I, 13-14. Similar loans for projects undertaken by organs of the central or local government had been granted for projects of special public value through the State Loan Bank but only in a few cases and then only against sufficient collateral ("Predstavlenie ministra finansov gr. E. Kankrina v komitet ministrov, 29 iiulia 1837 g.," *Krasnyi Arkhiv*, LXXVI [1936], 107).

was spent exclusively for the purposes indicated by von Gerstner.[96] By granting the loan and supervising its administration, the government was now playing a role in the affairs of the railway.

The expenses of building the railway continued to mount. By the end of December, 1837, a total of 4,500,878 rubles had been spent, and von Gerstner estimated that 672,620 rubles more would be needed to complete the railway, of which 398,000 rubles should be earmarked for the completion of the permanent terminal in St. Petersburg.[97] Thereafter the rate of expenditure fell, since the company had already made payment for most of the construction work and equipment, but expenses through April 30, 1838, had amounted to 4,733,700 rubles, leaving only 266,300 rubles of the capital of 5,000,000 rubles.[98] There were still works to be completed, moreover, even without building the permanent terminal on the Fontanka. A year later at the stockholders' meeting of April 16, 1839, it was announced that the railway had by then cost 5,281,667 rubles.[99] The company obviously had to resort to further borrowing. In the spring of the same year Nicholas I agreed to a request by the company to borrow an additional 250,000 rubles from the State Loan Bank, to be paid back within thirty-seven years at 6 per cent yearly interest.[100]

The total cost of the Tsarskoe Selo Railway in its initial form was, according to official sources, 5,349,480 rubles (1,528,423 silver rubles), or 213,978 rubles (61,136 silver rubles) per verst, that is, over 50 per cent more than the maximum amount of capital originally allowed (3,500,000 rubles).[101]

The Tsarskoe Selo Railway was expensive to build in comparison with some railways in Europe. But several European railways had cost more partly because, like the Tsarskoe Selo Railway, they had been built solidly and well with the very latest and

96. Von Gerstner, *Bericht über den Stand*, pp. viii-ix.
97. *Ibid.*, pp. ix-x, 11.
98. *Severnaia Pchela*, May 30, 1838, p. 473.
99. *Times* (London), May 30, 1839, p. 5, col. b.
100. *Kommercheskaia Gazeta*, April 4, 1840, p. 161. The company also obtained two small loans from privately owned banks (*Sbornik svedenii o zheleznykh dorogakh v Rossii* [St. Petersburg, 1867], I, 120).
101. *Sbornik svedenii o zheleznykh dorogakh v Rossii*, I, 119; A. I. Chuprov, "Pervaia zheleznaia doroga v Rossii," in *Iz proshlogo russkikh zheleznykh dorog* (Moscow, 1909), p. 10.

best equipment. For example, the Liverpool-Manchester Railway cost the equivalent of 460,000 rubles per verst to build and the London-Birmingham Railway cost 350,000 rubles per verst. But the St. Etienne–Lyons Railway in France cost only the equivalent of 163,000 rubles per verst, the Stockton-Darlington Railway 133,000 rubles per verst, and the Paris–Le Havre Railway 125,000 rubles per verst.[102]

Expenditures on the Tsarskoe Selo Railway had been greater than the estimates partly because of the rise in the price of English iron, partly because of the necessity to build more bridges than planned and to drain swampy areas, and partly because of the sums of money spent as bonuses to manufacturers and workmen in an effort to complete the railway by October 1, 1836. But the chief reason that von Gerstner exceeded the original estimates of costs, as with the Linz-Budweis Railway, was that with an eye to the future he insisted upon building the best sort of railway possible in respect to rolling stock, roadbed, and buildings, without regard to cost.

The Russian government, although it disagreed with von Gerstner on many points, never objected to his desire to build the Tsarskoe Selo Railway as well as possible. Indeed he set a standard by which the government continued to judge projects, and this standard was adhered to in building for the rest of the reign of Nicholas I. These construction methods increased the speed, capacity, and efficiency of the lines built, but also meant that a given sum of money could build fewer versts of railway. It is possible to wonder if a policy of building cheaper but more transportation facilities would not have served the interests of Russia better.

Russia had only the common problems of construction and operation to deal with in building and operating the Tsarskoe Selo Railway. Although attempts to acquire some of the private land resulted, as we have seen, in difficulties such as were so common in Western Europe, the greater part of the land was acquired easily and, when it had to be bought, was cheap.

Apart from the Ural and Caucasus Mountains all of European

102. P. P. Mel'nikov, "Svedeniia o russkikh zheleznykh dorogakh," ed. M. Krutikov, *Krasnyi Arkhiv*, XCIX (1940), 155. The high cost of land was of course partly responsible for this heavy expense of railway building in thickly populated areas like Lancashire.

Russia's topography was unusually favorable for the construction and low-cost operation of railways. To be sure, embankments had sometimes to be built a little high on the Tsarskoe Selo Railway since it was thought necessary to keep the roadbed level, and cuttings had to be avoided for fear that they would fill with snow. Also, although there were no heavy gradients to be dealt with, there were rivers and swamps to be crossed, and taking the easy way of going around an obstruction was not considered.

Most pioneering countries went to great lengths to keep their roadbeds level and straight. The English built cuttings, viaducts, bridges, and tunnels in profusion. In France the Corps des Ponts et Chaussées entirely ignored the economic considerations of what cities might be passed through to plan France's railways in straight lines. Prussia, on the other hand, followed the American example and bypassed many natural obstructions and built railways at much less cost per kilometer than other European countries.

The labor problems which have been mentioned in connection with the Tsarskoe Selo Railway were simple compared to those which arose when the St. Petersburg–Moscow Railway was built and which have become so well known through Nekrasov's poem "The Railway." The quantities of labor required by a railway of some length probably constituted a problem in every country, although this is a subject which in most cases remains to be investigated.

Engineers were largely obtained from abroad. The Institute of Transport Engineers founded by Alexander I provided native mining engineers for canals, drainage works, and roads, but either more confidence was placed in foreign engineers or there were not enough Russian engineers to go around. Rails and equipment, since they also were obtained from abroad and were usually the best obtainable, presented no problem beyond those of transport and expense.

Compared to the United States with its Allegheny mountain chain or Austria with its mountainous terrain or compared to those other pioneering countries, France, Belgium, and especially England with their many well built-up stretches of territory,

Russia seemed in a fortunate position for building railways. It was the country's size combined with a lack of capital that would constitute the big problem in Russia.

Part 2. The Operation of the Tsarskoe Selo Railway (April, 1838–December, 1841)

Because the volume and density of traffic could not be expected in Russia that could be expected in Lancashire or even the St. Etienne–Lyons region, after the construction of the Tsarskoe Selo Railway there were considerable experimentation with rates and schedules, planning of attractions to stimulate traffic, and measures to minimize operating and maintenance expenses. No effort was spared to attract traffic by fitting train service to demand, by insuring orderly operation, and by providing attractive facilities at Tsarskoe Selo and entertainment at Pavlovsk. Experimentation with rates and schedules was constant in many countries at this time, for it had been soon discovered that if very low rates were necessary to attract it the greatest volume of traffic did not always bring in the largest revenue. In the years immediately following its opening, the Tsarskoe Selo Railway proved popular enough and was prudently enough run in regard to operating costs to pay its expenses and yield a return sufficient to pay regular, if at first small, dividends. Furthermore, the operation of the "experimental" railway, in spite of two accidents, proved that railways could be practicable in Russia.

It was of great assistance in attracting traffic to the railway that from the very beginning of its regular operation the Tsarskoe Selo Railway enjoyed the patronage and protection of Nicholas I and his family. On April 12, 1838, the Tsar rode for the first time from St. Petersburg to Tsarskoe Selo and back, the trips requiring twenty-nine minutes and twenty-eight minutes, respectively. He expressed his complete satisfaction with the speed, comfort, and safety of the railway. On April 13, the Tsar rode by railway to Tsarskoe Selo again, this time taking the Empress and his family with him.[1] Thereafter the Tsar and his family gave official recognition to the railway by using it exclusively for travel to Tsarskoe Selo. Whenever Nicholas wished it, a locomotive and a single

1. *Severnaia Pchela*, April 16, 1838, p. 333.

134

carriage were placed at his disposal, and the trip from St. Petersburg was made in thirty to thirty-five minutes.[2]

Another "patron" of the Tsarskoe Selo Railway was Count A. K. Benckendorff, head of the Third Section. After von Gerstner's departure from Russia in January, 1838, Benckendorff took an ever greater direct interest in the affairs of the railway. By the spring of 1839, he was called its "president." It was Benckendorff's habit to have an interest in commercial enterprises, such as the Lübeck Steamship Company and several insurance companies. He generally became a director and appeared once a year to read the annual financial report. For his services he was given an annual salary and stock in the company, thereby amassing a considerable personal fortune. Of course, in the Russia of Nicholas I, it was advantageous for a new commercial enterprise to have the protection and patronage of the Third Section.[3]

The operations of the Tsarskoe Selo Railway were subject to strict supervision by this arm of the government. Not only were the documents of all passengers entering St. Petersburg checked,[4] but also agents called "commissars" supervised passengers at each station. While the train was in motion, the conductors were expected to watch the passengers. Smoking was forbidden in the carriages because of the aversion of Nicholas I to smoking in public. Smokers were expelled from the train and their names and places of employment were noted.[5]

In spite of police efforts the operation of the railway did not always proceed smoothly. The disorders caused by unruly crowds, which had been a problem during the first locomotive trials and in September and October, 1837, continued to plague the operation of the railway. Many passengers had trouble finding seats at the time of peak travel. For a seat on a train returning to St.

2. Österreichisches Haus-, Hof-, und Staatsarchiv, Vienna, letter of Count Karl Ludwig Ficquelmont to Prince Klemens Metternich, 1839, No. 17 (May 29/June 10).

3. See Sidney Monas, *The Third Section: Police and Society under Nicholas I* (Cambridge, Mass., 1961), p. 98; V. S. Virginskii, *Vozniknovenie zheleznykh dorog v Rossii do nachala 40-ykh godov XIX veka* (Moscow, 1949), p. 173.

4. See p. 100 above.

5. B. Velikin, *Peterburg-Moskva: iz istorii Oktiabr'skoi Zheleznoi Dorogi* (Leningrad, 1934), pp. 41-42.

Petersburg in the evening passengers often had to wait two hours or more.[6]

At the beginning of regular service (that is, after April 4, 1838) trains were operated with four classes, as in Belgium. The single fares between St. Petersburg and Tsarskoe Selo were 2 rubles 50 kopecks, 1 ruble 80 kopecks, 1 ruble, and 60 kopecks, respectively.[7] There were finally four stations: St. Petersburg, Moscow *Chaussée*, completed and opened to traffic on November 1, 1838,[8] Tsarskoe Selo, and Pavlovsk, opened to traffic on May 22, 1838. The attractions that were meant to draw the less lowly elements out to Pavlovsk were slow in getting started. The railway between Tsarskoe Selo and Pavlovsk, although one of the first stretches of track completed,[9] had not been opened to the public on October 30, 1837. Grand Duke Mikhail Pavlovich had forbidden its opening until the company had reached an agreement with the local authorities in Pavlovsk concerning regulations for handling crowds in an orderly manner.[10] As a result, the railway to Pavlovsk was opened only on May 22, 1838, at which time amusements meant for people of the upper and middle classes were provided. At first they consisted mainly of dining and dancing, with music supplied for the most part by local ensembles and military bands.[11] Because of the parks and amusement facilities at Tsarskoe Selo and Pavlovsk,[12] and because of the patronage of the imperial family and the encouragement of the Russian press, it became very fashionable to travel by railway

6. *Severnaia Pchela*, May 3, 1838, p. 390.

7. *Ibid.*, August 3, 1838, p. 696.

8. *Journal de St. Pétersbourg*, November 1/13, 1838, p. 524.

9. See p. 120 above.

10. Franz Anton von Gerstner, *Bericht über den Stand der Unternehmung der Eisenbahn von St. Petersburg nach Zarskoe Selo und Pawlowsk* (Leipzig, 1838), p. xxii.

11. *Severnaia Pchela*, May 30, 1838, p. 473; N. F. Findeisen, *Pavlovskii muzykal'nyi vokzal: Istoricheskii ocherk (1838–1912 gg.)* (St. Petersburg, 1912), p. 17.

12. The amusement facilities at Pavlovsk gave the Russian language its word for railway station—*vokzal*. Since the end of the eighteenth century in Russia the word *vokzal,* derived from the name of the famous Vauxhall Gardens in London, had meant "place of amusement." After 1838, it was also applied to the amusement facilities at Pavlovsk and hence to the adjoining railway station. In time it was applied to all railway stations (see Lucien Tesnière, "Les antécédents du nom russe de la gare," *Revue des études slaves,* XXVII [1951], 255-266).

in spite of the fact that—according to a foreign observer—most Russians had been opposed originally to the Tsarskoe Selo Railway.[13]

By the summer of 1838 the Tsarskoe Selo Railway had become the current enthusiasm. Pictures of its locomotives appeared in cheap, popular prints and on candy boxes and letter paper. In July, 1838, a play by one P. S. Federov was produced in St. Petersburg with the title *A Trip to Tsarskoe Selo by Railway*, the action of which took place on a train. When the steam locomotives were first used, to be sure, many of the peasantry and the common people of St. Petersburg were afraid of them.[14] But as the

13. John S. Maxwell, *The Czar, His Court, and People* (New York, 1848), p. 118. When news of the proposals made by von Gerstner in January, 1835, had filtered down to the educated public, the Russian press and public had begun to debate the railway question much more than previously. Von Gerstner's proposals and the idea of building railways in Russia met with qualified acceptance in the pages of the influential St. Petersburg newspaper *Severnaia Pchela* (*Severnaia Pchela*, March 2, 1835, pp. 195-196, and May 25, 1835, p. 460). But in April, 1835, an article was published in another periodical predicting that railways, built by self-seeking foreigners, would ruin the peasant carting industry and hurt the interests of the Russian landowner ("Mysl' russkogo krestianina-izvozshchika o chugunnykh dorogakh i parokhodnykh ekipazhakh mezhdu Peterburgom i Moskvoiu," *Zhurnal Obshchepoleznykh Svedenii*, III [1835], 177-178). The main attack against railways was made in October, 1835, when a supposedly scientific treatise was published claiming that railways in Russia would be "completely impossible, obviously useless, and extremely unprofitable" (N. Atreshkov [Otreshkov-Tarasenko], *Ob ustroenii zheleznykh dorog v Rossii* [St. Petersburg, 1835]). This work, which marked the height of anti-railway sentiment in the Russian press, met only with limited approval and even with sharp criticism by its reviewers (*Biblioteka dlia Chteniia*, XIII [1835], Sec. VI, 38-47; letter of V. F. Odoevskii to M. S. Volkov, May 4, 1837, in *Russkaia Starina*, XXVIII [1880], 804; cf. *Severnaia Pchela*, December 17, 1835, p. 1148).

After the first trials of the Tsarskoe Selo Railway in the autumn of 1836, the Russian press, except for one anonymous brochure (*Neskol'ko slov o zheleznykh dorogakh v Rossii* [Moscow, 1836]) showed nothing but a favorable attitude toward the Tsarskoe Selo Railway. The *Severnaia Pchela* and to a certain extent the *Sanktpeterburgskie Vedomosti* gave the construction of the railway and especially the trials extensive coverage, stressing the swiftness, safety, and pleasures of railway travel. One anonymous author even claimed that a railway journey would have the therapeutic value of a trip to Karlsbad ("Budushchnost' zheleznykh dorog," *Moskovskii Nabliudatel'*, XI [1837], 481).

This favorable attitude of the press, as well as the measures taken by von Gerstner during the period of construction, did much to improve the attitude of the public at least toward the Tsarskoe Selo Railway.

14. While the locomotive trials were being conducted, many people

common people became more familiar with steam locomotives, they became less afraid. Soon they were amusing themselves by watching trains come into St. Petersburg. The common people also began to ride on the railway in great numbers.[15]

Between April 4 and April 30, 1838, there was a total of only 13,923 passengers using the five trains daily in each direction.[16] But because of the increase in traffic produced by the approach of summer and especially the opening of the Pavlovsk station with its amusement facilities, in late May an extra pair of trains was added, and in the period from May 22 to June 21, 1838, there was a total of 116,694 passengers.[17]

As the summer drew to a close and the number of passengers began to decline, special attempts were made to continue to attract traffic. For instance, on Sundays in September there were fireworks and illuminations in Pavlovsk Park.[18] With the approach of autumn and winter, however, the number of travelers decreased still further, and trains were run throughout the autumn and winter of 1838–1839 on a reduced schedule.[19]

To attract passengers during the winter months, the company decided to hold a series of concerts by orchestras and choral groups in the *vokzal* at Pavlovsk. Pavlovsk thus gained the distinction of becoming one of the first centers in Russia for the performance of public concerts. Since the musical taste of the public was still unsophisticated, for the most part light music was performed. The first music director of these winter concerts was

---

crossed themselves as if they beheld demons. Rumors circulated among the populace that the devil sat inside the locomotives and forced the souls of departed sinners to propel them. A widow was supposed to have been visited by the ghost of her late husband, who had drowned himself. He told her that he was going to Semenovskii Square, where he and his fellow suicides were supplying power for the locomotives of the new railway (*Mechanics' Magazine*, October 21, 1837, p. 48; P. E. Gronskii, "Ocherk vozniknoveniia i razvitiia zheleznykh dorog v Rossii," *Zapiski Moskovskogo Otdeleniia Imperatorskogo Russkogo Tekhnicheskogo Obshchestva*, IV [1886], 10; *Vestnik Evropy*, LXXIX [1879], 800).

15. V. V. Salov, "Nachalo zheleznodorozhnogo dela v Rossii, 1836–1855," *Vestnik Evropy*, CXCVI (1899), 241; Findeisen, p. 17.

16. *Journal de St. Pétersbourg*, May 21/June 2, 1838, p. 241; *Severnaia Pchela*, May 30, 1838, p. 473.

17. *Journal de St. Pétersbourg*, July 9/21, 1838, p. 325.

18. *Severnaia Pchela*, September 10, 1838, p. 812, and September 23, 1838, p. 856.

19. *Ibid.*, November 30, 1838, p. 1088.

the composer and orchestra leader Josef Labitsky from Karlsbad in Bohemia, who stayed in Russia until January, 1840. Labitsky performed his own compositions and those of such contemporary composers as Johann Strauss and Lanner. Two pairs of special trains, running non-stop from St. Petersburg to Pavlovsk and return, carried those wishing to attend.[20]

These concerts were so popular that it was decided to hold them in the summer. Heinrich Hermann of Vienna was chosen as director of the summer concerts after he had given a short but highly successful series of concerts at Pavlovsk in January, 1839. The summer concerts, which lasted until early November, featured the same sort of music Labitsky's orchestra played, except that more serious works of the Russian composers Glinka and Dargomyzhskii were included, thereby helping to popularize them.[21]

In May, 1839, the railway suffered its first serious accident. On the evening of Sunday, May 21, a train left Pavlovsk about 1:30 A.M., over an hour late. It consisted of twenty-one carriages: five empty immediately behind the locomotive and sixteen full carriages. As the train was approaching the Tsarskoe Selo station, a coupling on one of the empty carriages broke. The momentum of the full carriages caused the empty carriages to be derailed. In the accident two officials riding in the empty carriages, the manager (*upravliaiushchii*) of the railway, Fassmann, and the conductor of the train, Busch, lost their lives, and a third official suffered a broken leg.[22] The accident caused panic among the passengers, and there was a rumor in St. Petersburg that 150 persons had been killed. This event for a short while reduced the number of people wishing to travel on the railway.[23]

Through the summer of 1839, however, the number of passengers traveling on the railway continued to be large. A full summer schedule was maintained.[24] In August and September,

20. *Ibid.*, January 19, 1839, p. 62.
21. Findeisen, pp. 30-31; *Severnaia Pchela*, October 12, 1839, p. 920.
22. *Journal de St. Pétersbourg*, May 25/June 6, 1839, p. 248.
23. A. V. Nikitenko, *Zapiski i dnevnik* (*1826–1877*) (St. Petersburg, 1893), I, 394-395; *Kommercheskaia Gazeta*, April 4, 1840, p. 161.
24. From May 17, 1839, there were nine pairs of trains each day between St. Petersburg and Tsarskoe Selo, with connecting service to Pavlovsk. In addition, on weekdays, there was one non-stop direct from St. Petersburg to Pavlovsk and return (*Journal de St. Pétersbourg*, May 18/30, 1839, p.

as in 1838, there were fireworks and illuminations in Pavlovsk Park on Sundays.[25] From late November, 1839, the railway started to run trains on its reduced winter schedule, with extra trains non-stop to Pavlovsk for concerts.[26]

The following summer, on the night of August 11, 1840, there was a major accident. The train scheduled to leave Tsarskoe Selo at 10 P.M. for St. Petersburg left an hour late at 11 P.M. Normally it would not have encountered any opposing train, but shortly after 11 P.M. a train of empty carriages left St. Petersburg for Tsarskoe Selo. The driver of the train from Tsarskoe Selo, an Englishman by the name of Robert Maxwell, was advised by verbal order that he was to go into a side track at the Moscow *Chaussée* station to meet this train. The management had to rely on such verbal orders because there was no block signaling or even a magnetic telegraph but only an "optical telegraph," which transmitted messages between St. Petersburg and Tsarskoe Selo by black spheres and lanterns mounted on posts placed at intervals of 1 to 2 versts, a method of communication which was, of course, subject to interference by bad weather conditions.[27]

Driver Maxwell, either through forgetfulness or confusion caused—it was rumored—by an overdose of vodka, proceeded at full speed past the Moscow *Chaussée* station, failing to notice that he had run through the side track back onto the main line. At a point 8 versts from St. Petersburg, there was a collision. Both locomotives and three carriages of each train were damaged. Six persons, including the fireman on the train from St. Petersburg, were killed, and seventy-eight passengers were injured.

The accident brought forth an outcry that the management as well as driver Maxwell was to blame for the accident because

231; *Severnaia Pchela*, May 20, 1839, p. 440). During the following summers this was considered rather too many except for special occasions.

25. *Severnaia Pchela*, July 21, 1839, p. 644, and August 19, 1839, p. 740.

26. *Ibid.*, November 23, 1839, p. 1060. From January 16, 1840, the public entertainments at Pavlovsk were suspended for the winter and were to be held only from spring to autumn from then on because the expense of the entertainments and the special trains was not being met during the winter months by admission fees and increased travel (*Kommercheskaia Gazeta*, April 4, 1840, p. 162; Findeisen, p. 26).

27. D. I. Kargin, *Nachalo signal'nogo dela na nashikh zheleznykh dorogakh* (Moscow, 1922), pp. 8-10.

they had not taken proper precautions.[28] For a while the public would not ride on the railway, which enraged the Tsar. He ordered that not only Maxwell but also several of the managerial personnel be arrested and was of the opinion that they ought to be punished for murder. Count Bobrinskii was hastily summoned from his estate in Kiev Province to give a personal accounting before the Tsar. But by the time the Count reached St. Petersburg, the Tsar's anger had somewhat abated. They made a trip together on the railway in perfect safety, and there was a reconciliation. The public, seeing that the Tsar was still willing to travel by railway and that no harm had befallen him, also regained its confidence.[29]

This accident led to several changes in the operation of the railway. Henceforth two drivers were to be on each locomotive as a safeguard. One or more flatcars loaded with bags filled with straw or sawdust were placed between the locomotive and the carriages to reduce any impact in case of collision. Previously trains had left St. Petersburg and Tsarskoe Selo simultaneously; henceforth trains were to leave St. Petersburg and Tsarskoe Selo at alternate hours. By orders of Nicholas I, no train was to leave a terminal until the train in the opposite direction had arrived.[30] Perhaps because of these precautions, there were no further accidents on the Tsarskoe Selo Railway during the years immediately following.[31]

During the summer of 1841 passenger travel was again increased by special events at Tsarskoe Selo. For instance, on June 29, there was a concert of forty French singers, for which a special train was run direct to Pavlovsk.[32] In the latter part of August, Nicholas sponsored horse races on several days. These drew large crowds, for which extra trains were run.[33] Because of

28. *Severnaia Pchela*, August 13, 1840, p. 721; cf. Prince P. A. Viazemskii, "Krushenie tsarskosel'skogo poezda," in *Polnoe Sobranie Sochinenii* (St. Petersburg, 1879), II, 276-281.

29. Maxwell, pp. 118-119; *Railway Times*, October 10, 1840, p. 870.

30. *Severnaia Pchela*, August 22, 1840, p. 752; Salov, p. 242.

31. For comments see the *Journal de St. Pétersbourg*, January 20/February 1, 1842, p. 1571.

32. *Severnaia Pchela*, May 7, 1841, p. 396, and June 28, 1841, p. 568.

33. *Ibid.*, August 13, 1841, p. 716; *Journal de St. Pétersbourg*, July 29/August 10, 1841, p. 1273.

the increased amount of traffic, the reduced winter schedule was introduced only on November 12 that year.[34]

During 1841, there was such an increase in third- and fourth-class travel that from October 1, 1841, the company began running carriages of these classes on Sundays and holidays on trains between St. Petersburg and Tsarskoe Selo, a policy which had been abandoned just three years previously after the first summer of operation. Such carriages had been serving only the utilitarian purpose of carrying the common people between St. Petersburg and Tsarskoe Selo on weekdays. They had never been used on trains meant especially for carrying the wealthier members of the public to places of amusement, that is, on the trains running between Tsarskoe Selo and Pavlovsk and those running directly from St. Petersburg to Pavlovsk.[35] Fares between St. Petersburg and Tsarskoe Selo were raised for third class to 1 ruble 40 kopecks (40 kopecks silver), and for fourth class to 80 kopecks (25 kopecks silver).[36] The company was also considering raising the first-class and second-class fares.[37]

All this care in adjusting the number of trains to the volume of traffic, all this effort to attract passengers, and the raising of fares resulted in only a small profit. In the years 1838 and 1839 the net profit was somewhat over 8 per cent of the capital of 3.5 million rubles. After something was set aside for spare capital and the necessary payments were made on the government loan, the sum of 140,000 rubles (40,000 silver rubles) was left in each of these years to be paid to the stockholders as a dividend of 4 per cent.[38]

34. *Severnaia Pchela,* November 7, 1841, p. 1000; *Journal de St. Pétersbourg,* November 11/23, 1841, p. 1455.

35. Failing always to include carriages for the common people was not confined to Russia. In England an Act of Parliament was needed in 1844 to oblige railways to run at least one train daily with third-class carriages, the so-called "parliamentary trains."

36. Fares for third and fourth class had already been raised on July 11, 1839, to 1 ruble 20 kopecks and to 70 kopecks, respectively (*Severnaia Pchela,* July 11, 1839, p. 608).

37. *Journal de St. Pétersbourg,* January 20/February 1, 1842, p. 1571.

38. Franz Anton von Gerstner, *Berichte aus den Vereinigten Staaten von Nordamerika über Eisenbahnen, Dampfschiffahrten, Banken und andere öffentliche Unternehmungen* (Leipzig, 1839), pp. 61-62; I. Gorlov, *Obozrenie ekonomicheskoi statistiki Rossii* (St. Petersburg, 1849), p. 268; *Kommercheskaia Gazeta,* April 4, 1840, p. 162. This dividend of 4 per cent

The number of passengers carried and the passenger revenues for the period April 4, 1838, to December 31, 1839, had corresponded roughly to von Gerstner's predictions, but freight revenue was far below.[39] Operation and maintenance costs were far above what von Gerstner had predicted[40] and were the main reason for the relatively low profits.[41]

Some of the biggest items of expense on the Tsarskoe Selo Railway were the repair of locomotives, wages (especially for foreign employees), and the use of imported English coke for fuel. Locomotive maintenance was an especially large item. The two Vulcan locomotives did not perform very satisfactorily and required many repairs. New axles and tires had to be imported from England, since the only factory in Russia which could produce such items charged twice as much as English manufacturers. The English locomotive drivers and other foreign personnel commanded even higher wages in Russia than they did in their homelands and received free lodging. Furthermore, losses were incurred through the incompetence and unreliability of some of these employees. Imported English coke and coal were used for heating purposes as well as for locomotive fuel. In the winter, when 100 per cent more coal was required (a great deal was needed, for one thing, to keep the water in the cisterns from freezing), the cost was very high. From 1837, all orders for equipment placed in England were handled through a London agent. Unfortunately the equipment often proved inferior. Twelve

on the invested capital was the same as the rate of interest on bank deposits in Russia.

39. A. I. Sokolov, *Nakanune 100-letiia: Pervaia russkaia zheleznaia doroga v proshlom* (Leningrad, 1925), p. 25.

40. As has been said, von Gerstner had also greatly underestimated the costs of operation and maintenance of the Linz-Budweis Railway (see R. Huyer, "Die Budweis-Linzer Pferdeeisenbahn," *Mittheilungen des Vereins für Geschichte der Deutschen in Böhmen*, XXXI [1893], 163, n. 1).

41. According to the London *Times*, the average number of passengers per train on the Tsarskoe Selo Railway was 121, compared with 143 passengers per train in Belgium, and only 40 passengers per train in the United States. But the operating expenses of the Tsarskoe Selo Railway in comparison with those of Belgium and American railways stood in a ratio of 36 : 21 : 20 (*Times* [London], July 9, 1841, p. 7, col. d). In other words, there were three times as many passengers per train on the Tsarskoe Selo Railway as on American railways, but operating expenses were almost twice as high, while the situation on Belgium railways was much more favorable both in respect to the number of passengers per train and operating costs.

carriage underframes ordered in England in 1837, for example, were so poorly made that they barely carried the load they were meant to carry.[42] Another source of expense was maintaining the amusement facilities at Pavlovsk, which in 1839 cost 157,090 rubles (44,883 silver rubles).[43]

In the years 1840 and 1841, although the novelty of the Tsarskoe Selo Railway had become less, the railway began to be put on a financially much more sound basis because it was being operated more efficiently. One reason was the hiring in 1839 of one of Count Toll's staff officers, a Colonel L'vov, as manager of the railway after his predecessor had lost his life in the accident of May 21, 1839. Colonel L'vov made many changes that led to efficiency and economy.

Until 1839 locomotives had been repaired in St. Petersburg and coaching stock in Tsarskoe Selo. From 1839, the repair shops were combined in St. Petersburg under a single supervisor. Also the locomotives were more efficiently maintained and required fewer repairs than previously. One of the unsatisfactory Vulcan locomotives was apparently retired from service, and, to take its place, another locomotive was ordered from Robert Stephenson and Company. This new locomotive was put into service in 1840. It consumed relatively little fuel and required almost no repairs. It was also able to pull a load of 6,800 poods at an average speed of 24 versts per hour.

Colonel L'vov also wanted to replace English engine-drivers and supervisory personnel, since they received inordinately high salaries, with Russians. These Russians would be borrowed from government service and placed under Colonel L'vov under conditions of military discipline, thereby increasing their efficiency and reducing expenses. However, the company did not succeed in finding enough Russians sufficiently trained to assume such duties. Afterward, Germans and Austrians, who received only half the salary received formerly by the Englishmen, began to occupy more and more of such positions as engine-driver and train conductor, as well as such posts as inspector and stationmaster.[44]

42. Von Gerstner, *Bericht über den Stand,* pp. xxxiii, xxxv-xxxvi.
43. *Kommercheskaia Gazeta,* April 4, 1840, p. 162.
44. Sokolov, p. 31.

Another economy was effected by returning to the use of wood as locomotive fuel. Locomotive fuel, which had cost the company 27,000 silver rubles in 1839 and 25,000 silver rubles in 1840, cost only 10,000 silver rubles in 1841.[45]

Scheduling of trains was also put on a more realistic basis, conforming even more to demand. Thus, in the summers of 1840 and 1841 there were fewer regularly scheduled trains than there had been in the summer of 1839, but for special events an ample number of extra trains were added.

Closing of the amusement facilities at Pavlovsk in the winter when they were not profitable also effected a needed economy.

In 1840 the net profits were still low (7.8 per cent), the lowest, in fact, since regular operation of the Tsarskoe Selo Railway had begun. Passenger revenues were less, perhaps because of the accident of August 11, or perhaps because the novelty of the railway was wearing off. Operating and maintenance costs were also smaller, but to a lesser extent than revenues.[46] However, the year 1841 was, from the financial point of view, the most success-ful year yet. The passenger revenues, although smaller than in 1839, were on a firmer basis, since the railway was being used less for excursions on summer Sundays in good weather and more for the daily needs of all classes of the population. As envisioned by von Gerstner, the wealthier residents of St. Petersburg began in increasing numbers to build or rent summer *dachi* in the Tsar-skoe Selo–Pavlovsk area.[47] Freight revenues, although they were the highest ever in 1841, remained only a small fraction of the amount originally estimated by von Gerstner.[48] While total reve-nues rose, even though not to 1839 levels, the expenses of opera-tion and maintenance were sharply reduced, producing the great-est net profit in the short history of the railway, about 11.5 per cent of the original capital of 3.5 million rubles. Unfortunately the payment of the fixed charges and of the expense of 35,000 rubles for repairing the rolling stock damaged in the August accident

45. *Kommercheskaia Gazeta*, April 4, 1840, pp. 161-162; *Journal de St. Pétersbourg*, January 20/February 1, 1842, p. 1571.

46. For details, see Sokolov, p. 25, and *Journal de St. Pétersbourg*, Jan-uary 20/February 1, 1842, p. 1571.

47. M. I. Semevskii, *Pavlovsk: ocherk istorii i opisanie, 1777–1877* (St. Petersburg, 1877), p. 293.

48. Sokolov, p. 25.

allowed a dividend of only 4 per cent, as in preceding years.[49]

As a result of the low dividends, the stock of the Tsarskoe Selo Railway, which had begun to depreciate in value when von Gerstner left Russia (it had been issued, it will be remembered, at 200 rubles, or 60 silver rubles), depreciated still further. As late as September, 1841, its value was only 108 rubles (31.5 silver rubles). Only in 1843, when a 7.5 per cent dividend was paid, did it rise to 224 rubles (64 silver rubles).[50] In subsequent years the Tsarskoe Selo Railway became more prosperous, but at the time of the decision to build the St. Petersburg–Moscow Railway no one could be sure of its future revenues.

Part 3. Further proposals by Franz Anton von Gerstner concerning railways in Russia (1836–1839)

Von Gerstner left Russia in January, 1838, before the Tsarskoe Selo Railway was running on a fixed schedule. He left allegedly for reasons of health and with the announced intention of returning the following summer, but discouragement must have played a role in his leaving. Although he had successfully managed to build the Tsarskoe Selo Railway, all of his plans to improve it or to build other railways were met with indifference if not hostility by the other directors of the railway and by the government. He had wished to make several improvements on the Tsarskoe Selo Railway and to extend it a short distance from Tsarskoe Selo to Izhora. He wished to build the other "experimental" railway from St. Petersburg to Peterhof and Oranienbaum and a railway between Moscow and Kolomna. He had also toyed with the possibility of building a short railway between Riga and Mittau. All these projects, except the railway between Riga and Mittau, were to be parts of the system of railways that von Gerstner still hoped to build in Russia. He was never to abandon this vision until his death in Philadelphia on April 12, 1840.

His projects for improving the Tsarskoe Selo Railway included moving the St. Petersburg terminal from its temporary location on Semenovskii Square to the site originally planned on

49. *Journal de St. Pétersbourg*, January 20/February 1, 1842, pp. 1571-1572.
50. Gorlov, p. 268; *Severnaia Pchela*, October 5, 1841, p. 880.

the square near the junction of the Fontanka and the Vedenskii canals, since this site, being nearer to the center of the city, was more heavily traveled and would attract more passengers. Furthermore, the passenger platform on Semenovskii Square, running diagonally across the square, was only 40 sazhens long and could accommodate only three hundred passengers at a time, with the result that often on days of heavy travel there was confusion which drove passengers away. The platform on the Fontanka would be 84 sazhens long, enough for any contingency. The terminal would also be able to expand on the larger site.[1]

In August, 1837, the directors of the company had been favorably disposed toward this proposal and had specifically stated that part of the government loan of 1.5 million rubles was to be used for this purpose. But nothing was done at that time, and in May, 1838, the directors of the company stated that if 300,000 rubles was spent for this purpose the total amount spent for the railway would exceed the capital of 5 million rubles. The plan was therefore rejected.[2] At the stockholders' meeting of April 16, 1839, it was decided to place the permanent St. Petersburg terminal at the cheaper site of the crossing of the Zagorodnyi Prospekt and the Vedenskii Canal, farther from the center of the city than the site on the Fontanka would have been, where it remained thereafter.[3]

Von Gerstner wished to make other improvements on the Tsarskoe Selo Railway to increase the efficiency of operation and bring greater profits. As early as March 30, 1836, the company had applied to the government for the cession of 1,500 to 2,000 desiatins (1 desiatin = 2.7 acres) of state and appanage land along the right of way, on which the company hoped to build *dachi* for the residents of St. Petersburg.[4] However, the com-

1. Franz Anton von Gerstner, *Bericht über den Stand der Unternehmung der Eisenbahn von St. Petersburg nach Zarskoe-Selo und Pawlowsk* (Leipzig, 1838), pp. xi-xii; Franz Anton von Gerstner, *Third Report on the Railroad from St. Petersburg to Zarscoe-Selo and Pawlowsk* (St. Petersburg, January 29, 1837), p. 10.

2. *Zheleznaia doroga ot S. Peterburga do Tsarskogo Sela i Pavlovska* (St. Petersburg, 1837), p. 16.

3. A. I. Sokolov, *Nakanune 100-letiia: Pervaia russkaia zheleznaia doroga v proshlom* (Leningrad, 1925), p. 16; *Sbornik svedenii o zheleznykh dorogakh v Rossii* (St. Petersburg, 1867), I, 119.

4. V. M. Verkhovskii, *Kratkii istoricheskii ocherk nachala i rasprostra-*

pany decided not to take any further action on this matter because of the additional capital outlay necessary.

Von Gerstner also made several minor proposals for increasing the revenues of the Tsarskoe Selo Railway: the formation of a contract with the government for the transport of mail and parcels, the posting of train schedules throughout the city of St. Petersburg, and the levying of tolls from pedestrians for the use of the bridge over the Obvodnyi Canal. The company, because of indifference or the fear of incurring additional expenses, took no action on any of these proposals.[5]

Von Gerstner also wished the company to apply to the government for permission to introduce a set of police regulations, modeled on those of the Paris–St. Germain Railway, in which the mutual rights and obligations of the Tsarskoe Selo Railway and the public would be explicitly stated. These police regulations would introduce greater punctuality and order into the operation of the railway and would improve its reputation in the eyes of the public. But the directors of the company failed to make such an application.[6]

Von Gerstner's main project for the Tsarskoe Selo Railway was a proposed extension 8 versts 120 sazhens in length from Tsarskoe Selo to Izhora, the first post-station on the *chaussée* to Moscow. He was of the opinion that the revenues of the Tsarskoe Selo Railway were based too much on summer passenger travel, and wished, therefore, to create additional sources of revenue, especially from freight traffic, that would have a year-round basis. Goods coming from Moscow on the *chaussée* could be reloaded at Izhora and sent by railway to a warehouse which he planned to build on the Obvodnyi Canal for further shipment to other parts of St. Petersburg or to Kronstadt for export. He also hoped that travelers coming from Moscow on the *chaussée* would prefer to complete their journey to St. Petersburg more quickly and cheaply by getting on the railway at Izhora. Above all, von Gerstner stated that the extension to Izhora should be regarded as the first segment of the railway to Moscow.[7]

neniia zheleznykh dorog v Rossii po 1897 g. vkliuchitel'no (St. Petersburg, 1898), pp. 37-38.

5. Von Gerstner, *Bericht über den Stand,* p. xxxviii.

6. *Ibid.,* p. xvi.

7. Von Gerstner, *Third Report,* pp. 22-24. Abroad, also, the Tsarskoe

Von Gerstner estimated that this extension would cost 1.6 million rubles, which could be raised by another government loan, with the property of the railway as collateral. Four extra locomotives, as well as twenty carriages and sixty freight wagons would be needed.[8]

On August 16, 1837, the stockholders voted overwhelmingly to postpone a decision on the Izhora extension until the railway to Tsarskoe Selo had been completed,[9] and the question was never raised again.

Von Gerstner fared no better with his proposal for the second "experimental" railway, to be built between St. Petersburg and Peterhof, with an extension to Oranienbaum. He felt that the Peterhof Railway would be a profitable undertaking because there was already heavy travel between St. Petersburg and Peterhof by the owners of the hundreds of *dachi* along the Gulf of Finland and by those wishing to visit the gardens of Peterhof. The extension to Oranienbaum would be a great convenience to passengers wishing to go to Kronstadt, who, instead of making the difficult and uncertain journey of 30 versts from St. Petersburg to Kronstadt by water, could go much more quickly by railway from St. Petersburg to Oranienbaum and travel only 6 versts by water from there to Kronstadt. Von Gerstner also suggested that since port facilities for merchant ships at Kronstadt had always been inadequate Peter the Great's plan of building a harbor for merchant ships at Oranienbaum might eventually be realized. When it should be, the railway to Oranienbaum would have great economic value for the transport of freight as well. If, in addition, the Oranienbaum Railway were connected with a St. Petersburg–Moscow–Nizhnii Novgorod Railway, the products of the Volga region could be delivered to Oranienbaum for export within a few days.[10]

This project for a railway to Peterhof and Oranienbaum had

Selo Railway was considered to be the first part of the railway between the capitals (see, for example, *Railway Magazine and Annals of Science*, No. 16 [June, 1837], p. 338).

8. Von Gerstner, *Bericht über den Stand*, p. 33.

9. *Zheleznaia doroga ot S. Peterburga do Tsarskogo Sela i Pavlovska*, pp. 19-20.

10. Franz Anton von Gerstner, *Pervyi otchet ob uspekhakh zheleznoi dorogi iz Sanktpeterburga v Tsarskoe Selo i Pavlovsk* (St. Petersburg, July 26, 1836), p. 20; von Gerstner, *Bericht über den Stand*, pp. xl-xli.

been tentatively authorized, along with the Tsarskoe Selo Railway, in the letter from Count Novosil'tsev to von Gerstner on December 21, 1835.[11] Von Gerstner had decided to build the Tsarskoe Selo Railway first because it would be easier to acquire the necessary land since it was mostly state and appanage land. The proposed routes of the Peterhof Railway, on the other hand, would have to run through many private estates and gardens along the Gulf of Finland, and some valuable buildings might have to be demolished. Von Gerstner was of the opinion that landowners would consent to this and cede their lands only when they were firmly convinced of the value of railways.[12]

Von Gerstner thought that the Peterhof Railway should be built by an interlocking company with the same directors as the Tsarskoe Selo Railway, the stockholders of which should have priority in buying stock in the Peterhof Railway. The Peterhof Railway should use the same passenger terminal in St. Petersburg as the Tsarskoe Selo Railway and the same locomotive sheds and repair shops. Within the limits of St. Petersburg it should use the same tracks. Both railways could pool their rolling stock in case of extraordinary traffic on one of the two lines. The same personnel could be used for dispatching trains, which would leave for Tsarskoe Selo and Peterhof at alternate hours.[13]

In the summer of 1836, the directors of the Tsarskoe Selo Railway asked permission of the Russian government to collect data on road traffic between St. Petersburg, Peterhof, and Oranienbaum, and this permission was granted on June 30.[14]

Also in the summer of 1836, after his return from Western Europe, von Gerstner made surveys, planning two possible routes, both using the tracks of the Tsarskoe Selo Railway for 1.5 versts within St. Petersburg. The first route was 37 versts 40 sazhens long and went inland south of the *chaussée* to Peterhof, rising 62 feet from St. Petersburg and falling 55 feet before reaching

11. See pp. 92-93 above.
12. Franz Anton von Gerstner, *O vygodakh postroeniia zheleznoi dorogi iz Sanktpeterburga v Tsarskoe Selo i Pavlovsk* (St. Petersburg, 1836), p. 21; von Gerstner, *Bericht über den Stand*, p. xl.
13. Franz Anton von Gerstner, *Vtoroi otchet ob uspekhakh zheleznoi dorogi iz Sanktpeterburga v Tsarskoe Selo i Pavlovsk* (St. Petersburg, October 7, 1836), p. 16; von Gerstner, *Bericht über den Stand*, p. xli.
14. Verkhovskii, pp. 40-41.

Oranienbaum, but with no gradient greater than 1:385. The second route surveyed was 36 versts 80 sazhens long and followed the *chaussée* to Peterhof at first but then ran directly along the shore of the Gulf of Finland, partly on an embankment built into the gulf itself. This second route would be perfectly level and would require fewer earthworks.[15]

Von Gerstner estimated the total cost of the Peterhof Railway at 8.4 million rubles, including nine locomotives, eighty carriages, and twenty freight wagons. No estimates were made of revenues or expenses, since von Gerstner hoped that those of the Tsarskoe Railway would provide a basis for planning.[16]

Von Gerstner was of the opinion that many investors both in Russia and abroad would be interested in investing in the Peterhof Railway; so on July 7-8, 1836, that is, about three weeks after his return from abroad, he published notices in the *Kommercheskaia Gazeta* and *Sanktpeterburgskie Vedomosti* announcing a stock company to build the railway. Von Gerstner stated that since work on the Tsarskoe Selo Railway was proceeding well he was availing himself of the exclusive right given by the Russian government in Count Novosil'tsev's letter of December 21, 1835, to build this second railway and that therefore permission was as good as granted. Surveys were under way and estimates of costs were being set up. Construction could begin in the spring of 1837, and the railway would be opened no later than July 1, 1838. Von Gerstner also invited Russian ironmasters to supply 150,000 poods of iron rails and 50,000 poods of cast-iron rail chairs, or twice these amounts if the railway were double-tracked.[17]

The notices attracted attention in England and caused the *Mechanics' Magazine* to print a notice to the effect that von Gerstner was planning to commence work on the railway to Peterhof and Oranienbaum in the spring of 1837.[18]

Von Gerstner's notices in the St. Petersburg newspapers attracted attention of a less favorable nature in official Russian circles. Nicholas I was angry that von Gerstner should have

15. Von Gerstner, *Third Report*, p. 29.
16. Von Gerstner, *Bericht über den Stand*, p. xli.
17. Von Gerstner, *Pervyi otchet*, p. 21; V. S. Virginskii, *Vozniknovenie zheleznykh dorog v Rossii do nachala 40-ykh godov XIX veka* (Moscow, 1949), p. 175.
18. *Mechanics' Magazine*, September 17, 1836, p. 432.

published these notices without asking official permission first. On August 4, the Tsar asked Lieutenant General Gorgoli, who had temporarily replaced Count Toll as head, whether von Gerstner had submitted a proposal for the Peterhof Railway to the Main Administration of Transport and Buildings. Gorgoli answered that von Gerstner had been informed that any further projects of his would not be considered until the Tsarskoe Selo Railway had been built and operated successfully.[19]

Von Gerstner gradually put aside his plan to build the railway to Peterhof and Oranienbaum, but he never actually gave it up. In October, 1836, he still hoped to start construction in February, 1837, and to complete the railway to Peterhof by July 1, 1838, and the extension to Oranienbaum by the end of the same year.[20] But by January, 1837, he was stating that he did not wish to start construction until the Tsarskoe Selo Railway had been completed and in operation for four weeks.[21]

One of the main difficulties that had faced von Gerstner in this railway project had been the problem of land. Nicholas I was opposed to allowing the fine estates and gardens along the Gulf of Finland to be ruined by the railway. On August 29, 1836, the Tsar stated that landowners along the proposed route knew nothing of von Gerstner's proposals and that he himself doubted if he would give his permission for construction of the railway if von Gerstner planned to build it through the Peterhof Gardens.[22] In the 1840's, in connection with projects of others for the Peterhof Railway, Nicholas was still loath to allow expropriation of lands along the proposed route.[23]

If Nicholas was reluctant to allow expropriation of the land necessary for the Peterhof Railway, the landowners along the proposed route would surely have been even more reluctant. Von Gerstner had obtained only with difficulty a few plots of private land for the Tsarskoe Selo Railway; these difficulties would have

19. Verkhovskii, p. 41.
20. Von Gerstner, *Vtoroi otchet*, p. 17.
21. Von Gerstner, *Third Report*, p. 28.
22. Verkhovskii, p. 42.
23. Public Record Office, London, Foreign Office 65 (Diplomatic and consular reports from Russia to England), Vol. CCCXXII. Andrew Buchanan to the Earl of Aberdeen, No. 45 (St. Petersburg, September 26 [N.S.], 1846).

been multiplied many times in obtaining land for the Peterhof Railway.

In point of fact, the railway from St. Petersburg to Peterhof and Oranienbaum was completed only after the death of Nicholas I, being opened to traffic in June, 1864.[24]

Another of von Gerstner's unrealized projects was to build a railway from Moscow to Kolomna, a town of about 10,000 inhabitants, located near the confluence of the Moskva River and the Oka River. This railway, unlike the Tsarskoe Selo and Peterhof railways, would—as a substitute for the very slow and inadequate water communications between the Oka River and Moscow—be potentially of great economic significance. The idea of building this railway had originally been suggested to von Gerstner in the autumn of 1834 by the military governor general of Moscow, Prince D. V. Golitsyn, who had been interested in improving the transportation system of the Moscow area since the 1820's.[25]

Von Gerstner saw this railway not only as a means of providing Moscow with better communications with the Oka River, but as part of a greater scheme. He hoped to establish a connecting steamboat service between Kolomna and Nizhnii Novgorod, so that travelers and goods from Moscow could reach Nizhnii Novgorod in twenty-four to thirty-six hours. He hoped also that the railway would serve to awaken public interest in a railway between the capitals, to which the Kolomna Railway would be connected, thus providing a through route from Nizhnii Novgorod to the Baltic.[26]

The railway was to be about 95 versts long and built in a straight line over nearly level terrain. The costs of construction were estimated at about 17 million rubles.[27]

While he was building the Tsarskoe Selo Railway, von Gerstner was making preliminary preparations for building the Moscow-Kolomna Railway. On March 30, 1836, Prince D. V. Golitsyn sent a letter to von Gerstner in England, stating that he was prepared to put such a railway under his protection and to give

24. *Sbornik svedenii o zheleznykh dorogakh v Rossii*, I, 121-122.
25. Von Gerstner, *Vtoroi otchet*, p. 17.
26. *Ibid.*, pp. 17-18; von Gerstner, *Third Report*, pp. 30-31.
27. *Severnaia Pchela*, November 20, 1839, p. 1052.

it every aid and urging von Gerstner to make surveys and estimates. Von Gerstner on his trip to Western Europe ordered surveying instruments in England and Austria for the railway as well as a locomotive to be delivered in the spring of 1837.[28]

Unfortunately for von Gerstner, Prince Golitsyn was abroad during the summer of 1836 when von Gerstner returned to Russia and was temporarily replaced by a Count Tolstoi. In early July von Gerstner applied to Count Tolstoi for surveying equipment and soldiers to help during surveying. Count Tolstoi reported to Minister of the Interior D. N. Bludov that he had no information on this subject and personally felt that a waterway between the River Moskva and the Volga would be more useful and that therefore he had not granted von Gerstner's request. Bludov, on the other hand, felt that von Gerstner's surveys could cause no harm and wished to instruct Count Tolstoi to grant von Gerstner's request. But on August 29 the Tsar said that there was no need to hurry and that one should wait to consult Prince Golitsyn upon his return from Europe.

By October, Prince Golitsyn had returned and reported to Bludov that he considered railways very useful in the great expanses of Russia and that he had agreed to von Gerstner's request to carry out surveys for a railway between Moscow and Kolomna, since on these surveys a project to assemble the necessary capital could be based.

Upon hearing Prince Golitsyn's report, Bludov and the Committee of Ministers on October 20 agreed to allow von Gerstner to carry out his surveys, as long as this permission was not considered an authorization to build the railway. If this authorization was eventually refused, von Gerstner would have no right to claim compensation for expenses incurred. This decision received imperial confirmation on October 30, and von Gerstner was informed on November 7, 1836.[29]

By February, 1837, surveying of the route was definitely under way. Von Gerstner himself stated later that he and other engineers under him made surveys until 1838 and that other preparations were made for starting construction on the railway.[30]

28. Von Gerstner, *Vtoroi otchet*, pp. 17-18.
29. Verkhovskii, pp. 41-43; von Gerstner, *Third Report*, p. 30.
30. *Railway Magazine and Annals of Science*, No. 12 (February, 1837),

But authorization for the Moscow-Kolomna Railway was never granted to von Gerstner. Even the second Hackworth locomotive, slated for delivery in 1837 and presumably meant for the Moscow-Kolomna Railway, was never delivered.

One of the reasons that authorization was never given was the opposition of Count Toll. This opposition to the Moscow-Kolomna Railway marks the real beginning of Toll's opposition to railways. He opposed even more strongly various projects for main-line railways submitted in the late 1830's.[31]

Von Gerstner also made a proposal to construct a railway between Riga and Mittau in the Baltic Provinces. Between these towns, which had a combined population of 63,000, there was already a lively traffic both of passengers and of freight. The railway would be 42 versts long, running along a nearly straight and level route. It would take a year to build.[32] Von Gerstner seems never to have taken any action on this project, perhaps because this railway, unlike all the others he proposed, did not fit into his general plan to provide Russia with a connected system of railways.

In connection with his various railway projects, in particular those for the Peterhof and Moscow-Kolomna railways, von Gerstner wanted very much to build a factory to produce rails in Russia. Despite the discouragement he had received on this score from the special committee earlier in the year,[33] on his trip abroad in the spring and summer of 1836 he entered into negotiations with John Cockerill in the hope that the Russian government would allow the two of them to set up a stock company for such a factory. Cockerill sent a representative to Russia to help von Gerstner negotiate this matter. On July 10, 1836, Count Kankrin and Major General Chevkin stated that the Russian government would assist such an enterprise, since it wished to help to develop the Russian metallurgical industry. The government even sent an agent to help Cockerill's representative locate a suitable site

---

p. 141; Franz Anton von Gerstner, *Berichte aus den Vereinigten Staaten von Nordamerika über Eisenbahnen, Dampfschiffahrten, Banken und andere öffentliche Unternehmungen* (Leipzig, 1839), p. 66.

31. See chap. v below.

32. Von Gerstner, *Vtoroi otchet*, p. 18.

33. Virginskii, *Vozniknovenie*, p. 146.

for the factory.[34] Von Gerstner quickly concluded a definite agreement with Cockerill, who sent two small industrial steam engines for the factory. Von Gerstner hoped to be producing rails by the summer of 1837 and to use these rails for the Peterhof and Kolomna railways. He hoped also to produce castings and eventually locomotives, using the puddling process and modern equipment in his factory.[35]

But this project, also, was fated never to be realized. It is to be supposed that von Gerstner, when he failed to receive any definite authorization for further railway construction, naturally did not set up a factory to produce rails.

Even after he left Russia, von Gerstner cherished his dream of giving Russia a system of railways. Writing from America in 1839, he said he hoped to return to Russia to build such a system and that he would be even more competent to do so, since he had learned much about railways in America. He pointed out that America was thinly populated, yet in ten years the equivalent of 300 million rubles had been spent to build the equivalent of 4,500 versts of railways. He asked why Russia, with three times the population, could not do the same, especially since railways would have a tremendous strategic value in Russia. Furthermore, American railways carried fewer passengers and less freight than a railway between the capitals would carry, and yet they were profitable. A railway between St. Petersburg and Moscow, as well as one between Moscow and Odessa later, could therefore be built much more substantially than American railways and still be profitable.

The Tsarskoe Selo Railway could form a segment of the St. Petersburg–Moscow Railway, and it and the projected St. Petersburg–Oranienbaum and Moscow–Kolomna railways would all fit into his plan. He repeated his suggestion that together with a fast steamboat service from Nizhnii Novgorod to Kolomna these railways would allow goods to be carried from the Volga area to Oranienbaum for export in a matter of days.[36] A railway of

34. Von Gerstner, *Pervyi otchet*, p. 14.
35. Von Gerstner, *Vtoroi otchet*, pp. 18-19; von Gerstner, *Third Report*, p. 32.
36. Von Gerstner, *Berichte aus den Vereinigten Staaten*, pp. 65-67.

roughly similar length then being built from Buffalo to Boston seemed comparable to him.[37]

One receives the impression that von Gerstner had antagonized his fellow directors by his insistence on excessively high standards for the Tsarskoe Selo Railway. In March, 1838, he had written that upon his return to Russia he wished no official role in the operation of the Tsarskoe Selo Railway, since his relations with the other directors in the months previous had not been pleasant, but he was still willing to act as a consultant.[38] Von Gerstner thought in terms of the future and was perhaps overly optimistic in appraising the potential success of his undertakings, while the other directors were concerned with immediate profits for the stockholders.[39] He was undoubtedly somewhat difficult in these matters. In building the Linz-Budweis Railway, he had also come into conflict with the stockholders and with his fellow engineers for much the same reason, but building railways on a large scale, and building them well, was for him a point of honor.[40]

Von Gerstner had the satisfaction at least of building the first public railway in Russia, the Tsarskoe Selo Railway, "the grandmother of Russian railways," as A. I. Stückenberg called it.[41] Russian writers both nearly contemporary with von Gerstner[42] and from later times[43] naturally consider the Tsarskoe Selo Railway the precursor of the St. Petersburg–Moscow Railway and of subsequent Russian railways. It was not just the plaything (*igrushka*) that it was so often called. As the first operational public railway in Russia it showed that railways could be built and operated there and it accustomed the people to their use.

37. *Ibid.*, p. 5.
38. Von Gerstner, *Bericht über den Stand,* pp. xxxvi-xxxvii.
39. Sokolov, p. 27.
40. Von Gerstner, *Bericht über den Stand,* p. xiv.
41. A. I. Shtukenberg, "Iz istorii zheleznodorozhnogo dela v Rossii: Nikolaevskaia doroga mezhdu Peterburgom i Moskvoiu," *Russkaia Starina,* XLVI (1885), 311.
42. I. Gorlov, *Obozrenie ekonomicheskoi statistiki Rossii* (St. Petersburg, 1849), p. 269.
43. See, for example, A. I. Chuprov, "Pervaia zheleznaia doroga v Rossii," in *Iz proshlogo russkikh zheleznykh dorog* (Moscow, 1909), p. 11; cf. P. E. Gronskii, "Ocherk vozniknoveniia i razvitiia zheleznykh dorog v Rossii," *Zapiski Moskovskogo Otdeleniia Imperatorskogo Russkogo Tekhnicheskogo Obshchestva,* IV (1886), 13.

It also brought up the problems connected with railways early and gave Russia experience in railway construction upon which to build. Had he not died in 1840, von Gerstner, rather than the American engineer, Major G. W. Whistler, might have been called upon to help build the St. Petersburg–Moscow Railway; but, until 1842, the question of whether the railway between St. Petersburg and Moscow would ever be built was still open.

Chapter V. Projects submitted by citizens for railways in Russia (1837–1839)

From 1837 to 1839 the Russian government did nothing to provide Russia with more railways; there was neither construction nor planning. But railways were nonetheless being much thought of and discussed. The press reflected the continuing interest,[1] and projects to build railways were submitted to the government, although all were rejected, largely because of the influence of Counts Kankrin and Toll.

1. In October, 1836, i.e., while the Tsarskoe Selo Railway was still under construction, F. Bulgarin printed an article written by him in *Severnaia Pchela* stating that further railway construction in Russia would be both possible and useful. He was of the opinion that railways should be built to connect the two capitals with each other as well as with Odessa and Kazan, since railways were superior to other forms of transportation and would therefore help Russian industry and agriculture (F. Bulgarin, "Patrioticheskii vopros: mogut li sushchestvovat' v Rossii chugunnye dorogi i budut li oni polezny?" *Severnaia Pchela*, October 12, 1836, pp. 930-932).

Discussion in the press became more frequent when the Tsarskoe Selo Railway had been opened to regular service in April, 1838. In the late spring of that year an article appeared, again in the *Severnaia Pchela*, stating that it was time to think of building a railway between St. Petersburg and Moscow via Novgorod. This railway would have great economic value and would cost less per verst than had the Tsarskoe Selo Railway ("O zheleznoi doroge iz S. Peterburga v Moskvu," *Severnaia Pchela*, May 30, 1838, pp. 475-476; May 31, 1838, pp. 479-480; June 1, 1838, pp. 483-484). This article led to a debate in the pages of the *Severnaia Pchela* during the summer of 1838 concerning the St. Petersburg–Moscow Railway. The main issues were whether to build the railway in a straight line or via Novgorod and how much the railway would cost ("O zheleznoi doroge mezhdu Peterburgom i Moskvoiu," *Severnaia Pchela*, July 2, 1838, pp. 587-588; *Severnaia Pchela*, July 21, 1838, pp. 651-652, and September 1, 1838, p. 784).

Opponents of railways were still expressing themselves in the press despite the successful operation of the Tsarskoe Selo Railway, although they were fewer in number and more restrained in their arguments. In 1838 one A. Pravdin published a pamphlet in which he claimed that railway construction in Russia would encounter financial difficulties and that conditions in Russia, unlike those in England and France, were not yet ripe for railway construction. In his opinion the only railway that could be built at that time was the St. Petersburg–Moscow Railway, and even that was a doubtful proposition financially (A. Pravdin, *O zheleznykh i tortsovykh dorogakh v Rossii* [Moscow, 1838]).

As the following account of them will show, these projects ranged from short lines, to be inexpensively built by an entrepreneur, to solidly built networks financed by the state. Whether large or small, these projects could not be embarked upon without at least the permission of the government, and since the bureaucracy as a whole was skeptical of the value of railways and since there was no large group of citizens actively promoting them in any case, any additional railway construction waited upon the Tsar's decision to build.

Nicholas I does not seem to have been very much interested in short lines, although he certainly did not oppose their construction. A short railway to link two rivers probably seemed worthy but did not particularly excite his interest. With his strong belief in centralized control, anything resembling a laissez faire policy permitting a great many little private lines to grow up in a haphazard manner as they had done in the United States and England would have been repugnant, but there were not enough interested entrepreneurs for this question to be raised.

On the other hand, plans for ambitious networks built by the state, attractive as they might be, could hardly win strong support from the Tsar, who had the responsibility for the state's finances. In Western Europe master plans for whole countries were being suggested in the early 1830's. As early as 1834 the Belgian government had started to build a network of trunk lines at the expense of the state. Since Russia's need for transportation from its rich agricultural regions to major cities and ports was so obvious, it was natural that citizens should suggest projects for individual railways, or even for whole networks, just as von Gerstner had done.

Governments elsewhere were also hesitating to embark on overall plans. Friedrich List only a few years before (1833) had published a pamphlet urging the execution of a plan for railways covering all of Germany. Fresh from a trip to the United States, he was fired by enthusiasm, but although he lived to see most of his plan carried out, at the time he had no success in getting the plan accepted. France had had the elements of a plan sketched out at about the same time, but it was 1842 before the Parliament could agree on measures to encourage construction. A plan for Russia would involve vastly greater distances than a plan for

France or Germany, so that Nicholas I's government would have greater cause for hesitancy than the governments in Western Europe. These large schemes for Russia came too early. Railways would have to be proven economic successes in a large number of places before the government could be expected to embark on expenditures as large as would have been necessary for any of them.

A project for the St. Petersburg–Moscow Railway was the one that appealed to Nicholas I. Such a project was uppermost in the minds of most people interested in railways, as articles in the press tend to show. But building the St. Petersburg–Moscow Railway involved an expense too great to be assumed lightly.

If the expense of building a long railway troubled the believers in railways, it troubled responsible officials still more. The high cost of construction and operation of the Tsarskoe Selo Railway made them wonder about the advisability of any further railway construction.[2] Some members of the government must have wondered by what amount railways hundreds of versts in length would exceed original estimates of construction costs if a railway only 25 versts in length exceeded them by more than 1.5 million rubles. Would the government be forced to grant correspondingly greater loans to allow such railways to be completed? The Tsarskoe Selo Railway, because of its shortness and because of the type of traffic over it resulting from its location, could neither prove nor disprove the potential economic value of other railways in Russia. Perhaps other members of the government might have been more venturesome had it not been for the influence of Count Kankrin and Count Toll. Nicholas I, still not convinced that his group of advisers was wrong, was too cautious to override their decisions.

Among those making proposals there were some who felt that, desirable as they might be in theory, railways would be too expensive to build over the great expanses of Russia and that the comparatively high cost of construction of the Tsarskoe Selo Railway gave weight to the contention that the expense would be prohibitive. To these men some form of steam traction seemed

2. V. M. Verkhovskii, *Kratkii istoricheskii ocherk nachala i rasprostraneniia zheleznykh dorog v Rossii po 1897 g. vkliuchitel'no* (St. Petersburg, 1898), p. 44; M. A. Polievktov, *Nikolai I: biografiia i obzor tsarstvovaniia* (Moscow, 1918), p. 279.

desirable, but perhaps on some inexpensive, simplified form of railway or on an advanced form of ordinary road. Some of the suggestions made were ingenious but quite impractical, for example, the "pillar railway" of I. K. El'manov[3] and the similar "prismatic railway" of K. V. von Hübenthal. Whereas El'manov envisioned the use of his invention only for mines and factories, von Hübenthal advocated the application of his on a nationwide basis.

Von Hübenthal thought that the main expense of railway construction was not rails but the embankment needed to make the roadbed level. He therefore suggested that in uneven terrain roads should be built upon a double row of pillars, much like an elevated railway. Along these rows of pillars were to be laid longitudinal beams hewn in the shape of a prism, along which steam locomotives would run. Conventional embankments could be used where they did not have to be built very high or where wood was scarce.[4]

Perhaps the most practical inventor of possible substitutes for railways was V. P. Gur'ev.[5] In the middle of the 1830's Gur'ev proposed to form stock companies to build a system consisting of a combination of "plank roads" (*tortsovye dorogi*), which were to be parquet pavements of hexagonal wooden planks, and of improved "winter roads." Steam traction could be used on both; on plank roads using steam traction two flat iron rails, seven inches wide and one inch thick, would be fitted into the plank surface so as to be level with it, like streetcar tracks into a pavement. These means of transportation would have the advantage, according to Gur'ev, of providing more rapid and reliable transportation while using as chief materials wood and snow, materials very abundant in Russia.[6]

3. V. S. Virginskii, "Zheleznodorozhnyi vopros v Rossii do 1835 goda," *Istoricheskie Zapiski*, XXV (1948), 163-164.

4. K. V. fon Giubental, "Prizimaticheskie dorogi, vmesto zheleznykh, v Rossii," *Severnaia Pchela*, March 9, 1839, pp. 215-216.

5. For a brief sketch of the life and career of Gur'ev, see A. S. Tanenbaum, *Vasilii Petrovich Gur'ev i ego idei o dorogakh dlia avtomobilei* (St. Petersburg, 1902).

6. V. P. Gur'ev, *Ob uchrezhdenii tortsovykh dorog i sukhoputnykh parokhodov v Rossii posredstvom kompanii* (St. Petersburg, 1837); V. P. Gur'ev, "Mysli o pervoi kompanii zimnikh dorog v Rossii," *Biblioteka dlia Chteniia*, XXXI (1838), Sec. IV, 1-17.

Gur'ev's proposals received some qualified praise in the Russian press and even awoke the interest of some in government circles, including the Tsar himself, who allowed them to be referred to a special committee. Also the government granted Gur'ev 15,000 rubles to publish a booklet explaining the advantages of plank roads, much as it had allowed von Gerstner to publish his *O vygodakh*.[7] In the end, however, Gur'ev's plans produced no permanent result, since by 1837 the Russian government and public were too interested in railways to consider seriously a form of transportation which did not represent very much of an improvement over *chaussées* and ordinary "winter roads." That the Russian government considered Gur'ev's proposals as seriously as it did shows how eager it was to find improved transportation at manageable cost.

Even before the completion of the Tsarskoe Selo Railway one or two projects for railway construction had been submitted to the government by men other than von Gerstner. In November, 1835, while von Gerstner's original proposals were still under discussion, a foreigner named de Riddel presented to Nicholas I a project to build a railway from St. Petersburg to Odessa, a distance of 1,806 versts. This project was too ambitious for this early time; even Mel'nikov agreed on this.[8] And in 1837 an anonymous project was submitted to the government for a railway using horse traction to link the Volga and Don rivers; three possible routes were suggested, all about 60 versts long. The government merely filed this modest proposal away in its archives.[9]

Late in 1837 a St. Petersburg merchant of the First Guild named E. I. Feigen submitted a memorandum to Nicholas I through Count Benckendorff which proposed to organize a private stock company, in which the government would participate, to build a railway using steam traction linking St. Petersburg, Tver, and Rybinsk and having a branch to Moscow. The original capital of the company would be 125 million rubles, with an expected yearly profit of 13.2 per cent.

Since Rybinsk was the starting point for passage through all

7. *Biblioteka dlia Chteniia*, XXIII (1837), Sec. V, 21-56; Gur'ev, *Ob uchrezhdenii*, p. 40.

8. P. P. Mel'nikov, "Svedeniia o russkikh zheleznykh dorogakh," ed. M. Krutikov, *Krasnyi Arkhiv*, XCIX (1940), 155.

9. V. S. Virginskii, *Vozniknovenie zheleznykh dorog v Rossii do nachala 40-ykh godov XIX veka* (Moscow, 1949), pp. 176-177.

three Volga-Neva canal systems and the railway would largely parallel the Vyshnii Volochek System, this was clearly a suggestion for supplementation of waterways by railways. Feigen asserted that the main source of revenue of the railway would not be the transportation of passengers but of freight. (Along this route this would necessarily have been the case, since the area traversed by the proposed railway had a sparse population.) Feigen stated that the main advantages of his railway would be the rapid and uninterrupted provisioning of St. Petersburg and a quicker turnover of capital for the Russian merchant.

In addition to concessions similar to those received by von Gerstner for the Tsarskoe Selo Railway, Feigen also requested a substantial amount of direct government aid in raising the necessary capital. The government was to take at least 25 per cent of the shares and was to guarantee the whole amount. Furthermore, the shares were to be equal to government financial paper and would be accepted as security (*v zalog*) in government contracts and deliveries.

On January 15, 1838, Nicholas I reported to Feigen through Count Benckendorff that he was favorably disposed to the project, but that he would have to consult Count Toll first. Count Toll rejected Feigen's proposal on the ground that such a railway was not necessary and would receive no revenue, since competing water transportation was cheaper.[10]

In March, 1838, the Moscow merchant and State Councilor A. V. Abaza submitted a project for the St. Petersburg–Moscow Railway which was the most detailed and well-reasoned project submitted in the years 1837-1839. Abaza was shrewd enough to submit his project to Nicholas I through the military governor general of Moscow, Prince D. V. Golitsyn, who was in favor of railways and who had encouraged von Gerstner in his efforts to build the Moscow-Kolomna Railway. On March 21, 1838, Prince Golitsyn sent Abaza's project to the Tsar together with a letter stating that he knew Abaza to be honest and a good businessman.[11] Golitsyn suggested that since the matter was of the utmost

10. D. I. Kargin, "Podgotovitel'nyi period k postroike nashei pervoi magistral'noi zheleznoi dorogi mezhdu stolitsami," *Tekhnicheskii Zhurnal Narodnogo Komissariata Putei Soobshcheniia*, Nos. 9-10 (1923), pp. 405-407.

11. Nicholas I formed such a good opinion of Abaza that, as we shall

importance a special committee should be formed to discuss it.[12]

In his project Abaza stressed the advantages the railway would have for the provisioning of St. Petersburg, for making Russian exports more competitive on the world market, and for the transportation of soldiers, matters of special interest to Nicholas I. Most important of all, Abaza stated, a railway would provide rapid communication by means of which Nicholas could make sure that his will was being carried out quickly and faithfully for the welfare of the Russian people.

The route of the railway would be St. Petersburg–Volochek–Tver–Moscow in a straight line bypassing Novgorod and Torzhok and would have a length of about 600 versts. The original capital of the company would be 120 million rubles and the expected yearly profits nearly 10 per cent. The railway, which would take six years to build, was to be constructed with two sets of tracks, one set using steam traction and the other horse traction. Steam locomotives would pull trains carrying passengers, mail, and perishables and could make the journey between St. Petersburg and Moscow in fifteen to twenty hours. Horses would pull wagons with heavier goods of lower value and could cover the distance between the capitals in six to twelve days.

Since the manufacture of rails and rolling stock had been an important issue in connection with the Tsarskoe Selo Railway, Abaza wished to solve the problem by inviting John Cockerill or someone else enjoying a European reputation to set up a factory to produce rails and to build and repair locomotives and other rolling stock, thereby avoiding the necessity of importing such equipment.

To raise the necessary capital of 120 million rubles, shares of stock were to be distributed in St. Petersburg and Moscow and also in the provinces. If all shares were not taken within a year, those left over would be offered to foreign investors, but Abaza hoped that there would be enough patriotic Russians to take all the shares. Abaza realized that if this amount of capital was to be raised within Russia the small investor with little capital on hand

see presently, he called upon him later to help gather information concerning a possible St. Petersburg–Moscow railway and for his help in the planning when the railway was about to be built.

12. "Pis'mo moskovskogo voennogo gen.-gubernatora kn. D. V. Golitsyna Nikolaiu I, 21 marta 1838 g.," *Krasnyi Arkhiv*, LXXVI (1936), 107-108.

and desiring a profit immediately would have to be attracted to the enterprise. Therefore, although each share would cost 600 rubles, it could be paid for in six yearly installments. The stockholders would receive a 5 per cent yearly dividend from the very beginning. For the first three years this would require 7 million rubles to be supplied from the capital of the company. But in three years, when the railway had been opened from St. Petersburg to Volochek, this dividend could be paid from its revenues.

Abaza was aware that these measures might not by themselves be enough to raise the necessary capital. Therefore, like Feigen, he asked for aid from the government. But he knew that even though the government was willing to make concessions to railway enterprises, it was still ill-disposed toward the idea of making financial sacrifices to help them. Therefore he did not ask for a direct government loan or subsidy; neither did he ask that the government take any large number of shares of stock, or that it guarantee a profit on the capital. He did ask for an indirect government loan: every landowner mortgaging his land and serfs with the government Mortgage Councils (*Opekunskie Sovety*) and wishing to be a stockholder would receive an additional 50 rubles per serf over and above the original amount of the mortgage loan. This sum was to be deposited in the name of Abaza's company, which would issue stock for it. (Here was a shrewd businessman's appraisal of the finances of the typical members of the landowning class and his idea of a means by which they could become stockholders in the new railway, which otherwise would be impossible.) He also asked that stock in the company would be accepted as security in government contracts, deliveries, and purchases. In addition, he asked for what amounted to the patronage and protection of Nicholas I and the Russian government. The Tsar should participate personally in Abaza's company and should take a few shares of stock in his own name to encourage others to do the same.

Abaza was of the opinion that the larger amount of revenue would come from passengers, not only first-class passengers traveling in closed carriages but also migratory workers from the Moscow area going to seek work in St. Petersburg. But he also estimated a considerable revenue from freight, including most of the goods formerly transported by road between the capitals.

The larger part of the goods transported between the Volga and St. Petersburg would continue to go by water, but certain categories of goods needing rapid shipment to St. Petersburg for export would be carried by railway, as would other goods occasionally in event of abnormally low water or an early winter. Goods being transported to St. Petersburg from Morshansk, Orel, and other Oka landings via Nizhnii Novgorod and Rybinsk, and consisting mostly of expensive items like wheat and tallow, would be carried instead by the Moskva River to Moscow and thence by railway to St. Petersburg. Tallow and hemp from Kursk and Orel, which were customarily shipped by "winter road" to the Gzhat landings, would be shipped to Moscow, 100 versts nearer, and thence by railway to St. Petersburg.[13]

On March 25, 1838, Nicholas I, favorably impressed by Abaza's project, established a special committee consisting of Count Toll and Count Kankrin, Count Benckendorff, Minister of the Interior Bludov, and General A. P. Ermolov, who was to act as chairman. These last two members were men with some breadth of outlook and probably were chosen by Nicholas with the hope of giving what appears to have been an unusually well-conceived project a better chance of acceptance, since their forward-looking attitude would balance the conservatism of Toll and Kankrin, while Benckendorff could be counted on to follow the Tsar's lead.

Count Toll[14] and Count Kankrin[15] both gave unfavorable reports on Abaza's project. The special committee as a whole placed less emphasis than they on the dubious value of railways in general and more emphasis on the financial risks involved, but refused to give approval to the project. Abaza's company might suffer losses and might not be able to operate or even complete the railway. To survey the proposed route might take more than the two years planned, and the company then would not com-

13. "Proekt uchrezhdeniia aktsionerogo obshchestva ustroistva zheleznoi dorogi ot St. Peterburga do Moskvy, 21 marta 1838 g.," *Krasnyi Arkhiv,* LXXVI (1936), 108-117; I. P. Borichevskii, "Predlozheniia chastnykh lits ob ustroistve zheleznykh dorog postupivshie v G. U. P. S. i P. Z. do 1860 goda," *Zhurnal Putei Soobshcheniia,* XXXIX, kn. I (1863), 136-137.

14. "Zamechaniia glavnoupravliaiuschego putei soobshcheniia i publichnykh zdanii gr. Tolia na proekt A. Abazy, aprel' 1838 g.," *Krasnyi Arkhiv,* LXXVI (1936), 118-119.

15. "Zamechaniia ministra finansov gr. E. Kankrina na proekt A. Abazy, aprel' 1838 g.," *Krasnyi Arkhiv,* LXXVI (1936), 119.

plete the railway within six years, the period for which provision had been made for payment of dividends pending the beginning of operation of the railway, which would cause losses to stockholders and perhaps ruin the company. Unforeseen difficulties and delays might appear before the end of the six-year period during which the company expected to receive all its capital, and stockholders might withdraw before they had paid all the installments provided for and deprive the company of necessary capital.

Even the slightest doubt of the success of an enterprise requiring such large sums obligated the Russian government to refuse the help and protection requested by Abaza. If the government did allow the company to be founded eventually, it should not guarantee its success. If the government took part in the company, it would encourage others to do the same, and in the event of the company's failure, the loss to the stockholders would give rise to complaints against the government which would not be without justification. In Europe and America railways were new and unproven, and it was not yet known how much they would cost or how profitable they would be. It would be better to wait to see how railways fared in other countries and to wait for and examine new methods of construction which might reduce expenses. These conclusions of the special committee were forwarded to Nicholas.[16]

Later in the year Abaza published a pamphlet in which he reiterated basically the same arguments he had used in the project he had submitted to the Russian government.[17] In trying to

16. "Mnenie komiteta po predlozheniiu A. Abazy, 5 aprelia 1838 g.," *Krasnyi Arkhiv*, LXXVI (1936), 119-122; Borichevskii, pp. 138-140.

17. "A. A." [A. V. Abaza], *Mysli moskovskogo zhitelia o vozmozhnosti uchredit' obshchestvo na aktsiiakh dlia sooruzheniia zheleznoi dorogi ot S. Peterburga do Moskvy* (St. Petersburg, 1838). Reprinted in *Severnaia Pchela*, October 8, 1838, pp. 907-908; October 10, 1838, pp. 911-912; October 11, 1838, pp. 915-916; October 12, 1838, pp. 919-920. Among other things Abaza stated in this pamphlet that, since in Europe and especially America the introduction of railways had caused prices of the kind of raw materials Russia produced to be lowered, Russian products would be out-priced in world markets and Russia would lose part of its export trade if it did not build railways. He pointed out that the population of the two capitals, as well as their trade and industry, had grown in the previous thirty-five years, with the result that freight traffic had more than doubled and was still increasing, and, even if the government spent huge sums to improve waterways, their capacity would still be limited. Abaza posed the question whether railways in Russia might not bring more bene-

promote his scheme Abaza gained the support of Count A. A. Bobrinskii. In his memoirs A. I. Del'vig notes that the effort of these two men, especially when they served on the commission set up by Nicholas I in March, 1841, to study the possibilities of the St. Petersburg–Moscow Railway, was one of the main causes of the eventual authorization of that railway in January, 1842.[18]

Feigen and Abaza were able men who could see the advantages railways could bring to their class. There had been other merchants, such as the "capitalists" in Morshansk who were interested in N. M. Gamaleia's project to connect Morshansk and the mouth of the river Tsna, who had seen the possibility of advantages for themselves in railways. The need was, of course, especially obvious in an area rich in natural resources but poor in water transportation. It is also true that in January, 1842, the merchant class of Moscow sent a delegation of fifteen men to Nicholas I to thank him for his interest in the welfare of Russian trade shown by his authorization of the St. Petersburg–Moscow Railway.[19] But Count Ficquelmont reported that some of the strongest opponents of railways were merchants, both Russian and foreign, who profited from the fact that the expense caused by the slowness of trade concentrated this trade in the hands of a few who had sufficient capital to meet the expense. These merchants argued that rapid communications were not necessary.[20] Probably there was no strong support among the merchants to uphold the Tsar in his desire to build railways. In any case, the merchant class was small.

Feigen and Abaza each proposed one railway of limited length. As merchants they kept their gaze on their own needs and the likelihood of profit for themselves. Two other authors of projects for railways, A. Golievskii and N. N. Murav'ev, were not of the merchant class. Their projects were both for whole systems of railways that could only, because of the expense, be built di-

fits than in Europe, since Russian waterways were frozen for half the year and "winter roads" had serious deficiencies.

18. Baron A. I. Del'vig, *Moi vospominaniia* (Moscow, 1912–1913), I, 241.

19. Verkhovskii, p. 59.

20. Österreichisches Haus-, Hof-, und Staatsarchiv, Vienna, letter of Count Karl Ludwig Ficquelmont to Prince Klemens Metternich, 1836, No. 21 (May 5/17).

rectly by the government; their view of needs and profit was far wider than that of the merchants.

On December 17, 1837, A. Golievskii, a retired lieutenant, submitted his memorandum with proposals for a system of railways to be built at government expense. The system would consist of two main railways, would have a total length of over 3,600 versts, and would take nine years to complete. The first railway would be built St. Petersburg–Novgorod–Borovichi–Vitebsk–Mogilev–Chernigov–Kiev–Belaia Tserkov-Tiraspol–Odessa (1,830 versts), with a branch from Belaia Tserkov to the Austrian border (430 versts). The second main railway would be built from Moscow to Vitebsk, where it would meet the railway between St. Petersburg and Odessa. From Vitebsk it would be built to Warsaw via Wilno, Grodno, and Bialystok (1,360 versts). Since the second railway would also connect with the Gzhat landings, it would link that rich area with the ports of St. Petersburg and Odessa. This system of railways would link the capitals, even if indirectly, but its primary importance would be in helping Russia's export trade by giving the richest agricultural areas of Russia access to Baltic and Black Sea ports. The stretch St. Petersburg–Novgorod–Borovichi could also supplement the Vyshnii Volochek System.

Golievskii said that he suggested that the Russian government finance this railway system because private companies might fall under foreign control. To reduce the amount of capital necessary, the government would require every five hundred peasants in the fifteen provinces served by the railways to produce one worker equipped with an ax and shovel. These workers would be provisioned by landowners along the railway. To raise the necessary capital, which would total 100 million rubles, or about 25,000 rubles per verst, the poll-tax-paying population would pay a special tax of 14.5 kopecks per person yearly. Thus, this system of railways was to be financed largely by a variation of the peasant road tax.

Golievskii's project was reviewed by the Main Administration of Transport and Buildings, first by its Commission of Projects and Estimates and then by its Council, both of which were of the opinion that Golievskii's estimates were unrealistic and without basis and that therefore his project did not merit further attention and should be rejected.[21]

This decision was confirmed by the Committee of Ministers April 22, 1838, with Count Toll adding the remark that, although Russia needed better communications, this did not mean that railways should be built.[22]

Another project which proposed a whole system of railways to be built at government expense was submitted late in 1838 by State Secretary N. N. Murav'ev. Murav'ev was a landowner in, and later governor of, Novgorod Province and was the father of the famed Murav'ev-Amurskii.

Murav'ev, like Abaza, was in a position to be able to gain the attention of Nicholas I. On December 5, 1838, he sent a letter with a memorandum directly to the Tsar. Murav'ev began by stating that Russia's population was growing rapidly and the country would need better communications. Canals and *chaussées,* started in the reign of Alexander I and expanded since then, would not be adequate and therefore a system of railways should be built. Railways were being built abroad and were beginning to satisfy the transportation needs of other countries. In Russia the Tsarskoe Selo Railway had opened the eyes of all men to the desirability of railways, but it was only a "toy," while railways in the rest of Russia would serve the daily needs of a growing population.

Murav'ev envisioned a whole system of railways, but the St. Petersburg–Moscow Railway was the most important and should be built first. It should go via Novgorod and should have six (!) tracks, three for steam traction and three for horse traction, with one of each to be used only as a spare track. This railway would take fifteen years to build. When the capitals had been linked by a railway, other railways could be built to such places as Polangen on the Prussian border, Kovno, Warsaw, and Kalisz, to Odessa, to Kazan, and even to Mozdok in the Caucasus.

All these railways were to be built by the state, since it would

21. Virginskii, *Vozniknovenie,* pp. 192-193; S. A. Urodkov, *Peterburgo-Moskovskaia Zheleznaia Doroga: Istoriia stroitel'stva (1842–1851 gg.)* (Leningrad, 1951), pp. 55-56.

22. Verkhovskii, pp. 53-54; N. A. Kislinskii, *Nasha zheleznodorozhnaia politika po dokumentam arkhiva Komiteta Ministrov* (St. Petersburg, 1902), I, 18.

have the interests of all the people more at heart than would any private company and would not indulge in harmful speculation. Furthermore, all rails and locomotives should be manufactured in Russia by the state. The St. Petersburg–Moscow Railway would cost 300 million rubles, which could be issued from the Assignat Bank. A yearly profit of 100 million rubles could be expected, since all valuable goods carried by the Vyshnii Volochek and Tikhvinskii systems would go by railway.[23]

Nicholas I forwarded Murav'ev's memorandum to Count Toll on December 9, and Toll had his report ready on December 25. In this report Toll agreed with Murav'ev that the increasing population and developing industry of Russia made improved communications necessary. But the question of what kind of improved transportation was not so simple, and it could not be said that railways should be built everywhere, since sometimes roads and waterways would produce the greatest advantages. Railways were most advantageous where there was a lively sale of manufactured products, the demand for which fluctuated according to business conditions. When there was a great demand at the place of marketing, there had to be either a large supply of goods on hand or else rapid and uninterrupted communications with the place of manufacture. A perfect example would be the Liverpool-Manchester area, where a railway had been built. Toll claimed that a similar situation did not exist in Russia, an agricultural country which could depend upon canals supplemented by "winter roads." For agricultural products and raw materials rapid transportation was not necessary. St. Petersburg was linked to the Volga basin by three good water systems, which were being improved. These improvements would cost less than a railway and would allow these three water systems to meet all the requirements of St. Petersburg for the foreseeable future.

As for the construction of railways by the government, Count Toll stated that the government budget would not allow this, since it was sufficient only to meet the necessities of the state. If railways were to be built, they should be built by stock companies with the government checking all projects in advance before authorizing the railway. Concerning Murav'ev's plan for a

23. Tsentral'nyi Gosudarstvennyi Istoricheskii Arkhiv v Leningrade, fond 1263 (1839); delo 1249, pp. 432-441. Hereafter cited as TsGIAL.

railway between St. Petersburg and Moscow, Toll was of the opinion that Murav'ev's estimates were so indefinite and inaccurate that such a giant undertaking could not be based upon them.[24]

The Committee of Ministers met on January 10, 1839, to discuss Murav'ev's memorandum. It found that the proposals contained nothing new and that Murav'ev's contentions were so general that they did not call for further discussion. The committee also found that because of the great distances in Russia and a lack of capital, which was not sufficient for other branches of industry, railway construction could not be undertaken by the Russian government except with greater caution than was necessary in other European countries. Also, where railways should be built in Russia had not yet been decided. Some wished a railway between the capitals, others a railway between St. Petersburg and Rybinsk. These alternatives had to be considered in respect to possible economic and social consequences. Also, expenses and revenues had to be estimated carefully. A delay of two or three years would be less harmful than a mistake in calculations. In foreign countries railways were not always useful, and where they were it was more for transporting passengers than freight. It was therefore necessary to wait until these questions had been decided abroad. Then, using the experience of other countries, railways could be built in Russia without special losses. Therefore Murav'ev's proposal was rejected, but the issues which he had raised were to be studied further by Kankrin and Toll.[25]

On January 20, 1839, Murav'ev submitted a second memorandum to Count Toll. In this memorandum he tried to answer the Count's report of December 25, 1838. Murav'ev asserted strongly that railways could be useful in non-industrial countries, since raw materials also often needed rapid transportation for export. He contended that railways would be fifteen times faster and four times less expensive than canals. Railways should be built to follow navigable waterways through agricultural areas. Thus the St. Petersburg–Moscow Railway would run along the Volkhov River to Novgorod and then along the meadows bordering Lake Il'men, from the vicinity of which St. Petersburg would receive much of its requirements for fodder. When rail-

24. *Ibid.*, delo 1248, pp. 244-250.   25. *Ibid.*

ways were in operation, canals would be used only at the time of the spring floods.

This second memorandum from Murav'ev was received by the Committee of Ministers at its meetings of January 24, and 31, 1839. Count Toll repeated his earlier arguments and offered as proof that railways would be a more expensive means of transportation than canals the practice in Western Europe, where only passengers and expensive goods were carried by railway. The committee therefore reaffirmed its decision of January 10, 1839.[26]

Murav'ev, refusing to be satisfied with this decision, on February 21, 1839, submitted a third memorandum directly to the Committee of Ministers, thereby avoiding Count Toll. Murav'ev reasserted that only railways could unite the far-flung expanses of Russia so that one could travel from St. Petersburg to Warsaw in one and a half days, to Tiflis in two and a fourth days, and to Irkutsk in six days. Murav'ev still considered the St. Petersburg–Moscow Railway to be the basic railway from which others could be built. The entire system would be over 20,000 versts in length. From Novgorod, on the St. Petersburg–Moscow Railway, a railway could be built to Pskov, Riga, and Polangen on the Prussian border. From Pskov another railway could be built to Wilno, Grodno, Warsaw, and Kalisz and from Wilno to Minsk, Zhitomir, and Odessa. Another railway would link Rybinsk, Tver, Briansk, and Orel. Railways would radiate from Moscow. One railway would be built to Orel, Kursk, Kharkhov, Stavropol, and Vladikavkaz. Another railway would connect Moscow with Penza and Saratov, with a branch from Penza to Samara and Tambov. But Murav'ev's most daring idea was to build a railway from Moscow to Nizhnii Novgorod and Kazan and thence to Omsk, Tomsk, and Irkutsk. By this suggestion, Murav'ev became the first Russian to propose what over a half-century later was to become the Trans-Siberian Railway.

Except for the railways to the Caucasus and Siberia, this system was to cost 6,000,000 rubles for every 100 versts, or a total of 405,000,000 rubles. Revenues would be 537,500,000 rubles for

26. *Ibid.*, delo 1250, pp. 388-394.

every 100,000,000 poods carried. These estimates were not supported by any figures drawn from experience elsewhere.[27]

Murav'ev kept sending memoranda to the Committee of Ministers, handing in two additional memoranda on March 14 and 23, 1839. In these statements Murav'ev added little, if any, new data but continued to stress the desirability of railways in principle, especially in comparison to canals. He did, however, suggest that railways be financed, not from the Assignat Bank, as he had recommended before, but by laying a special tax on state and proprietary peasants or by obtaining a loan from England. These last three memoranda were rejected by the Committee of Ministers, as the first two had been.[28]

Approximately at the same time that Murav'ev was making these proposals, one A. Safonov in an article in *Syn Otechestva* was also proposing that the Russian government build a whole system of railways, but Murav'ev's proposals were much more grandiose and his emphasis on the government's role much more definite.[29]

Safonov, Golievskii, and Murav'ev advocated construction of railways by the government because they were beginning to

27. Borichevskii, pp. 141-142.   28. Urodkov, pp. 58-60.

29. Safonov argued that the lack of communications was especially evident in the rich provinces south of Moscow. Safonov therefore thought that not only the St. Petersburg–Moscow Railway should be built, but also a whole network. The most important railway to be built would be between St. Petersburg, Moscow, Tambov, and Saratov to unite "surplus" and "deficit" Russia and to facilitate trade with the Caspian Sea region and with Central Asia. This railway would allow the area around Tambov to send its products to St. Petersburg for export. Perishables from Taurida, cattle from the Ukraine, and salt from Lake Elton could be sent to the northern parts of the empire. Coal deposits along the Volga and Don rivers could be exploited, saving Russia's forests and providing fuel for the steppe area. The other main railways to be built would be Moscow-Kursk-Kremenchug-Odessa and Kursk-Sevsk-Smolensk-Riga, which would give the granaries of Kursk, Kharkhov, and Poltava a chance to send their products to Odessa or Riga for export.

Safonov felt that all railways should be built solidly with two tracks and the best quality of roadbed and bridges. The three main railways to be built initially would cost about 200 million rubles, a considerable sum, but Safonov thought that such railways would increase the wealth of Russia by much more than the amount spent. When the first three railways had been built and earned profits, the government could use the profits to build other railways, and make Russia rich and prosperous (A. Safonov, "Ob ustroistve v Rossii zheleznykh dorog," *Syn Otechestva*, IX [1839], Sec. III, 138-151).

realize that more capital would be required to build a whole net of railways in Russia, or even a railway between St. Petersburg and Moscow, than could be raised by private means. In any case, to avoid large risks to stockholders or the use of foreign capital the Russian government should provide the necessary capital.

Some few members of the nobility shared the pro-railway views of Murav'ev. One early partisan of railways among the Russian nobility was N. S. Mordvinov, a large landowner and president of the Free Economic Society. Mordvinov was also one of the earliest Russians to favor large-scale industrial development of Russia.[30] As early as December, 1827, he had submitted to Nicholas I a memorandum stating that railways would be the best of the alternatives for improving transportation in Russia, since they would have more capacity than roads and would be faster than canals. If steam traction was used on railways, a freight train could travel, he said, 300–400 versts a day, thereby delivering goods from Ekaterinburg, Astrakhan, and Odessa to St. Petersburg in six to ten days.[31] Some others, S. I. Mal'tsov, Count A. A. Bobrinskii, and Prince P. G. Oldenburg had supported von Gerstner in 1835–1836 and had been previously interested in his work or in railways in general.[32]

Although it is difficult to be entirely sure about public opinion, especially in a country where the press was rigidly controlled, most of the nobility probably did not share these enlightened views. Count Ficquelmont reported in the spring of 1836 (after the construction of the Tsarskoe Selo Railway had begun) that nearly all Russian landowners were against railways. Many wanted the advantages of industrialization in theory, and wished that Russia could be as advanced as other European countries, but they feared that railways and the resulting mobility of the lower classes of the towns and of the peasant masses would give the people ideas too advanced for their station in life. These land-

30. For Mordvinov's views on industrial development see Helma Repczuk, "Nicholas Mordvinov (1754–1845): Russia's Would-Be Reformer" (unpublished Ph.D. dissertation, Columbia University, 1962), pp. 146-170.

31. N. S. Mordvinov, "Soobrazheniia pri razsmotrenii rospisi na 1828 god," *Arkhiv grafov Mordvinovykh,* ed. V. A. Bil'basov (St. Petersburg, 1901–1903), VII, 70.

32. P. E. Gronskii, "Ocherk vozniknoveniia i razvitiia zheleznykh dorog v Rossii," *Zapiski Moskovskogo Otdeleniia Imperatorskogo Russkogo Tekhnicheskogo Obshchestva,* IV (1886), 11; see chap. iii above.

owners felt that the best guarantee of Russia's internal security was the difficulty of communication between the peoples of the various parts of the empire coupled with the ease with which the Russian government could extend its actions everywhere. In Count Ficquelmont's opinion, the basic fear of the Russian landowner was that the introduction of railways into the country would lead to the emancipation of the serfs.[33]

There seems to have been some fear, too, among the Russian nobility that railways would undermine the Russian monarchy. In 1834, the author of an article on American railways in *Biblioteka dlia Chteniia* felt it necessary to refute the view frequently held in Europe that railways and industry prospered best under a republican form of government, and stated that the American spirit of enterprise was independent of political forms and resulted from the love of profit alone. The author quoted a member of the American House of Representatives, who said that the United States was building so many railways in order to turn itself more quickly into a monarchy.[34]

Some landowners must have feared the introduction of railways into Russia because they had interests in competing forms of transportation. The *Obshchestvo Dilizhansov*, which would presumably lose many of its passengers to a railway built between the capitals, had among its stockholders many influential members of the nobility. Also, the nobility would naturally fear the possible ruin of the peasant carting industry, which would bring the loss of valuable *obrok*. A British diplomat no doubt had

33. Österreichisches Haus-, Hof-, und Staatsarchiv, Ficquelmont to Metternich, 1836, No. 21 (May 5/17).

Before the opening of the Tsarskoe Selo Railway, there had also been other more colorful objections. The anonymous author of an article in *Biblioteka dlia Chteniia* published early in 1835 remarked that Russian landowners feared that their lands would be divided and that they would suffer from the intrusion of travelers, whom they compared to hordes of Arabs and Bashkirs. They feared that their woods and fields would be set on fire, that birds and animals would be driven away, and that their livestock would not reproduce. These landowners were said to have feared that if they themselves rode on the railway they would be suffocated by smoke or deafened by noise and might even lose their lives in wrecks ("Chugunnye dorogi," *Biblioteka dlia Chteniia*, VIII [1835], Sec. III, 106-107; "Budushchnost' zheleznykh dorog," *Moskovskii Nabliudatel'*, XI [1837], 477-478).

34. "Chugunnye dorogi v Amerike," *Biblioteka dlia Chteniia*, VI (1834), Sec. VII, 27-28.

these possibilities in mind when he remarked in 1842 that many Russians with capital were against railways.[35]

In other countries of Europe at this time it seems also to have been only the occasional enlightened landowner or the exceptionally far-seeing merchant who advocated railways. The pressure for railways was more likely to come from the new industrial bourgeoisie, who had to get coal and raw materials to their factories, an element largely lacking in Russia.

Nor were there any strong propagandists for railways in Russia like Friedrich List or Friedrich Harkort. Russia's intellectuals (although there was an occasional exception such as A. S. Khomiakov) were not usually interested in railways.[36] They had no way of knowing that a transportation revolution would bring an industrial revolution that would change the whole face of Russia.

By early 1839 Nicholas I probably felt that no progress was being made in reaching a decision concerning the railway question. Only a few men had submitted railway projects to the government, and it must have been obvious that they were only isolated individuals without experience in railway building and without broad support. The Tsar saw also that members of his government intrusted with the discussion of these projects were ill-disposed toward railways. Previously he had made no suggestions of his own but had only been receptive to those of others. Perhaps in an effort to have discussion on railways continued, he decided to make a proposal of his own.

In January, 1839, Nicholas I suggested a railway over the route from St. Petersburg to Rybinsk. Such a railway, built to supplement the three canal systems and going more directly, certainly might have expected a large volume of traffic because of the large and increasing amount of goods coming from the Volga. Therefore, on January 22, 1839, when the minutes of the

35. Public Record Office, London, Foreign Office 65 (Diplomatic and consular reports from Russia to England), Vol. CCLXXX. Lord Stuart de Rothesay to the Earl of Aberdeen, No. 20 (St. Petersburg, February 2 [N.S.], 1842).

36. See Alexander Gerschenkron, "The Problem of Economic Development in Russian Intellectual History of the Nineteenth Century," in *Continuity and Change in Russian and Soviet Thought*, ed. Ernest J. Simmons (Cambridge, Mass., 1955), p. 17.

January 10 meeting of the Committee of Ministers rejecting Murav'ev's first proposal to build a railway between St. Petersburg and Moscow were presented to Nicholas, he wrote on it: "It would not be superfluous, however, to commission Count Toll now to study all necessary considerations for the construction of a railway from Rybinsk to St. Petersburg, since the advantages of this road, it seems, would be incontestable."[37] Nicholas I may have thought of this railway either because of E. I. Feigen's project or because of the allusion to such a railway in the report of the Committee of Ministers of January 10. Although the Tsar did not state so specifically, it seems that he was considering having the railway built at the expense of the state.

Count Toll submitted a report to Nicholas I on April 12, 1839, in which he stated that a railway between St. Petersburg and Rybinsk would be at least 600 versts long and would cost 150,-000,000 rubles, even if horse traction alone were used. The costs of operation, including a profit of 8 per cent, would be 28,665,083 rubles yearly. As for revenues, Toll claimed that 24,000,000 poods of goods to St. Petersburg and 700,000 poods from St. Petersburg might be carried yearly by the railway, but to meet expenses rates of 1 ruble 16 kopecks per pood would have to be charged if horse power were used, and 2 rubles 16 kopecks per pood if steam traction. Even the cheaper rate was two times

37. Verkhovskii, p. 46. Nicholas I's suggestion for a railway connecting St. Petersburg and Rybinsk gave rise to a debate in the press as to the relative expense and potential economic benefits of the St. Petersburg–Rybinsk and St. Petersburg–Moscow routes (*Severnaia Pchela*, March 23, 1839, p. 264; "Eshche pis'mo iz Moskvy o zheleznoi doroge," *Severnaia Pchela*, May 9, 1839, pp. 403-404; "Moskovskii Zhitel'," "Pis'mo iz Moskvy o kolomenskoi zheleznoi doroge," *Severnaia Pchela*, November 20, 1839, pp. 1051-1052). But after November, 1839, either because of discouragement stemming from the lack of activity on the part of the government or because of official pressure, the Russian press almost ceased to discuss railways. There was an occasional notice on foreign railways (see, for example, "Zheleznye dorogi v Germanii," *Otechestvennye Zapiski*, XI [1841], Sec. VII, 12-13). But the only article of any consequence was that written in 1840 by F. Bulgarin, in which he "dreamt" that he had returned to Russia after an absence of ten years and beheld a railway between the capitals, financed by the state, which was bringing increased prosperity to all classes of the population and was developing agriculture and industry (F. Bulgarin, "Poezdka v Moskvu vo sne," *Severnaia Pchela*, April 20, 1840, pp. 347-348).

the amount charged by the Tikhvinskii System.[38] It was therefore highly doubtful if any freight, except a few express goods, would be carried by railway. Toll supported this contention by showing that the St. Etienne–Lyons Railway, which depended mainly on coal for its revenue, made little if any profit, while the Liverpool-Manchester Railway, which depended mainly on passengers, showed a large profit. On the St. Petersburg–Rybinsk Railway passenger revenue would be negligible, since the only prospective passengers would be migratory workers going to St. Petersburg. But they traveled via the Tikhvinskii System in their own boats almost without expense, so they would not use the railway. Hence, because of this lack of freight and passenger revenue, the St. Petersburg–Rybinsk Railway would be completely unprofitable.

Count Toll also tried to frighten Nicholas by raising the specter of social change if railways were built in Russia. He quoted—or rather misquoted—the Frenchman Michel Chevalier as claiming that in Europe and America railways were "the most democratic institution which one could devise for the transformation of society." Toll wrote that he was of the same opinion. Waterways would not spread democratic ideas and inclination but would allow economic activity to expand within the Russian Empire and contribute more to the public welfare than any railway.[39]

On April 13, 1839, Nicholas, having received Toll's report on the previous day, stated he agreed that where there were already good waterways they should be preferred to railways, but that the question of railways in Russia had not been finally decided.[40]

The years 1838–1839 marked the high point of the successful resistance by members of Nicholas I's government to the introduction of railways into Russia. While von Gerstner had received tentative authorization to build the St. Petersburg–Moscow Railway in December, 1835, and had built Russia's first

38. This system, it will be remembered, charged the highest rates of the three water systems linking the Volga region and St. Petersburg and therefore carried the fewest goods, but was the shortest and fastest of the three systems (see p. 12 above).

39. Verkhovskii, pp. 48-49; Borichevskii, pp. 142-143.

40. TsGIAL, fond 1263 (1839), delo 1261, p. 505.

railway between St. Petersburg and Tsarskoe Selo–Pavlovsk, all projects submitted by others in the years up to 1839 were rejected by the government. Men like Feigen, Abaza, Golievskii, and Murav'ev lacked von Gerstner's knowledge and experience, and Nicholas I, although still very much interested in railways, must have had doubts about allowing such tremendous undertakings. At his bidding considerable attention had been given to the projects of Abaza and Murav'ev. The special committee studying Abaza's project and the Committee of Ministers studying Murav'ev's project no doubt rendered their decisions on what they considered the merits of these projects, which were admittedly in some respects indefinite and in Murav'ev's case unrealistic. Except for Count Kankrin and Count Toll, most members of Nicholas' government showed themselves to be cautious and conservative rather than opposed to railways.

Doubts about railways were felt mainly on financial grounds. In 1838–1839 the technical feasibility of railways in Russia was not an issue. The question of the social effects of railways had been hardly an issue in 1835–1836—at least officially—and was no more of an issue officially in 1838–1839, although raised once or twice as a bête noire by Count Toll. It is true, however, that Count Ficquelmont observed again in 1839, as he had in 1836, that members of the Russian government were still opposed to railways because they feared that more rapid movement of people would make governing more difficult and would set in motion new forces with which they might not be able to deal effectively.[41] Be that as it may, in 1838–1839 the question of the financial feasibility of railways in Russia remained, as previously, the main issue. The fear was simply that if costs were too great and revenues too small the Treasury would have to pay something as a return on the capital to stockholders and for costs of operation and maintenance and would thereby increase appreciably the government debt.[42]

During this period the strong opposition of Count Kankrin and Count Toll more than any other factor accounted for the doubts that led to the lack of positive action. Count Kankrin, who

41. Österreichisches Haus-, Hof-, und Staatsarchiv, Ficquelmont to Metternich, 1839, No. 17 (May 29/June 10).

42. A. D. Shumakher, "Pozdnye vospominaniia," *Vestnik Evropy*, CXCVI (1899), 105.

in the period 1835–1836 had been able to exert only an indirect influence against railways, now, as a member of the special committee judging Abaza's project and as a member of the Committee of Ministers judging Murav'ev's project, could make the weight of his anti-railway views felt more directly. The advice of Count Toll as head of the Main Administration of Transport and Buildings was naturally always heeded.

From early 1835, when von Gerstner made his first proposal to build railways in Russia, until his retirement from his post as minister of finance in 1844, Kankrin voiced his opposition to all proposals.[43] He, it will be remembered, had been a member of the committee that met on February 28, 1835, to discuss von Gerstner's original proposals and had raised objections to them, and when Nicholas I left him out of the special committee to conduct further negotiations, Kankrin submitted memoranda to the committee giving more detailed objections.

These memoranda summed up his objections to railways. He stated in them that railways were not always useful. The railway between the capitals would not be profitable because of the small amount of goods moved along the route due to the cheapness of competing water transportation. To bring bulky goods from Nizhnii Novgorod to St. Petersburg by railway would be prohibitively expensive. The ruin of the peasant carting industry would bring losses to both landowners and the government and cause unrest among the populace. If the populace became unused to carting and railway traffic were ever interrupted, there might be food shortages. Count Kankrin stated that the introduction of steam traction would mean exhaustion of forests, since Russia had no coal supply. To transport soldiers, a great number of carriages would be needed, which otherwise would be useless. He concluded that it would be impossible at that time to cover Russia with a system of railways and that even the proposal to build a railway from St. Petersburg to Moscow and Kazan was premature by several centuries.[44] Mel'nikov remarked that many

43. Kankrin had also opposed the introduction of steamboats because, he said, passengers and goods were so few that the time had not yet arrived when steamboats could be profitable (S. M. Seredonin, *Istoricheskii obzor deiatel'nosti Komiteta Ministrov* [St. Petersburg, 1902–1905], II, part 2, 178).

44. Verkhovskii, pp. 25-26.

of these arguments were not peculiar to Kankrin but were wide-spread among the Russian public.[45]

In November, 1835, Count Kankrin stated that railways could be profitable only when there was a large volume of passengers of the middle class (a class that was understood to be smaller in Russia than elsewhere) and not where there was mainly freight traffic.[46] At another time he stated that the present fashion of building railways in other countries was already beginning to decline, since railways could serve more for unnecessary pleasure trips than for the transportation of goods over long distances.[47] In December, 1835, Kankrin objected to any duty-free import of rails for von Gerstner's St. Petersburg–Moscow Railway. He also opposed the authorization of the Tsarskoe Selo Railway. When it was authorized, he is said to have remarked, "Well, there is a tavern in Pavlovsk and there will be a railway running to it. That is useful."[48]

While the Tsarskoe Selo Railway was being built, Count Kankrin of necessity accepted the accomplished fact. On April 7, 1836, he wrote in reference to the Tsarskoe Selo Railway Company's petition to import rails and other iron products free of duty that he considered it his duty to ask imperial permission for this in order to allow completion of the railway by the scheduled time.[49]

45. Mel'nikov, "Svedeniia," *Krasnyi Arkhiv*, XCIX (1940), 150-151.
46. The tenor of the memorandum of which this statement was a part and which was in connection with the proposed law on the formation of stock companies was characteristically cautious. He stated that the Russian government for the protection of the private investor should not allow any stock company to introduce any innovation against which objections had been raised in Western Europe and which had been shown to bring little or no profit or which had failed outright. It was better to forbid the formation of ten companies than to permit one which might do harm to the public. Speculation should also be prevented, since it drew off capital from constructive enterprises. The stock of a company should not be concentrated in a few hands but spread among the population (Ministerstvo Finansov, *Ministerstvo Finansov, 1802–1902* [St. Petersburg, 1902], I, 345-346).
47. Oscar Matthesius, *Russische Eisenbahnpolitik im XIX. Jahrhundert, 1836–1881* (Inaugural dissertation, Berlin, 1903), p. 18.
48. S. I. Mal'tsov, "Iz vospominanii S. I. Mal'tsova," *Zapiski Moskovskogo Otdeleniia Imperatorskogo Russkogo Tekhnicheskogo Obshchestva*, IV (1886), 40.
49. "Predstavlenie ministra finansov gr. E. Kankrina v komitet ministrov, 7 aprelia 1836 g.," *Krasnyi Arkhiv*, LXXVI (1936), 104-105.

On July 29, 1837, it became Count Kankrin's duty to study the request of the Tsarskoe Selo Railway Company for a government loan of 1.5 million rubles and to submit a report on the matter to the Committee of Ministers. He agreed with the contention of the company that the funds which it had on hand were insufficient for the completion of the railway and that a foreign loan would be desirable. He was of the opinion that the Treasury, however, could not make such a large loan, especially since an exception would have to be made to the rules of banking because of the lack of attachable property in possession of the company. He felt that the future revenues of the railway would be too small to constitute sufficient collateral. Kankrin concluded his report by stating that opinion abroad was divided on the future value of railways and that they were a phenomenon of the time presenting no proof of success. He did not wish, he said, to give a decisive opinion on the question of the loan, but suggested that it be submitted to the judgement of the Committee of Ministers.[50]

Count Kankrin presumably feared that if this concession was not made, the railway could not be completed. Losses to stockholders and imperial displeasure both had to be avoided. Even so, for him to assume the sole responsibility for a government loan for such a purpose was abhorrent. All through his career he was against providing government loans to industry, either directly or through the banking system, maintaining that such loans did more harm than good. Such loans diverted funds from the state banking system that were needed for other purposes, and Kankrin also was afraid that merchants would engage in harmful speculation and would not have the essential technical and business skills needed to make productive use of the borrowed funds.[51]

In the discussion of von Gerstner's other projects Kankrin seems to have taken little if any part. In July, 1836, as has been mentioned, he did give his approval and offered government aid to von Gerstner for setting up a factory in Russia to produce

50. "Predstavlenie ministra finansov gr. E. Kankrina v komitet ministrov, 29 iiulia 1837 g.," *Krasnyi Arkhiv*, LXXVI (1936), 107.

51. Walter M. Pintner, "Government and Industry during the Ministry of Count Kankrin, 1823–1844," *Slavic Review*, XXIII (1964), 48-54.

rails and other iron products, since, he said, that would help Russia's metallurgical industry.

In March and April of 1838, Count Kankrin was able to exert considerable influence as a member of the special committee discussing Abaza's project for the St. Petersburg–Moscow Railway. His arguments apparently definitely affected the decision of the committee. In the discussion of other proposals submitted during this period Kankrin seems to have let Count Toll make most of the pronouncements against the project, while he remained passively in agreement, and lent Count Toll his moral support.[52]

Even when later he was traveling abroad for his health and using railways to travel from one watering place to another, he continued to make peevish remarks in his diary about railways. In October, 1840, in Germany he wrote that he found railway journeys very irritating, since the train went through empty regions with fewer buildings and plants than one would find beside highways. Also the train went too fast and made him into a "machine" just by sitting in the carriage. Kankrin felt that now travelers would feel colder to strange regions and would lose their enjoyment of nature. Railways were also ruining the innkeeping business because there was less travel on highways.[53]

Kankrin felt that countries in Europe such as Austria and Prussia were making concessions to this illness of the times only because they felt compelled to keep up with their neighbors and did not wish to fall behind in trade and industry. As a matter of fact, railways were primarily a luxury for needless passenger travel and would lose their popularity when the expense and what he considered the inconveniences of railway travel manifested themselves. Yet Kankrin was at times realistic enough to know that his was wishful thinking, that European countries would continue to build railways and that in Russia itself the St. Petersburg–Moscow Railway would eventually be built. He asked himself in a resigned mood: who could fight against rail-

52. Kargin, *Tekhnicheskii Zhurnal*, p. 421, n. 1.
53. *Aus den Reisetagebüchern des Grafen Georg Kankrin, ehemaligen kaiserlich russischen Finanzministers, aus den Jahren 1840–1845* (Braunschweig, 1865), I, 141-142.

ways when they seemed to be a trend of the times? He congratulated himself on having done so successfully several times.[54]

Although a general discussion of Kankrin's political and economic theories cannot be entered into here,[55] it should be remarked that he was not opposed to all change, merely distrustful of it. He believed first of all in a stable society and a balanced budget. Kankrin's attitude was not blindly negative. He was not against the industrialization of Russia in principle, but many of his financial policies discouraged the growth of industry. When an ambitious project was put forward, his attitude was determined by its immediate effect on government expenditures and revenues, not by its possibly beneficial long-range effects.[56]

In 1839 Count Ficquelmont stated that Kankrin opposed railways because the financing of a railway between the capitals costing 200 million to 500 million rubles would remove that amount of capital from Kankrin's control, since, he said, the financing of this railway would be done without Kankrin's playing a role. If the railway was successful, capital would flee banks controlled by Kankrin seeking greater profits, especially if the government offered some guarantee to the investor, who then would no longer have to seek the comparative safety of one of Kankrin's banks to protect and increase his money. This flight of bank deposits would also deprive the Treasury of needed revenue.[57] If Ficquelmont was correct, Kankrin's sentiments should not be attributed to his desire for power but to his real concern for the finances of the government. Well aware of the scarcity of both private and public capital in Russia, Count Kankrin was apprehensive of this use of capital.

54. *Ibid.*, I, 23, 272; II, 31.
55. For Count Kankrin's own exposition of his political and economic theories, see Graf E. Cancrin, *Die Oekonomie der menschlichen Gesellschaften und das Finanzwesen* (Stuttgart, 1845). For secondary works dealing with this subject, see Walter M. Pintner, "Count Kankrin's Administration, 1823–1844" (unpublished Ph.D. dissertation, Harvard University, 1962), and I. N. Bozherianov, *Graf Egor Frantsevich Kankrin, ego zhizn' literaturnye trudy i dvadtsatiletniaia deiatel'nost' upravleniia Ministerstvom Finansov* (St. Petersburg, 1897).
56. Pintner, "Kankrin," pp. 91-94; Pintner, *Slavic Review*, XXIII (1964), 59-60.
57. Österreichisches Haus-, Hof-, und Staatsarchiv, Ficquelmont to Metternich, 1839, No. 17 (May 29/June 10).

Kankrin firmly believed that railway construction consumed capital which should be spent on the "productive forces" of a country, especially agriculture. In his book published in 1845 he stated that with the steady growth of Europe's population, the first objective should be to provide cheap grain rather than to build railways. The productive forces of the countries of Europe did not warrant expenditure for railways, except in the case of England, where much money had already been invested in agriculture. Of course, when the productivity of a country was greatly increased, the question of what was the best means of carrying its products to market would arise. However, transportation should not be improved at the expense of productivity, which would be the case if railways were built first.[58]

In the years 1838–1839 it was Count Toll who led the opposition to railways. His opposition had more effect than Count Kankrin's at this time, if only because he was more often and more directly involved in the discussion of the projects submitted. In considering von Gerstner's original proposals to build railways in Russia, Toll had reacted critically to them and had tried to limit the concessions given. As a member of the special committee of 1835–1836, he had played the role of a perfunctory bureaucrat doing his duty and had seemed to decide with quite an open mind the issues presented to him on their merits. He had been absent for some of the time and had let others, especially Michael Speransky, make most of the decisions. But in the period which followed Toll apparently automatically expressed his opposition to every railway project submitted to him. He was instrumental in the rejection of the projects of Feigen, Golievskii, Abaza, and Murav'ev, and of the proposal of Nicholas I for a railway between St. Petersburg and Rybinsk.

Count Toll's primary concern, unlike that of Count Kankrin and many others, was not the financial soundness of railways,[59] although he used financial arguments. Toll's main concern was that the building and improvement of Russia's waterways should take precedence over the building of railways, the same stand

58. Cancrin, pp. 95-96; cf. Bozherianov, p. 233.
59. On February 28, 1835, Count Toll had stated that the profitableness of railways was the concern of the stockholders alone. (See p. 83 above.)

that General Destrem had taken in 1831.[60] From the beginning of his career as head of the Main Administration of Transport and Buildings in 1833, Toll had paid the greatest attention to the improvement of waterways, neglecting in their favor the improvement of roads.[61]

Count Toll was quoted in his obituary in May, 1842, as having said that agriculture was the main industry in Russia, and bulky agricultural goods, concentrated by "winter roads" at a few river landings, were marketable only when they could be transported farther at low prices. Toll had therefore wished to improve waterways, since they provided the cheapest form of transportation.[62]

Count Toll feared that railways more than roads might compete with waterways, or even supplant them, and that the Russian government might spend money either directly or indirectly on railways that otherwise would be spent on waterways. With his enthusiasm for waterways Toll had come (at least indirectly) into conflict with Nicholas I, whose interest was in improving roads. The budget of the Main Administration of Transport and Buildings had already been reduced several times because Toll's policies were not in favor with the Tsar.[63] Toll's fear of road and, even more, of railway competition for funds was especially evident in connection with projects for a railway which was to parallel an already existing waterway or for which some sort of government aid was requested. Right at the outset in 1835 Count Toll had rejected the proposal of N. M. Gamaleia to build a railway from Morshansk to the mouth of the river Tsna because he did not want to see a railway competing for traffic with the river Tsna, since the Main Administration of Transport and Buildings had spent considerable sums on improving navigation there.

Perhaps von Gerstner had avoided Toll's opposition in his original proposals because he had not stressed that his St. Petersburg–Moscow Railway would attract freight traffic from waterways.

60. See p. 65, n. 1 above.
61. V. M. Shiman, "Imperator Nikolai Pavlovich. Iz zapisok i vospominanii sovremennika," *Russkii Arkhiv*, No. 1 (1902), p. 470.
62. *Severnaia Pchela*, May 12, 1842, p. 416.
63. Shiman, p. 470.

Also he had not asked the Russian government to give his enterprise any direct financial aid, which might have diverted funds from the improvement of waterways.

But the situation was different in respect to other railway projects. Toll was opposed to von Gerstner's proposal for a Moscow-Kolomna Railway because it would parallel and compete with navigation on the Moskva River on which extensive improvements were being made. Toll was opposed to Feigen's project because he had chosen the route of his railway, St. Petersburg–Tver–Rybinsk, expressly to enter into competition with existing waterways, and was also asking for financial support from the government. Abaza's project also called for some financial support, and Abaza stated that his railway would attract some goods from waterways, even if most would continue to be transported by water. Murav'ev's proposals in his first memorandum stated that a large part of the goods carried by the Vyshnii Volochek and Tikhvinskii systems would be carried by a railway between St. Petersburg and Moscow. Murav'ev also wished the government to spend 300 million rubles on this enterprise. In later memoranda Murav'ev stressed even more emphatically the advantages of railways over waterways and stated that waterways would be largely supplanted by railways, which would be built intentionally to parallel them. As for the suggestion of Nicholas I for a railway between St. Petersburg and Rybinsk, Toll must have been really upset when even the Tsar was suggesting a railway that was meant to supplement an existing waterway and was presumably intending to build it with government funds. Therefore Toll tried especially hard to show him that this railway would be totally unprofitable and in addition might lead to social change, while improved waterways would bring economic benefits to Russia without any danger to the existing order.

Nicholas I seems to have been less enthusiastic about the projects put forward by Russians in the years 1837–1838 than he had been about von Gerstner's project, perhaps because von Gerstner as a skilled railway builder with a good reputation was more likely to be able to carry out his projects. Nevertheless, when any project was submitted to the government and Nicholas heard of it, he impatiently demanded discussion of it by his government and seemed to hope to see construction started.[64]

Nicholas I, unlike many rulers in Western Europe, could have ordered the acceptance of one of the projects by decree, yet he deferred to the advice of his advisers. While Western European countries were gaining momentum in railway building, Russia failed to advance, largely because of the resistance of Count Kankrin and Count Toll. The Tsar respected and followed Count Kankrin's advice in most financial matters, for this assertive public servant had early won his trust and esteem. Nicholas I was rigid in his attitude toward people as in everything. His confidence, once placed, was not easily shaken. Kankrin was undoubtedly able and had achieved substantial results in putting the government's finances in order. He was also older than Nicholas, and a legacy from the reign of the brother whom the Tsar revered. Furthermore, Nicholas really had little understanding of finance,[65] and a railway of any length was, after all, a large financial undertaking.[66]

In the period 1838–1839 every proposal submitted was referred eventually to Count Toll. One writer characterized Toll as an authority in technical matters, independent, and of impeccable character.[67] It was natural that Nicholas I should defer somewhat to his judgment also, especially since he was the head of the Main Administration of Transport and Buildings. Until January, 1839, Nicholas did not challenge Count Toll's decisions. It was in that month that the Tsar made his own suggestion that although Murav'ev's plan for a railway between the capitals was unacceptable, a railway between St. Petersburg and Rybinsk should be profitable. When, in a memorandum to the Tsar on March 15, 1839, Toll repeated his arguments about waterways once more, Nicholas answered the memorandum with the following statement: "I do not know how to settle this question, but I admit that I incline more to consider railways extremely use-

64. Mel'nikov, "Svedeniia," *Krasnyi Arkhiv,* XCIX (1940), 161.
65. See Pintner, "Kankrin," pp. 30-31.
66. Up to the time of the authorization of the Tsarskoe Selo Railway the only important matter on which Nicholas had overruled Kankrin was the reform program for state lands (Pintner, *Slavic Review,* XXIII [1964], 47, n. 3).
67. "Zapiski senatora K. I. Fishera," *Istoricheskii Vestnik,* CXII (1908), 434.

ful in facilitating internal trade."[68] In April upon receiving Toll's unfavorable report on the St. Petersburg–Rybinsk railway, the Tsar immediately ordered Toll to send two reliable officers of the Corps of Transport Engineers to study railways in America.[69] The engineers chosen by Toll were in America in the years 1839–1840, and the information they gathered helped Nicholas I make the decision to build the St. Petersburg–Moscow Railway.

If Nicholas I's ministers had been as eager as he for railways, or if perhaps there had been strong pressure from some segment of the population, more than four years would not have passed between the completion of the Tsarskoe Selo Railway and the beginning of the St. Petersburg–Moscow Railway. The extremely cautious reaction of the committee to Abaza's proposal seems to betray the strength of the influence of Toll and Kankrin on men like Bludov and Ermolov. When even the more forward-looking men on the committees he appointed could be induced to worry so about every untoward financial contingency and to vote against taking any action, Nicholas must have despaired of getting moral support. Bludov, Ermolov, and others like them repeatedly remarked that if Russia waited, when railways *were* finally built, it would be possible to enjoy that one advantage of backward countries, profiting from the mistakes of the pioneers.

Nicholas I, in spite of his own feeling that railways in Russia would be useful and profitable, must have still had doubts himself. The arguments of the opponents of railways, such as Counts Kankrin and Toll, were not unreasonable in the context of the time and must have carried much more weight in the Russia of the late 1830's than they would have later when railways had proven themselves successful both in Russia and abroad. Railways had not been uniformly successful abroad. Speculation in railway stocks had been partially responsible for a financial panic in the United States in 1837. Although many railway projects in England had been successful, some had not. Many European governments were still doubtful about the advisability of building railways. Railway construction had not yet progressed very far in many countries, and had not even been started in others. Even if railways were successful abroad, the opponents of railways were

68. Verkhovskii, p. 48.
69. TsGIAL, fond 1263 (1839), delo 1261, p. 505.

correct in stating that this would be no guarantee that they would be useful and profitable in Russia. They might even fail outright, as Count Kankrin suggested. The prevailing view even abroad was that railways could be profitable only by carrying primarily first-class passengers and such goods as manufactured wares. In backward Russia there might not be sufficient revenues from these items. Railways there would have to rely heavily upon third-class travel and the transportation of agricultural products and other raw materials. In other words, the question could well be raised whether railways, which had been only partially successful in more advanced countries, could be successful in economically and socially backward Russia, or whether one should rely instead upon already existing means of transportation. By January, 1839, the Tsar, impatient with his ministers and advisers, was ready to take the initiative in finding an answer to this question.

Chapter VI. Events leading to the final approval of the St. Petersburg–Moscow Railway (January, 1839–February, 1842)

Although Nicholas I took two years to decide to exercise his absolute power in the matter of the St. Petersburg–Moscow Railway after it seemed clear that his ministers were not likely to change their position, he was not during this time undergoing any change in his own attitude, which had been consistently in favor of railways from the beginning. He was merely conscientiously making sure that he was making no mistake in following his desires before embarking on a huge undertaking. Once reasonably sure in his own mind, he was not too cautious to take action in the face of a great deal of contrary opinion.

A series of events helped him to make his decision. First of all, early in January, 1839, a few days before he made his suggestion about a railway from St. Petersburg to Rybinsk, Nicholas had taken the opportunity, despite his grave doubts, to advance the cause of railways in Russia by signing a decree authorizing the construction of a railway which was to be built by a Polish company and was to run from Warsaw to the Austrian border. The authorization was at the urging of Nicholas I's viceroy in Poland, General I. F. Paskevich, Prince of Warsaw, but the permission for the building of the Warsaw-Vienna Railway and the responsibility that the government had to assume for it was without doubt one factor in Nicholas I's moving closer to his decision to build the St. Petersburg–Moscow Railway. Count Ficquelmont reported early in the summer of 1839 that he felt this railway would decide the question for the rest of Russia, since the Russian government could hardly refuse to a Russian company what it had already granted to a Polish company.[1]

The Warsaw-Vienna Railway was significant for the future development of other railways in the Russian Empire also be-

1. Österreichisches Haus-, Hof-, und Staatsarchiv, Vienna, letter of Count Karl Ludwig Ficquelmont to Prince Klemens Metternich, 1839, No. 17 (May 29/June 10).

cause the contract—which was between the Bank of Poland, acting in behalf of the government, and the company building the railway, but which was ratified by Nicholas I—represented another step in the formulation of a railway policy by the Russian government, since it contained several important departures from the policy previously followed.

The Warsaw-Vienna Railway was originally conceived by Prince Paskevich. It has often been thought that the Warsaw-Vienna Railway was meant to serve primarily strategic purposes,[2] but Prince Paskevich seems to have thought more of its economic value. In the 1830's Prince Paskevich was much concerned about the dependence of the trade of the Kingdom of Poland on Prussia, through which this trade had to pass to reach Danzig and the Baltic. A Prusso-Polish treaty allowing the transit of Polish trade had expired in 1834, and Prussia had refused to renew it, presumably to force Poland into the German *Zollverein*. Negotiations for a new treaty dragged on without result, with Prussia making impossible demands. Meanwhile Paskevich thought of new trade routes which would allow Poland to export its goods either by way of Austria or by way of the Russian Baltic ports of Windau or Libau.

When in 1837–1838 the Kaiser Ferdinands–Nordbahn was being built from Vienna toward Austrian Galicia, Paskevich thought of extending a railway, which he had already planned to build between Warsaw and Niwka,[3] to the Austrian border to join the new Austrian railway.[4] Thereby, Polish trade would have access to the Adriatic,[5] and costs of transportation would be no

2. See, for example, P. P. Migulin, *Russkii gosudarstvennyi kredit* (*1769–1899*) (Kharkov, 1899–1904), I, 258.

3. Niwka was a mining center in a mineral-rich area of southern Poland.

4. The so-called Kaiser Ferdinands–Nordbahn was being built north from Vienna through Moravia toward Bochnia in Galicia. A railway running south from Vienna to the port of Trieste on the Adriatic was also under consideration. The idea of linking Vienna with Bochnia and Trieste had been conceived as early as 1829 by one Franz Xaver Riepl, a colleague of von Gerstner at the Wiener Polytechnikum (*Geschichte der Eisenbahnen der Österreichisch-ungarischen Monarchie* [Vienna, 1898], I, 130, 134 ff.).

5. The railway would also serve to transport northward the salt, grain, iron, and coal from Galicia and the southern part of the Kingdom of Poland (*Severnaia Pchela*, September 20, 1841, p. 835).

more than to Danzig, while Poland would be freed of its commercial dependence on Prussia.[6]

Prince Paskevich began to look for an entrepreneur who would build such a railway. On June 10, 1838, Fuhrmann, the head of the Government Finance Commission, reported to Paskevich that the Warsaw banker Peter Steinkeller would form a company to build the railway.[7] On November 14, 1838, a contract for the construction of the line was signed between the company that Steinkeller had formed and the Bank of Poland, acting in the name of the government of the Kingdom of Poland. The government made the concessions to the railway company that had come to be expected, and two new provisions, hitherto not fully applied to any railway project, were added. The railway was to remain the property of the stockholders only until all the capital had been extinguished (with a premium of 10 per cent) by a sinking fund to be supplied by profits in excess of 10 per cent yearly and was then to become the property of the government. The government for its part guaranteed a yearly dividend of 4 per cent to the stockholders, to be paid from Treasury funds through the Bank of Poland. Taking into account the likely fear of investors of unsettled conditions in Poland, the government further promised that this dividend would be paid punctually to all investors, regardless of nationality, in peace or in war.[8]

The first of these new provisions was not entirely without precedent, since in December, 1835, von Gerstner had been informed that his projected St. Petersburg–Moscow Railway would revert to the state at the end of fifty years. However, at the time it had not been stated how the capital would be extinguished. In the case of the Warsaw-Vienna Railway no definite term for the expiration of the privilege was set, but provision was made for the extinction of the capital. The government's guarantee of a 4 per cent yearly dividend was entirely without precedent and represented a reversal of policy, not only toward private railway companies but also toward other kinds of stock companies as

6. A. P. Shcherbatov, *General-Fel'dmarshal kniaz' Paskevich: ego zhizn' i deiatel'nost'* (St. Petersburg, 1888–1904), V, part 1, 189-191.

7. For details of the government's negotiations with Steinkeller, see *ibid.*, V, part 2, 376-381.

8. *Railway Times*, February 1, 1839, p. 154; *Dnevnik Zakonov Tsarstva Pol'skogo*, XXVI, No. 105 (September 27/October 9, 1840).

well. For the first time, except for the loans made to the Tsarskoe Selo Railway (1837–1839), the Russian government was offering direct financial aid to a railway undertaking after having rejected this idea in connection with von Gerstner's St. Petersburg–Moscow Railway and the railway projects of the years 1837–1838. It was the first such guarantee of a private railway company by a government in Europe.[9] The guarantee was presumably made 4 per cent to correspond to the rate of interest which an investor would receive if he deposited his money in a state credit institution.[10]

When on January 6, 1839, the assistant secretary of state of the Kingdom of Poland, J. Turkull, presented Nicholas I with Prince Paskevich's petition that the Tsar sign a decree ratifying the contract between Steinkeller's company and the Bank of Poland, Nicholas, ever cautious, replied that he considered the matter too important to decide by himself. He thereupon forwarded Paskevich's papers to the Department of Polish Affairs of the State Council with instructions that it was to make its report within a day.

The department met on January 7. Since the usefulness of the railway had already been decided by the Tsar, it limited itself in its discussion to the financial aspects of the problem. Count Kankrin, who was present, stated that the project was too risky for the government to be able to give a guarantee of 4 per cent. The Department of Polish Affairs considered the estimates Steinkeller had given not sufficiently supported by data and feared that the revenues of the railway would not cover costs of construction. Nevertheless the department returned Paskevich's papers to Nicholas I for signature. It did suggest, however, that Paskevich have the right, in case he should share the department's doubts, to stop the construction of the railway and refer the whole matter again to St. Petersburg.

On January 7, 1839, Nicholas I signed the decree affirming the

9. Such a guarantee had been proposed in France in 1837 for the projected Lyons–Marseilles Railway, but had not been granted. This proposal attracted immediate attention in Russia (see *Biblioteka dlia Chteniia*, XXIII [1837], Sec. V, 38). The first such guarantee was given in France only in 1840 for the Paris–Orléans Railway.

10. N. A. Kislinskii, *Nasha zheleznodorozhnaia politika po dokumentam arkhiva Komiteta Ministrov* (St. Petersburg, 1902), I, 20-21.

contract between Steinkeller's company and the Bank of Poland and giving the guarantee of a 4 per cent yearly dividend on the original capital of 21 million Polish florins (equivalent to 3.1 million silver rubles),[11] but he ordered that a copy of the proceedings of the meeting of the Department of Polish Affairs be forwarded to Paskevich with a statement that he was in agreement with its suggestion.[12]

Nicholas I probably desired the railway in order to further indirectly the cause of railways in other parts of the Russian Empire and perhaps for strategic reasons—he certainly did for economic reasons. In a private letter to Paskevich on January 28, 1839, he wrote that he considered the railway very useful if the Austrian government did not close its borders, as the Prussian government had, which could frustrate all their plans.[13] However, Nicholas seems to have had his doubts about the financial success of this railway, just as he had doubts about that of other railways, doubts which had been assiduously cultivated by his advisers, and therefore, gave Paskevich the right to stop construction of the railway if he should consider it necessary.

But Prince Paskevich allowed construction of the railway to be started.[14] Soon Steinkeller went to England to make arrangements for the distribution of stock through Harman and Company of London, which was to dispose of most of the shares. Colonel C. J. Barnett, British consul in Warsaw, thought that the Bank of Poland, which was also to distribute the shares, would not succeed in doing so, since it did not enjoy the confidence of the majority of the Polish public. Colonel Barnett later reported that Steinkeller had returned to Warsaw on April 4, 1839,[15] and that he said that he hoped to raise all the capital

11. For the full text of this decree, see *Dnevnik Zakonov Tsarstva Pol'skogo*, XXIII, No. 79 (January 7/19, 1839).

12. V. M. Verkhovskii, *Kratkii istoricheskii ocherk nachala i rasprostraneniia zheleznykh dorog v Rossii po 1897 g. vkliuchitel' no* (St. Petersburg, 1898), pp. 50-51; Shcherbatov, V, part 1, 192-193.

13. Shcherbatov, V, part 2, 384.

14. Prince Paskevich could afford to manifest independence of spirit in the territory that he governed all the more because he had been Nicholas' regimental commander. Nicholas is said to have liked to address him as "father commander" and heap rewards upon him (Nicholas V. Riasanovsky, *Nicholas I and Official Nationality in Russia, 1825–1855* [Berkeley, 1959], p. 43).

15. Shortly after his return from England, Steinkeller proposed two

in London soon (in actuality the shares were not selling well).[16]

Work on the railway was started in the spring of 1839 and was to last four years. The railway was to be built with a single track, but the roadbed and the stone parts of bridges were to be built to take a second track later.[17] The gauge of the railway was to be 4 feet 8.5 inches (1,435 mm.), i.e., the "standard" gauge common to the railways of England and most of Western Europe, including Austria and Prussia. The Warsaw-Vienna Railway was built to this gauge to facilitate connection with the Kaiser Ferdinands–Nordbahn.[18]

Steinkeller had originally planned to use horse traction and tram rails to save costs, but the government insisted that steam traction and ordinary rails be used, which raised costs considerably.[19] Still, costs were kept down by the level terrain over which the railway was built and by the abundance of cheap labor. Although, viewed as a whole, costs of land were not high because

other railways in connection with the Warsaw-Vienna Railway, but nothing came of these. His proposal for a railway from Warsaw to Nizhnii Novgorod was considered by Count Kankrin and Count Toll to be premature because of its length and because Steinkeller had failed to furnish any estimates. But the railway proposed by Steinkeller from Jurburg (Jurbarkas) on the Niemen River to the Russian Baltic ports of Windau or Libau aroused the interest of both Kankrin and Toll, because it would help Polish trade to avoid transit duties levied by Prussia, since it would divert trade on the Niemen River from the Prussian ports of Königsberg, Tilsit, and Memel to Russian ports. Paskevich was instructed to tell Steinkeller to draw up a project and then to report to Count Kankrin. Nicholas confirmed this instruction on May 28, 1839 (Verkhovskii, pp. 54-55; Public Record Office, London, Foreign Office 65 [Diplomatic and consular reports from Russia to England], Vol. CCLV; Colonel C. J. Barnett to Viscount Palmerston, No. 6 [Warsaw, April 22 (N.S.), 1839]). Nothing further seems to have come of this project, although in November, 1839, it was reported in the London Times that Russian engineers were surveying the route from Jurburg to Windau and Libau for a railway. At the same time, doubt was expressed in this article that a railway would be built because the writer thought that the water routes would still be cheaper because they were more direct (Times [London], November 11, 1839, p. 3, col. d).

16. Public Record Office, F.O. 65, Vol CCLV. Colonel C. J. Barnett to Viscount Palmerston, No. 4 (Warsaw, February 13 [N.S.], 1839), and No. 6 (Warsaw, April 22 [N.S.], 1839).

17. V. V. Salov, "Nachalo zheleznodorozhnogo dela v Rossii, 1836–1855," Vestnik Evropy, CXCVI (1899), 256.

18. Oscar Matthesius, Russische Eisenbahnpolitik im XIX. Jahrhundert, 1836-1881 (Inaugural dissertation, Berlin, 1903), p. 19, n. 2.

19. Ibid., p. 21; Kislinskii, I, 22, n. 1.

the state was ceding its land without charge,[20] there seems to have been difficulty in persuading owners of private land to cede it at a reasonable price, for in 1840 the Council of Administration of the Kingdom of Poland reaffirmed the right of the railway to take private lands and laid down rules whereby these lands could be taken without delaying work on the railway.[21]

Everything taken together, the Warsaw-Vienna Railway Company was soon in financial difficulties because of expenses which exceeded the original estimates. Also, the stock of the company was still not selling well. The government tried to help by granting a subsidy of 4 million florins and by postponing twice the deadline for the distribution of all the stock. But during the financial crisis of 1841 additional funds were hard to obtain. Therefore, on May 31, 1842, Steinkeller's company declared that it was unable to continue and dissolved itself without having opened any part of the railway to traffic.[22]

The British consul in Warsaw, DuPlat, reported that he considered that Steinkeller had tricked the government into authorizing the Warsaw-Vienna Railway and guaranteeing its capital by giving ridiculously low estimates of construction costs which proved to be twice as high as originally estimated.[23] In justice to Steinkeller, it should be kept in mind that the failure of his company was not entirely his fault, since the government had raised costs by insisting on steam traction and more expensive rails, and since it had been so difficult to distribute all the stock of the company.

In January, 1842, Baron Solomon Rothschild, who headed the committee in charge of the construction of the Kaiser Ferdinands–Nordbahn, had written to Prince Paskevich that he was planning a railway from Leipzig to Bochnia via Oswiecim and had urged Paskevich to hasten the completion of the Warsaw-Vienna Railway to the Austrian border to make both railways

20. *Journal de St. Pétersbourg*, September 20/October 2, 1841, p. 1367.

21. *Dnevnik Zakonov Tsarstva Pol'skogo*, XXVI, No. 105 (September 27/October 9, 1840).

22. Verkhovskii, pp. 51-52; Matthesius, *Russische Eisenbahnpolitik*, p. 21.

23. Public Record Office, F. O. 65, Vol. CCCXXVI. DuPlat to the Earl of Aberdeen, No. 34 (Warsaw, November 26 [N.S.], 1846).

more valuable. Paskevich forwarded the letter to Nicholas I, suggesting that the Bank of Poland make any advances necessary.[24] Steinkeller's company had nevertheless been allowed to fail a few months later. But this possibility of finally achieving a connection with a railway in Austria induced the government after a time to resume construction of the railway. In October, 1843, by imperial decree, construction was ordered to be continued at the expense of the Treasury with the government reimbursing the investors for the capital already spent, with an additional payment of 4 per cent of this amount.[25]

Work on the railway was started again in 1844 under the direction of Russian and some English engineers. By the autumn of 1846 the railway was opened to Czestochowa, 216 versts from Warsaw, and was operating profitably and bringing economic benefits to the area which it served.[26] The remaining part of the railway to the Austrian border was opened to traffic on April 1, 1848. The total length of the railway was 287.5 versts, with a 19.5-verst branch to Lowicz. The total cost of construction was 7 million silver rubles.[27] This meant that the cost of construction per verst was just under half that of the Tsarskoe Selo Railway, but it was more than twice the original estimate made by Steinkeller in 1838.

With the opening of the Warsaw-Vienna Railway to the Austrian border, the Russian Empire received its first international railway connection, at first only with Austrian Galicia but after September, 1848, with Vienna. It was not until 1856, however, that Vienna could be reached without going through Prussian territory.[28]

24. *Times* (London), February 12, 1842, p. 4, col. f.
25. Verkhovskii, p. 52.
26. Public Record Office, F.O. 65, Vols. CCCXVI, CCCXXVI. DuPlat to the Earl of Aberdeen, No. 16 (Warsaw, June 15 [N.S.], 1845), and No. 34 (Warsaw, November 26 [N.S.], 1846).
27. Verkhovskii, p. 52.
28. In 1845 the Free State of Cracow had authorized construction of a railway 65 kilometers in length to be built from Cracow to the Prussian border via Trzebinia–Szczakowa–Myslowice, with a branch 1.6 kilometers in length from Szczakowa to Granica on the border of the Kingdom of Poland. In spite of the annexation of the Free State of Cracow by Austria in 1846, the railway between Cracow and the Prussian and Polish borders was opened in October, 1847. This railway connected with the Warsaw-Vienna Railway after April 1, 1848, at Granica. It connected also with the

Of even greater importance than the Warsaw-Vienna Railway for the development of railways in Russia was the order given by Nicholas I to Count Toll on April 13, 1839, to send two reliable engineers of the Corps of Transport Engineers to America to study railways. S. I. Mal'tsov quoted the Tsar as saying about this time, "I am sure that we can build railways in Russia. They built them in America. I shall send someone there to look at them, and then we shall begin."[29] The Tsar hoped that reliable information on American railways, where so many conditions were like those in Russia, would elucidate all the questions which had previously kept the government from deciding to allow railways to be built in Russia.[30]

Count Toll's choice fell on Colonel N. O. Kraft and Lieutenant Colonel P. P. Mel'nikov, who were in America from June, 1839, to June, 1840.[31]

Kraft since 1825 had been engaged in hydraulic works, especially projects for the uniting of the Volga and Don rivers and for the avoidance of the Dnieper Rapids by means of a canal. In 1837 he had been made a professor at the Institute of Transport Engineers.[32] His only previous experience with railways had come when he was sent to Austria in 1835 to gather information on von Gerstner's role in the building of the Linz-Budweis Railway. Mel'nikov also had been engaged primarily in hydraulic works, but had been the first native Russian engineer in the

---

Prussian Oberschlesische Bahn, which went to Breslau and Berlin. From this latter railway a branch was completed on September 1, 1848, from Kosel in Upper Silesia to Oderberg (Bohumin), which the Kaiser Ferdinands–Nordbahn had reached in 1847. Thus the Warsaw–Vienna Railway had a connection with Vienna but only by a route through Prussian territory. It was not until March, 1856, that a direct railway link between Oderberg and Cracow was completed, thereby providing a route entirely avoiding Prussian territory (*Geschichte der Eisenbahnen der Österreichisch-ungarischen Monarchie*, I, 204, 288, 304).

29. S. I. Mal'tsov, "Iz vospominanii S. I. Mal'tsova," *Zapiski Moskovskogo Otdeleniia Imperatorskogo Tekhnicheskogo Obshchestva*, IV (1886), 40.

30. See the comments of P. P. Mel'nikov in "Svedeniia o russkikh zheleznykh dorogakh," ed. M. Krutikov, *Krasnyi Arkhiv*, XCIX (1940), 164.

31. Verkhovskii, p. 49.

32. S. M. Zhitkov, *Biografii inzhenerov putei soobshcheniia* (St. Petersburg, 1889–1902), I, 46; A. M. Larionov, *Istoriia Instituta Inzhenerov Putei Soobshcheniia Imperatora Aleksandra I-ogo za pervoe stoletie ego sushchestvovaniia, 1810–1910* (St. Petersburg, 1910), p. 96.

Corps of Transport Engineers to become seriously interested in railways.[33] In 1831 Mel'nikov had started to teach practical mechanics at the institute. A part of this course dealt with steam engines, especially their application to railways, a subject with which he had therefore become familiar. In 1835 he published a pamphlet entitled *O zheleznykh dorogakh* (*On Railways*), the first work of the sort in the Russian language. From June, 1837, to September, 1838, Mel'nikov had been sent to Western Europe along with another engineer of the Corps of Transport Engineers, S. V. Kerbezd, to study various types of communications. He traveled through England, France, Belgium, and Germany, talking with many famous engineers, including George and Robert Stephenson and Isambard Kingdom Brunel, the engineer of the Great Western Railway.[34]

Mel'nikov had returned home from Western Europe convinced that railways would be especially useful to facilitate administration and for the transportation of passengers. He had come to the conclusion that a country with a full system of railways would be as if it were sixteen times smaller in respect to administration and communication. Yet in 1837–1838 Mel'nikov, like most engineers of that time, was not yet convinced that railways would have great advantages for the transportation of freight. The disadvantages of canals, their slowness and the interruption of traffic by ice in winter, seemed to him outweighed by their cheapness. Furthermore, if canal transportation was made faster, Mel'nikov felt that canals might be used to carry passengers from the poorer classes of society. He made the reservation, however, that his judgment should not be considered final, since more powerful locomotives might be built which could pull large amounts of freight at high speeds. Such transportation of freight by railway might be especially useful in Russia.[35]

33. For a biographical sketch of Mel'nikov see Zhitkov, I, 52-75. Mel'nikov was to advocate the building of railways in Russia throughout his long and distinguished career. He continually advocated other forms of improved transportation, too, especially river steamboats. He became minister of the ways of communication (1862–1869) at the time of the railway building boom under Alexander II.

34. Mel'nikov, "Svedeniia," *Krasnyi Arkhiv*, XCIX (1940), 138, 160-161; Zhitkov, I, 53-55.

35. Mel'nikov, "Svedeniia," *Krasnyi Arkhiv*, XCIX (1940), 138-139; P. P. Mel'nikov and S. V. Kerbezd, "Ob otnositel'nykh vygodakh razlichnykh

Mel'nikov returned to Russia from America in September, 1840, with his previous conviction about the value of railways for carrying passengers and high-priced goods confirmed, but now also convinced that railways would have great value in Russia for carrying all kinds of freight, since in America the introduction of railways carrying low-priced goods in connection with river steamboats had had a very beneficial effect on that country's economy. Railways in Russia, as in America, could reduce the great distances of the country and operate uninterruptedly during all seasons of the year.

Thirty years later Mel'nikov wrote that he had met many Americans who pointed out that the economy of the United States had been developed by railways in the previous ten years and suggested that Russia should follow the example of America as soon as possible. Railways would not only increase the value of Russia's trade and industry, as they had those of European countries, but would even create this trade and industry, since Russia, although rich in natural resources, suffered from a lack of markets for its products because of a lack of adequate transportation. The Russian government should first construct the most important railways on its own account. Mel'nikov's American acquaintances maintained that the capital invested by the Russian government would soon be paid back through direct revenues, the reduction of other government expenditures, and the general increase in the national wealth. Secondary railways could then be built by private enterprise. The private investor would be willing to invest his money if the government would give a suitable guarantee.[36]

Mel'nikov's first step after his return from America was to start writing a long report on his experience there, especially on the mass of technological data which he had gathered, data which would be useful among other things for setting up estimates of costs for a railway between St. Petersburg and Moscow. Mel'nikov's report on railways and river steamboats in America eventually filled six thick volumes, but it was largely ignored,

sistem vnutrennykh soobshchenii," *Zhurnal Putei Soobshcheniia,* III, kn. III (1840), 206-227.

36. Mel'nikov, "Svedeniia," *Krasnyi Arkhiv,* XCIX (1940), 139, 165.

except for several sections which were printed in 1842 in the *Journal of Transport* (*Zhurnal Putei Soobshcheniia*).[37]

Early in 1841, the *Journal of Transport* had published an excerpt from Mel'nikov's report on his trip to Western Europe in 1837–1838. This excerpt dealt with Belgian railways. In this article Mel'nikov discussed several matters which would have significance for Russia. Mel'nikov wrote that when Belgium gained its independence from Holland in 1830 the Belgians wished to develop the port of Antwerp as an outlet for their own trade and for goods originating in Germany. In previous years, much money and effort had been spent on Belgium's waterways, but in 1833, the Belgian government had decided to link the Rhine with Antwerp by a railway rather than by a canal, since a railway would cost no more to build and could be built more quickly, would provide more rapid and cheaper transportation for passengers and high-priced goods, and could be operated throughout the year. It was also felt that a railway would be advantageous because it would stimulate branches of Belgian industry such as metallurgy more than a canal would.

Mel'nikov observed that the Brussels-Antwerp Railway had cost four times less to build than the Liverpool-Manchester Railway because the terrain was less difficult and because the Belgians had been able to learn from the mistakes of the English, and that in spite of low fares the profits of the Belgian railway were twice as large as those of the English one. The number of passengers was twice as large, even though the cities of Brussels and Antwerp did not stand in such close relationship to each other as did Manchester and Liverpool.

Mel'nikov wrote that railways in Belgium built by the state cost less than others because some costs inevitable for private companies could be avoided. The Belgian government then gained indirectly through increased trade activity and the growth of industry and public enlightenment, as well as by the assurance

37. P. P. Mel'nikov, "Opisanie v tekhnicheskom otnoshenii zheleznykh dorog severo-amerikanskikh shtatov," *Zhurnal Putei Soobshcheniia* (1842), II, kn. I, 19-85, kn. II, 95-197, kn. IV, 285-374; III, kn. I, 1-70, kn. II, 85-156.

of peace and order within the country, even if the direct profits from most of its railways were small for the first few years.[38]

Mel'nikov, firmly convinced after his trip to America that the St. Petersburg–Moscow Railway was desirable and necessary, did not wish to limit himself to writing reports and publishing articles, but wished to persuade his superiors that the railway should be built. Although he had been sent abroad at Nicholas' request, in the autumn and winter of 1840-1841, Mel'nikov was faced with the difficulty of gaining access to high government officials who would be sympathetically disposed toward his arguments. In October, 1839, Toll had suffered a stroke which left him partially paralyzed and unable to perform his duties.[39] On April 13, 1840, Nicholas I granted him permission to tour the spas of Germany to recover his health.[40] During his absence his duties as head of the Main Administration of Transport and Buildings were to be performed by Lieutenant General A. P. Deviatin. General Deviatin had the reputation of being an intelligent and able man with a good deal of technical knowledge,[41] but he proved to be, like Count Toll, a staunch opponent of railways; Mel'nikov could find no support from his superiors in the Main Administration of Transport and Buildings. He of course would have liked to talk directly to Nicholas I, but he had no means of gaining an audience. Mel'nikov therefore made the acquaintance of Count A. A. Bobrinskii, who would presumably be sympathetic and have access to the Tsar. Mel'nikov told Count Bobrinskii about his experiences in America and said that

38. P. P. Mel'nikov, "Zheleznye dorogi v Bel'gii," *Zhurnal Putei Soobshcheniia*, I, kn. I (1841), 1-28.

39. A. Sushkov, "Vospominaniia o grafe K. F. Tole," *Chteniia v Imperatorskom Obshchestve Istorii i Drevnostei Rossiiskikh pri Moskovskom Universitete*, LV (1865), 219.

40. On April 13, 1840, Count Kankrin was also granted imperial permission to go abroad for six months (N. Dubrovin, [ed.], *Sbornik istoricheskikh materialov, izvlechennykh iz Arkhiva Sobstvennoi Ego Imperatorskogo Velichestva Kantseliarii* [St. Petersburg, 1876–1917], IX, 22.

41. He managed the affairs of the Main Administration of Transport and Buildings once or twice more when Toll was absent and after Toll's death on April 23, 1842 (Dubrovin, IX, 21-22; Baron A. I. Del'vig, *Moi vospominaniia* [Moscow, 1912–1913], II, 5-6).

he thought that the St. Petersburg–Moscow Railway was possible and should be built. Count Bobrinskii agreed to talk to Nicholas I but thought that his advocacy of the railway would be more effective if he could find some well-known bankers who would make a concrete proposal.[42]

Meanwhile Nicholas had sent Major General K. V. Chevkin, the chief of the Corps of Mining Engineers, to England. Chevkin was ordered to study the English railway system and to make the acquaintance of prominent English railway engineers, with the idea of perhaps engaging them later to build the St. Petersburg–Moscow Railway. Chevkin also was to study French and German railways.[43]

In late 1840 Nicholas I consulted his Committee of Ministers several times on the possibility of building the St. Petersburg–Moscow Railway. Nearly all of the committee spoke out against the building of the railway with perhaps more forcefulness than in the period 1838–1839, stating that the railway would be impossible and useless. Again the opposition to railways was led by Count Toll, who had returned from his journey abroad. Count Toll used arguments that he had not previously used. He asserted that local difficulties would be more insuperable than any in America. It would be impossible to build the railway through the swamps in Novgorod Province and over the Valdai Hills. Even if it could be built, winter snows and frosts would hinder operation in northern Russia. If railways could operate successfully in the American climate, it should be remembered that the coldest part of America had a climate like that of Kharkov Province, i.e., the southern part of Russia. Toll also produced his usual argument that Russia needed cheaper, not faster transportation, and therefore water communications between the capitals should be built. The minister of state domains, Count P. D. Kiselev, presented the arguments that coachmen along the Moscow *Chaussée* would be deprived of their means of livelihood and that Russia's forests would be exhausted in supplying the necessary amount of locomotive fuel. Other ministers stated that the railway would

42. Mel'nikov, "Svedeniia," *Krasnyi Arkhiv*, XCIX (1940), 166–167.
43. *Railway Times*, September 26, 1840, p. 806, and October 31, 1840, p. 928.

lead to the leveling of social classes, since all classes of society would ride side by side in the same railway carriage.[44]

Then, early in 1841, Count Bobrinskii approached the Tsar with a project devised by him and A. V. Abaza to build a railway from Rybinsk to the river Tvertsa where it crossed the Moscow *Chaussée*. The estimated cost of this railway was only 6 to 7 million silver rubles, since less expensive horse traction and tram rails were to be used. Nicholas I, when presented with this project, did not discuss it, but wished to discuss with Bobrinskii the possibility of building the St. Petersburg–Moscow Railway instead.[45] As a result of their discussion Bobrinskii came to feel more than ever that what was needed was a proposal by someone who had a reputation as a railway builder and who could raise the necessary capital, thus providing a certain authoritativeness to balance the opposition of men like Toll and Kankrin. Bobrinskii, feeling that the time was now ripe, therefore wrote to the Leipzig bankers Dufour and Harkort, with whom he had dealings concerning his own affairs, suggesting that they make a proposal to the Tsar to build the St. Petersburg–Moscow Railway.[46]

Albert Dufour-Feronce and Gustav Harkort were Leipzig bankers and merchants who had been active since 1833 in the building of the Leipzig-Dresden Railway in Saxony. Both Dufour and Harkort had been founders and later two of the first directors of the company building the railway.[47] By 1839 the Leipzig-Dresden Railway had been completed, and Dufour and Harkort, like von Gerstner before them, were seeking new spheres of activity. Russia seemed to them, as it had to von Gerstner, to afford excellent opportunities for pioneers in building railways. They must have been acquainted with von Gerstner's attempts to build railways in Russia and with his Tsarskoe Selo Railway, many of the shares of which had been distributed in Saxony. Von

44. A. I. Shtukenberg, "Iz istorii zheleznodorozhnogo dela v Rossii: Nikolaevskaia doroga mezhdu Peterburgom i Moskvoiu," *Russkaia Starina*, XLVI (1885), 314-315; *Postroika i eksploatatsiia Nikolaevskoi Zheleznoi Dorogi (1842–1851–1901 gg.): Kratkii istoricheskii ocherk* (St. Petersburg, 1901), pp. 5-6.

45. "Zapiski senatora K. I. Fishera," *Istoricheskii Vestnik*, CXII (1908), 444.

46. Mel'nikov, "Svedeniia," *Krasnyi Arkhiv*, XCIX (1940), 167.

47. See *Die Leipzig-Dresdner Eisenbahn in den ersten 25 Jahren ihres Bestehens* (Leipzig, 1864), pp. 5-31.

Gerstner had also published in Leipzig his *Bericht über den Stand der Unternehmung der Eisenbahn von St. Petersburg nach Zarskoe-Selo und Pawlowsk* in 1838 and his *Berichte aus den Vereinigten Staaten von Nordamerika* in 1839. In both works he had talked of building the St. Petersburg–Moscow Railway, perhaps with the intention of interesting German capitalists in the scheme.

Dufour and Harkort had in fact submitted proposals to build the St. Petersburg–Moscow Railway in the spring of 1839. The Russian government had rejected these proposals, just as they had those of less experienced entrepreneurs.[48] This was, of course, just at the time when Kraft and Mel'nikov were starting off to America to study conditions there. But when in 1841 Count Bobrinskii got in touch with them, they came to St. Petersburg and submitted a lengthy memorandum in French, describing their previous achievements, especially the Leipzig-Dresden Railway, and stating the advantages that a railway between the capitals would bring to Russia.

Dufour and Harkort asked for a privilege to build the St. Petersburg–Moscow Railway and to form a company to which this privilege would be transferred and which would begin to function when 10 per cent of the necessary capital was actually on hand. The members of this company, as well as the stockholders, would be largely German capitalists; the company would therefore have its headquarters in Leipzig. However, it would have a board of directors in St. Petersburg which would direct operations within Russia. Dufour and Harkort proposed to help the board of directors set up its administration and train officials and artisans. During the period of construction, Dufour and Harkort would come every year to St. Petersburg to report the desires of the stockholders in Germany to the directors. The Russian government could set up a commission to supervise the activities of the board of directors and could take part of the stock of the company to participate directly in the company and assure itself that its interests would be protected.

Dufour and Harkort asked the Russian government for many of the same concessions that had been granted to the Tsarskoe

48. Verkhovskii, p. 53.

Selo and Warsaw-Vienna railways.[49] They also asked for a guarantee such as Peter Steinkeller had obtained for the Warsaw-Vienna Railway of at least a 4 per cent yearly dividend on the as yet undetermined amount of capital needed. But Dufour and Harkort were not content to let the extinction of the capital depend, as it had on the Warsaw-Vienna Railway, on profits over 10 per cent. They asked for a definite arrangement to guarantee the extinction of the capital and a premium on the shares. They suggested three possible forms of guarantee by the government for regular payments that would lead to government ownership at a stated time.[50] The Russian government could gain possession of the railway at any time before the expiration of the privilege if it bought all the shares, paying the premium on the shares due by that year. As compensation for their efforts, Dufour and Harkort would receive a banker's commission of 1 per cent of the capital and an additional 1 per cent in shares of stock.

Dufour and Harkort had made no surveys of the proposed route of the railway. They therefore suggested that as soon as the privilege had been granted, the Russian government set up a commission to conduct these surveys, with the company paying the expenses.

Dufour and Harkort did not state when the railway would be completed or how much capital would be necessary. They also did not state what obligations the government should demand of their company. They did not display von Gerstner's eagerness, but suggested that the government set up a special committee of officials, merchants, and industrialists to study whether the St. Petersburg–Moscow Railway would be useful for Russian trade and industry. This committee, not they, would also determine the best methods of construction and make estimates of po-

49. See p. 100, n. 89, and p. 195 above.
50. The government was to guarantee yearly (1) a dividend of 4.5 per cent, 1 per cent for the extinction of the capital, and 1 per cent for the premium, so that each share would increase in value every year by that amount, and the privilege would last forty-seven years; or (2) a dividend of 4.5 per cent, 1.5 per cent for the extinction of the capital, 1 per cent for the premium, and the privilege would last for thirty-seven years; or (3) a dividend of 4 per cent, 2 per cent for the extinction of the capital, with the annual premium decreasing gradually from 2 per cent to 1 per cent over the thirty-six years during which the privilege would last.

tential costs, revenues, and profits to prove that the railway would be profitable.[51]

On March 8, 1841, Count Benckendorff wrote to Count Toll that the Tsar wished a committee to be formed to review a project for building the St. Petersburg–Moscow Railway from the technical and commercial standpoints. This committee was to be under the chairmanship of Count Benckendorff (henceforth this committee will be referred to as the "Benckendorff Committee"), and the other members were to be Major General Chevkin, Colonel Kraft, Lieutenant Colonel Mel'nikov, and Count Bobrinskii. (At the command of the Tsar, A. V. Abaza was added to the committee on March 27.) The Benckendorff Committee, the proceedings of which were to be secret, was to invite prominent merchants from St. Petersburg and Moscow for consultation. When it had presented its conclusions, they would be forwarded to Count Kankrin and Count Toll and then to the Committee of Ministers for further consideration.[52]

Mel'nikov later wrote that the Tsar obviously chose men sympathetic to railways to form a committee that might meet the expected opposition of the Committee of Ministers, especially Toll, Kankrin, and Count A. G. Stroganov, the minister of the interior.[53]

At the first meeting of his committee Count Beckendorff divided the tasks to be accomplished among its various members. To Mel'nikov, Kraft, and Chevkin, all of whom had studied rail-

51. I. P. Borichevskii, "Predlozheniia chastnykh lits ob ustroistve zheleznykh dorog, postupivshie v G.U.P.S. i P.Z. do 1860 goda," *Zhurnal Putei Soobshcheniia*, XXXIX, kn. I. (1863), 143-145; Mel'nikov, "Svedeniia," *Krasnyi Arkhiv*, XCIX (1940), 167-168.

52. "Otnoshenie upravliaiushchego III otdeleniia gr. A. Benkendorfa k glavnoupravliaiushchemu putei soobshcheniia i publichnymi zdaniiami gr. Toliu 8 marta 1841 g.," *Krasnyi Arkhiv*, LXXVI (1936), 126.

53. Mel'nikov, "Svedeniia," *Krasnyi Arkhiv*, XCIX (1940), 169. There is considerable doubt whether Count Benckendorff was personally in favor of railways. According to a foreign observer, he had feared that railway construction in Russia might lead eventually to the emancipation of the serfs (Österreichisches Haus-, Hof-, und Staatsarchiv. Ficquelmont to Metternich, 1836, No. 21 [May 5/17]). However, Benckendorff, regardless of his personal feelings, was so close to the Tsar that he would support whatever he thought Nicholas might want. When Count Benckendorff was put in charge of a project, the Tsar could be certain that great effort would be made to carry out his will.

ways abroad, was intrusted the assignment of setting up estimates of costs and revenues. Abaza, with the help of a merchant named Butorin, was told to study commercial considerations. Count Bobrinskii was to conduct all further negotiations with Dufour and Harkort.[54]

On May 30, 1841, Abaza submitted a report on the commercial advantages of the St. Petersburg–Moscow Railway. In this report, the first to be made by any member of the Benckendorff Committee, Abaza stressed that a more rapid turnover of capital made possible by more rapid transportation would make the prices of goods, especially grain, cheaper, benefiting the Russian population and making Russian goods more competitive on the world market. In contrast to his position in 1838 Abaza put more emphasis on the value of the St. Petersburg–Moscow Railway as a freight carrier than as a means of transporting passengers. Apparently on hearing Mel'nikov tell of the success of American railways in carrying freight he had been flexible enough to alter his opinion.

With this freight traffic in mind, Abaza proposed that after the St. Petersburg–Moscow Railway had been built, a railway should be built from Moscow to Tula, Orel, Kursk, Kharkhov, and Alexandrovsk (a town on the Dnieper River beyond the Dnieper Rapids). From Alexandrovsk there would be a connecting steamboat service to Odessa. Another railway should be built from Nizhnii Novgorod via Moscow to Warsaw, where it would connect with the railways of Europe. These two railways would allow all of Europe's trade with Asia to be funneled through Moscow or Nizhnii Novgorod.[55]

During the summer of 1841, while the work of the Benckendorff Committee was still in progress, Nicholas I considered it necessary to give Dufour and Harkort a preliminary and conditional indication of the financial terms of the privilege which might eventually be granted them. On July 11, 1841, the Tsar appointed another committee to work on drafting these terms and to conduct further negotiations with Dufour and Harkort. From the Benckendorff Committee, Count Benckendorff, Count

54. *Ibid.*
55. V. S. Virginskii, *Vozniknovenie zheleznykh dorog v Rossii do nachala 40-ykh godov XIX veka* (Moscow, 1949), pp. 212-213.

Bobrinskii, and General Chevkin were chosen. But Count A. G. Stroganov, the minister of the interior, General Deviatin, and F. P. Vronchenko, the deputy minister of finance, were also included.[56]

On July 30, 1841, this committee reported to Dufour and Harkort that they might eventually receive permission to build a double-tracked railway between St. Petersburg and Moscow, using steam traction and capable of transporting at least 200,000 passengers and 24 million poods of freight yearly on financial terms slightly less attractive than those they had proposed.

Their company could start its activities when one-tenth of the capital was actually on hand. To help them attract the capital, the Russian government undertook to guarantee a yearly profit of 4 per cent on a capital of no more than 43 million silver rubles, plus an additional 2 per cent for the extinction of this capital and the premium on the shares, i.e., a total yearly guarantee of 6 per cent. This guarantee was to take effect only from the day of completion of the railway. This last stipulation may have been inspired by a similar condition in the guarantee given by the French government for the Paris–Orléans Railway in 1840.[57] Another source of inspiration may have been the fact that by the summer of 1841 the Warsaw-Vienna Railway, to which a 4 per cent guarantee had also been given, was in serious financial difficulties and had opened no part of the railway to traffic. The committee stated that the privilege was to last thirty-seven years, after which ownership of the railway was to revert to the Russian government. The government would have the right to acquire the railway before the expiration of the thirty-seven-year privilege by buying all the shares of stock, and paying the premium which would have accumulated. Any profits in excess of the yearly 4 per cent dividend and the 2 per cent for the extinction of the shares and the premium on them would form a fund to be applied to the more rapid extinction of the still unredeemed shares. The founders of the company would receive a banker's commission of 1.5 per cent of the capital (instead of the 2 per cent originally requested), .5 percent of the shares and 1 per cent of the capital used for construction.

These terms were reported to Dufour and Harkort on July

56. *Ibid.*   57. Kislinskii, I, 22, n. 2.

30, 1841. On August 1, they asked that the guarantee be given not just from the day of the opening of the railway but from the time of the deposit of the money for the shares. Dufour and Harkort also still insisted on a banker's commission of 2 per cent. When the government refused to accede to these demands, negotiations were suspended.[58]

In spite of the suspension of negotiations with Dufour and Harkort, the Benckendorff Committee, which in July, 1841, had been changed into a commission, continued with its work and on September 15, 1841, was able to submit its report. This report (hereinafter referred to as the *Donesenie*) finally convinced Nicholas I that the St. Petersburg–Moscow Railway would be useful and profitable and that he should at last order it to be built.

The *Donesenie* tried to refute especially the argument that the St. Petersburg–Moscow Railway would cost too much to build and operate and would produce too little revenue to be a financial success. It contained a very detailed report, using official statistics wherever possible as well as information on the experience of railways abroad from reliable sources. The Benckendorff Commission emphasized that it was purposely making its estimates of costs higher than they would probably be and its estimates of revenues lower. It admitted that its estimates were only approximate but claimed that they should be near enough to be reliable.[59]

The Donesenie stressed that the experience of America and Europe showed that the opponents of railways in Russia were wrong in believing that railways were only an expensive luxury unsuited for carrying heavy goods. Railways abroad had been originally used mainly for carrying passengers, but recently revenues from freight had become an important or even major factor in the profitableness of railways. This was especially so in America, where railways profitably carried large amounts of low-priced bulky raw materials. In America railway building was taking place in spite of the simultaneous building of canals. Railways were often being built both parallel to and instead of canals, since they offered a more rapid and convenient means of

58. Borichevskii, pp. 146-148.
59. "Donesenie Nikolaiu I komissii po ustroistvu zheleznoi dorogi mezhdu Peterburgom i Moskvoi, 15 sentiabria 1841 g.," *Krasnyi Arkhiv*, LXXVI (1936), 127.

communication not subject to stoppage by freezes in the winter. The same would be the case in Russia, where the Tsarskoe Selo Railway had functioned successfully for the previous three winters without a single stoppage of traffic.

The *Donesenie* stated that in the northern part of Russia railways would have great advantages over waterways and roads, especially for the transportation of freight. Goods would be shipped from producer to consumer more quickly, making marketing easier and goods cheaper. The Russian merchant, with quicker and easier transportation at his disposal, could employ his capital on more enterprises every year, which could help the development of various branches of Russian economic activity.

The railway would help Russia's internal and export grain trade. Rybinsk, the main supplier of St. Petersburg, could deliver grain and other goods by water to Tver or Shosha, whence they could be quickly transported to St. Petersburg. Moscow would become the second supplier of St. Petersburg. Thus, in the event of a harvest failure on the Lower Volga, the central provinces around Moscow could supply St. Petersburg quickly via Moscow and the railway. Moscow could become a center for the storage of grain, which could be shipped where needed. As for the export trade in grain, if the St. Petersburg–Moscow Railway was built, grain from the provinces around Moscow could be quickly shipped abroad to take advantage of high prices caused by any harvest failure in Western Europe.

The St. Petersburg–Moscow Railway would bring direct advantages to the state. Russia's forests would be conserved by the fact that fewer barges would have to be built. The competition of Moscow and Rybinsk as grain markets would mean that the Treasury could obtain supplies at more advantageous prices. Also, government expenses for the transportation of various sorts of goods and for supplying military forces in and around the capitals as well as for the transportation of the post would be reduced considerably.

The St. Petersburg–Moscow Railway would prevent an excessive concentration of factory workers in both capitals. This concentration was harmful for national morality and caused losses to manufacturers, since the maintenance of these workers cost more in the capitals. If a railway was built between the capitals, factories could be spread out along the railway, since their products would have quick and cheap access to markets.

The *Donesenie* concluded that one of the main advantages of the St. Petersburg–Moscow Railway would be to bring St. Petersburg, the administrative, commercial, and cultural center of the empire, nearer to the interior of Russia. Without a railway most traffic on the waterways connecting St. Petersburg and the interior of the country flowed mainly toward St. Petersburg, while little traffic flowed in the opposite direction. If, on the other hand, a railway were built, St. Petersburg, which was only the head of Russia, would become, along with Moscow, the heart of Russia.[60]

In debates concerning previous railway projects, one of the most important issues had been the costs of construction and whether they would greatly exceed the original estimates, as the Tsarskoe Selo Railway had done. Mel'nikov, who with Kraft and Chevkin was to prepare the estimates for the Benckendorff Commission, had the advantage of the knowledge he had gained on his American trip and used this information in setting them up.[61] Although Mel'nikov's estimates were based on the experience of American railways, he proposed that the St. Petersburg–Moscow Railway be built more solidly and elaborately than most railways of that time. In his report for the Benckendorff Commission he outlined the methods that later were employed in the construction of the St. Petersburg–Moscow Railway. In his desire to build the Railway better than most railways in America, and even most in Europe, Mel'nikov was the spiritual heir of von Gerstner.

The *Donesenie* proposed that the St. Petersburg–Moscow Railway be built as a steam railway with two tracks, because it was anticipated that the volume of traffic would be large. The railway would be as straight as possible, and would avoid Novgorod and Torzhok. The length of the railway would be 590 versts, but costs were estimated for a railway 620 versts in length.

Earthworks would be the largest single item of expense. These estimates were based upon the costs of similar earthworks for the Moscow *Chaussée*, which paralleled the proposed route of the railway, except from Chudovo to Volochek. Unlike those in

60. *Ibid.*, pp. 140-144.
61. Mel'nikov, "Svedeniia," *Krasnyi Arkhiv*, XCIX (1940), 169.

America, the gradients of the railway would be light, so that locomotives could pull larger loads, especially in the direction in which most traffic would move, from Moscow to St. Petersburg. Total costs of earthworks were estimated at 10,437,900 silver rubles for 5,163,708 cubic sazhens of embankments and cuttings, an estimate which was one-third higher than the cost of similar works on English railways and three times that for Belgian railways. On the earthworks was to be laid a three-foot layer of gravel or other material for drainage to protect the tracks against moisture or frost. This would cost an additional 3,624,300 silver rubles.

Bridges and drainage pipes would cost 3,467,000 silver rubles, including 1,000,000 silver rubles for the three long bridges across the Volkhov, Msta, and Volga rivers. These bridges were to be wooden, but were to rest on stone pillars. Buildings would cost 2,915,200 silver rubles, including 1,000,000 silver rubles for station buildings in the capitals.

The superstructure would cost 9,046,900 silver rubles, including 6,867,500 silver rubles for 4,807,000 poods of iron rails. This price was one and a half times that of English rails, which would allow Russian ironmasters to supply as much of the total amount required as they were able. Some foreign rails would have to be used because not enough iron could be produced in Russia to cover all the demand for rails.

A machine shop for building locomotives and other rolling stock would be established in St. Petersburg as well as a locomotive repair shop in Moscow and a carriage repair shop in Volochek. The Benckendorff Commission wished a strong effort to be made to insure that as much of the rolling stock as possible should be produced in Russia. It would be necessary to order 362 steam locomotives, costing 3,984,900 silver rubles, and 9,100 eight-wheeled carriages and freight wagons, costing 3,827,100 silver rubles.

There would be miscellaneous expenses for such items as surveys, the acquisition of land, clearing of forests, etc., which would amount to 2,112,200 silver rubles, making the total estimated cost of construction 39,114,500 silver rubles. To this sum had to be added an additional 10 per cent to pay the banker's commission and the dividends of the stockholders during the period of construction, making the total estimated amount of capital necessary for the construction of the railway 43,026,000 silver rubles, or for a railway of 600 versts, 71,666 silver rubles per verst. This cost per verst was more than the average cost of European railways,[62] and over 10,000 silver rubles more per verst than the cost of the Tsarskoe Selo Railway.

The Benckendorff Commission in its *Donesenie* tried to set up reliable estimates to show that there would be sufficient revenues from both passengers and freight to make the St. Petersburg–Moscow Railway a profitable undertaking. The number of first- and second-class passengers was estimated from the number of passengers traveling yearly between the capitals by various kinds of carriage, with the assumption that if the railway was built and offered quicker travel and cheaper fares, travel between St. Petersburg and Moscow would increase threefold. Also, a large number of third-class passengers would be migratory workers from the Central Provinces going to St. Petersburg to seek seasonal work who would find it cheaper and more convenient to use the railway than to travel on foot. Therefore, the total number of passengers was conservatively estimated at 270,-000. The *Donesenie* pointed out that in Europe, whenever cheap travel by railway was offered, passenger travel between two points increased often ten times, or even more. In Europe the yearly number of railway passengers between two cities was generally equal to or greater than the combined population of these two cities. St. Petersburg and Moscow had a combined population of over 850,000 and there were 700,000 people living in the area between the capitals. The *Donesenie* therefore asserted that the estimate of the yearly total number of passengers for the St. Petersburg–Moscow Railway was very conservative.

There would also be a considerable amount of revenue from the post, both official and private, and from parcels and small express goods, as well as from travelers' baggage and occasional private carriages carried on flatcars. A large amount of revenue would come from the transportation of cattle from southern Russia, since drovers could save money on feed and could prevent the loss of weight of their livestock if transportation by railway were available from Moscow to St. Petersburg.

62. "Donesenie," *Krasnyi Arkhiv*, LXXVI (1936), 127-130.

The *Donesenie*, however, estimated that the main source of revenue would not be from passengers, express goods, or cattle, but from the transportation of those raw materials such as grain and hemp which were the chief products of Russia. This view represented a departure from most of the previous thought on the subject both in Russia and abroad. Von Gerstner in his prospectus for the Tsarskoe Selo Railway had stated that railways could be profitable only by carrying passengers.[63] As mentioned above, Mel'nikov had held the same view before his trip to America. Abaza, in his original proposal to build the St. Petersburg–Moscow Railway in March, 1838, had thought that the main source of revenue would come from passengers, although he had estimated a considerable revenue from freight. But views were changing.

The *Donesenie* made a detailed report on the places of origin and approximate amounts of goods that would be carried by the St. Petersburg–Moscow Railway. It was estimated that the 6 million poods of goods currently carried between the capitals by the Moscow *Chaussée* would be carried by the railway, since railway transportation would be over five times as fast and only half as expensive as road transportation. The St. Petersburg–Moscow Railway would also carry 1 million poods of relatively high-priced goods customarily transported via the Tikhvinskii System to the Nizhnii Novgorod Fair. If goods were shipped by railway from St. Petersburg to Tver or Shosha and from there via the Volga to Nizhnii Novgorod, shipment would be much faster and only half as expensive; therefore the goods formerly moved by the Tikhvinskii System from St. Petersburg to the interior would be carried by railway.

The *Donesenie* predicted that the largest source of freight revenue would come from a part of the goods which at the time was being transported from the interior of Russia to St. Petersburg via the Vyshnii Volochek, Tikhvinskii, and Mariinskii systems. The Vyshnii Volochek System especially would lose traffic to the St. Petersburg–Moscow Railway. The *Donesenie* stated that a large part of these goods would continue to be transported

63. Franz Anton von Gerstner, *O vygodakh postroeniia zheleznoi dorogi iz Sanktpeterburga v Tsarskoe Selo i Pavlovsk* (St. Peterburg, 1836), p. 53.

by water, but some could be more advantageously shipped by railway, especially high-priced export goods. In addition, the railway would offer an altenative form of transportation in the event of the complete stoppage of water transportation by low water or an early winter. The *Donesenie* therefore estimated that of the yearly total of 22.5 million poods of freight to be carried by the St. Petersburg–Moscow Railway, 15.5 million poods could be taken from the three water systems linking the interior of Russia with St. Petersburg. (The estimate did not include goods from between Tver and St. Petersburg.) This estimate was in contradiction to Count Toll's main contention that all goods transported to St. Petersburg from the interior of Russia would continue to be carried by waterways as the cheapest form of transportation. These goods taken from waterways would be largely agricultural products such as grain, hemp, and tallow brought either by "winter road" or by tributaries to the Upper Volga and Oka landings from the central agricultural provinces to the south, which were rich and productive but which had poor communications with the outside world. There would also be a considerable amount of the same sort of goods from the Middle Volga region. Goods originating from the Lower Volga would provide a relatively small proportion of the total.[64] The St. Petersburg–Moscow Railway was thus conceived as primarily having economic value for only part of Russia, not for the country as a whole.

In summary, the *Donesenie* estimated a yearly total of 270,000 passengers,[65] giving a revenue of 2,110,000 silver rubles, 80,000 cattle at 5 silver rubles a head, yielding a revenue of 400,000 silver rubles, and 22.5 million poods of freight,[66] yielding a revenue of 3,220,000 silver rubles. Thus the total yearly revenue of the St. Petersburg–Moscow Railway was estimated at 5,730,000 silver rubles.[67]

64. "Donesenie," *Krasnyi Arkhiv*, LXXVI (1936), 133-140.
65. Fifty thousand first-class passengers at a fare of 15 silver rubles each, 100,000 second-class passengers at 10 silver rubles each, and 120,000 third-class passengers at 3 silver rubles each.
66. Three million poods from St. Petersburg to Moscow, 1 million poods from St. Petersburg to Tver, 14.5 million poods from Moscow to St. Petersburg, and 4 million poods from Tver to St. Petersburg.
67. "Donesenie," *Krasnyi Arkhiv*, LXXVI (1936), 133.

Costs of operation and maintenance, which had been higher than anticipated on the Tsarskoe Selo Railway and which had cut considerably into its profits, were estimated for the St. Petersburg–Moscow Railway at 13 per cent higher per verst than the costs for the Tsarskoe Selo Railway of the previous year, 1840. The main cost of operation would be for locomotive fuel, which would cost 565,700 silver rubles yearly. Wood would be used, since it was abundant in Novgorod and Tver provinces, through which the railway would run. Imported coal would be used only in case of necessity. Locomotive maintenance, the cost of which would be reduced by having a repair shop in Moscow, would amount to 504,500 silver rubles a year. Repairs of other rolling stock would amount to 394,100 silver rubles. The salaries of foreign locomotive drivers and firemen and conductors would cost 630,000 silver rubles yearly, but these costs could be reduced when Russian personnel had been trained to take the places of the foreigners. The maintenance of the roadbed and other structures would amount to 559,400 silver rubles, with the salaries of maintenance personnel an additional 241,900 silver rubles. Administration and unforeseen expenses were estimated at 250,500 silver rubles, making the total yearly operation and maintenance costs of the St. Petersburg–Moscow Railway 3,150,000 silver rubles.[68]

The *Donesenie* thus estimated a yearly profit of 2,580,000 silver rubles, or nearly 6 per cent of the capital necessary for construction. If there were such a profit, the railway would pay for itself within thirty-seven years.[69]

Nicholas I received the report of the Benckendorff Commission on September 15, 1841, and immediately forwarded it for examination to Deviatin (Count Toll had been absent again for reasons of health since the preceding April),[70] and to Count A. G. Stroganov, minister of the interior, with orders that both men were to deliver their conclusions no later than October 15. If they needed help or explanations, they were to consult with those able to provide the necessary information. The Tsar said that the matter of building the St. Petersburg–Moscow Railway

68. *Ibid.*, pp. 130-132. 69. *Ibid.*, p. 140.
70. Dubrovin, IX, 35.

would be discussed in his presence when both reports had been delivered.[71]

Deviatin formed a committee of the Main Administration of Transport and Buildings with General Destrem as chairman, and with General Rokasovskii, Colonel Golovinskii, Major Kerbezd, and the State Councilor Pereverzev from the Ministry of the Interior as the other members. This committee was to check the technical and statistical information and the conclusions of the *Donesenie*. The committee began its work on September 22, finishing it by October 10. It found that costs of construction would be only 37,474,755 silver rubles and costs of operation only 2,172,702 silver rubles, both sums considerably less than those estimated by the *Donesenie*. The committee estimated, however, that there would be a yearly total of only 180,000 passengers (40,000 first-class, 80,000 second-class and 60,000 third-class), giving a revenue of 1,500,000 silver rubles. Thirty thousand cattle rather than 80,000 would bring a revenue of 150,000 silver rubles. As for freight, the committee estimated that only 7,800,000 poods yearly would be carried by the railway. It agreed with the Benckendorff Commission that 6,000,000 poods of freight would be taken from the Moscow *Chaussée* (this was the only estimate of revenue made by the *Donesenie* that the committee did not reduce) and that 800,000 poods then going to the Nizhnii Novgorod Fair via the Tikhvinskii System would be carried by railway (instead of the 1,000,000 poods estimated by the *Donesenie*). But the committee stated that, instead of the 15,500,000 poods of freight estimated by the *Donesenie*, only 1,000,000 poods of tallow would be taken by the railway from the three water systems connecting the interior of Russia. All other goods would continue to be carried by these waterways. Therefore total revenues from freight would be only 1,332,000 silver rubles. With these lower estimates of revenue from both passengers and freight, the total yearly revenues would be only 2,962,000 silver rubles, or 2.11 per cent of the capital spent on construction.[72]

The committee of the Main Administration of Transport and

71. Mel'nikov, "Svedeniia," *Krasnyi Arkhiv*, XCIX (1940), 172.
72. "Zakliuchenie komiteta pri glavnom upravlenii putei soobshcheniia i publichnykh zdanii, 10 oktiabria 1841 g.," *Krasnyi Arkhiv*, LXXVI (1936), 145-147.

Buildings reduced severely the estimates of the number of third-class passengers and the number of cattle to be carried by the railway, perhaps figuring that the lower classes of society and cattle drovers would prefer to travel as they previously had and would not realize the value of the railway, even if it would be to their advantage to use it. But most important of all, the committee seems to have held Count Toll's view that very few goods would be transported by railway from the interior of Russia to St. Petersburg because water transportation would still be cheaper. Mel'nikov thought that the committee came to such a conclusion only not to displease Toll or Deviatin.[73]

General Destrem, who had been chairman of the committee, submitted a special report that was much more optimistic about the possible success of the railway. Mel'nikov states as his opinion that Destrem had changed his mind and become a partisan of the St. Petersburg–Moscow Railway because he was after all an intelligent and enlightened man and understood the significance of the data which Mel'nikov had brought from America, and in addition, guessed which way the Tsar's sympathies were inclining.[74] Destrem's report estimated construction costs of 40,571,722 silver rubles and yearly costs of operation and maintenance of 2,890,426 silver rubles. Revenues from 400,000 passengers and 14,800,000 poods of freight would be 6,922,000 silver rubles, giving a yearly profit of 4,031,574 silver rubles or nearly 10 per cent.[75]

Count Toll, who had returned to his duties in October,[76] upon forwarding the report of the committee of the Main Administration of Transport and Buildings and the special report of General Destrem to Count Benckendorff, asked permission to submit a special report of his own by the end of October. In this special report, Count Toll attacked the conclusions of the *Donesenie* and the committee where they had been in agreement. Toll claimed that costs of construction should be estimated for a railway of 625 versts, not 620 versts. He claimed that the estimated costs of the earthworks were too low and that too little attention had been paid to the costs of the acquisition of land. Toll concluded

73. Mel'nikov, "Svedeniia," *Krasnyi Arkhiv*, XCIX (1940), 173.
74. *Ibid.*   75. *Ibid.*, p. 176.
76. *Severnaia Pchela*, October 29, 1841, p. 964.

his report by stating that freight rates would have to be four and one-half times higher than those proposed. With such high rates, the railway could attract few goods from waterways or even the Moscow *Chaussée*. Therefore revenues would be much less than even the costs of operation and maintenance.[77]

Count A. G. Stroganov, the minister of the interior, also delivered a special report at the request of the Tsar to Count Benckendorff on October 11, 1841. Together with his official report, he sent a private letter in which he expressed the desire to have his report placed in the archives. Count Stroganov stated that since Russia was not accustomed to railways, such a large and dangerous undertaking as the St. Petersburg–Moscow Railway would not be feasible, especially since Russia was not yet mature enough as a country nor its people skilled enough to enter upon such a large work; in short, the railway would be impossible to build. Even if it were possible, its usefulness would not be proportionate to the huge sums spent upon it, and even if it were useful, its operation would be impossible because of the difficulty of setting up adequate police supervision over such a long distance through such sparsely populated territory. Count Stroganov estimated that the railway would earn at most a profit of 3.5 per cent, and more likely only 2 per cent, which would not make it a profitable venture. He considered the estimates made by the *Donesenie* only preliminary and without basis, so that, even if Nicholas I were not convinced that the railway was impossible, useless, and unprofitable, a final decision on this most important question still demanded the elucidation of many complicated and novel questions. Until these questions had been answered, caution demanded that such an undertaking costing hundreds of millions of rubles should not be entered upon. Count Stroganov concluded his report by adding that one should consider carefully before building a railway which would benefit only a few private interests in the capitals at the expense of the poorer districts, where there were no communications at all.

In October, 1841, Count L. A. Perovskii replaced Count Stroganov as minister of the interior. Perovskii, like Count Stroganov, submitted a special report on the St. Petersburg–Moscow Railway on November 2. He repeated Count Stroganov's arguments that

77. Mel'nikov, "Svedeniia," *Krasnyi Arkhiv*, XCIX (1940), 176-177.

the railway would be useless, impossible, and unprofitable. But he added some ideas of his own. He stated that the closer connection brought about by the railway between the interior of Russia and foreign lands by way of St. Petersburg would result in a strong influx of foreign ideas into Russia's central provinces.[78] However, like most of the members of the Russian government who were opposed to railways, Perovskii stressed, above all, the financial difficulties the railway might entail. Perovskii stated that if the Russian government considered the railway useful and inevitable, it should accept the proposals of the bankers (Dufour and Harkort, that is), but it should be willing to pay for the losses of the railway and in the event of its complete failure should be willing to pay for all expenses incurred by its builders. But if the government planned to see the railway built only in the hope that it would be profitable, then it should not be built, since it was doubtful if there would be sufficient revenue to make it profitable.[79]

The conclusions of the committee of the Main Administration of Transport and Buildings together with the special reports of General Destrem and Count Toll and the reports of Count Stroganov and Count Perovskii were forwarded to Count Benckendorff for examination by his commission. The commission, after examining all these reports, submitted a twenty-five-page report upholding its earlier contentions about the value, timeliness, and profitableness of the St. Petersburg–Moscow Railway. It was especially emphatic in trying to counter the arguments that the railway would produce too little revenue from the transportation of freight. The Benckendorff Commission's report was finished on December 24, 1841, and was handed to Nicholas I on the same day.[80]

Nicholas I now was ready to have the matter discussed in his presence. Earlier in December Dufour and Harkort, with whom

78. The question of the effect of the railway on the internal order in Russia was more present in the minds of Stroganov and Perovskii than of others, since they, as heads of the ministry in charge of the police, were responsible for keeping order. In spite of their opposition to the railway, however, there seems to have been an undercurrent of resignation to the fact that the railway would probably be built.

79. Mel'nikov, "Svedeniia," *Krasnyi Arkhiv*, XCIX (1940), 172-174.

80. *Ibid.*, pp. 172-173, 177.

negotiations had been suspended since the preceding August, had been asked to return to St. Petersburg to settle preliminaries for building the St. Petersburg–Moscow Railway. They left Leipzig for St. Petersburg on December 25 (N.S.), 1841.[81]

Nicholas I called for a special meeting (*soveshchanie*) of the Committee of Ministers, over which he himself would preside. This meeting was set for January 13, 1842. Several members of the Committee of Ministers submitted written reports in advance. Count Kankrin in his written report made his usual statements against railways but added the new arguments that much of the grain carried by railway would be lost in transit, and that the capacity of the railway would be too small to carry a significant amount. Prince P. M. Volkonskii, minister of the imperial court and appanages, stated that Russia was not yet ready to build such a railway, which would be useful only later. Count P. D. Kiselev, the minister of state domains, was generally in favor of the railway but was of the opinion that its proposed route should be surveyed more thoroughly and that it should be built via Novgorod and Torzhok. Count A. I. Chernyshev, the minister of war, was also not against railways but felt that the Moscow-Kolomna Railway should be built before the St. Petersburg–Moscow Railway. I. V. Vasil'chikov, chairman of the State Council, held the same view.[82]

In addition to the ministers submitting written reports, there were present at the meeting of the Committee of Ministers on January 13, 1842: Grand Duke Alexander Nikolaevich; Count Toll; Count Benckendorff; Count V. V. Levashev, chairman of the Department of Economy of the State Council; Prince A. S. Menshikov, head of the naval staff; L. A. Perovskii, the minister of the interior; General Destrem; General Chevkin; Count Bobrinskii; F. P. Vronchenko, the deputy minister of finance.

At the meeting of January 13, 1842, Nicholas I proposed the following questions for discussion: (1) Would the construction of the St. Petersburg–Moscow Railway be useful for Russia, especially for uniting St. Petersburg with the heart of Russia? (2) What could be the obstacles to building the railway? (3) Should the railway be built by a private company or by the

81. *Railway Times*, January 8, 1842, p. 41.
82. Virginskii, *Vozniknovenie*, pp. 222-223.

state? (4) How could the financing be done most advantageously?

These questions were argued by all members of the Committee of Ministers. Toll nearly lost control of himself in arguing vehemently against building the railway. Count Kankrin stated again that railways were useless and transitory. Other ministers attacked the estimates of the *Donesenie*. Prince Menshikov, citing the example of European railways, said that the estimate of the costs of construction was too low, but the Tsar interrupted him, stating that he believed the estimates to be correct. That ended the discussion on that matter.[83]

Nicholas I, having heard the arguments of his ministers, the majority of whom were against building the St. Petersburg–Moscow Railway or at least wished to postpone its construction until a later time, announced his decision. He stated in a firm tone that he considered the St. Petersburg–Moscow Railway both possible and useful and that construction should start as soon as possible. The railway was to be built at the expense of the Treasury, not by a private company. Measures would be taken to choose the most suitable route of those proposed, after which detailed surveys would be made. To meet expenses of construction, a loan would be floated or other measures would be employed, depending upon a later report of the minister of finance. The construction of the railway was to be administered not by the Committee of Ministers or by the Main Administration of Transport and Buildings (both of which bodies Nicholas considered hostile to the railway), but by a special committee under the chairmanship of Grand Duke Alexander Nikolaevich. A construction commission was to serve under the special committee. The minutes of the meeting of January 13, 1842, were signed by Nicholas I on January 16, with a note that the decisions reached at this meeting were to be carried out.[84]

Thus, having considered the possibility of building the St. Petersburg–Moscow Railway since 1834, Nicholas I finally ordered its construction, overriding the majority of his ministers and advisers. The St. Petersburg–Moscow Railway would become a

83. *Ibid.*; "Zapiski senatora K. I. Fishera," *Istoricheskii Vestnik*, CXII (1908), 445.

84. "Zhurnal osobogo soveshchaniia komiteta ministrov 13 ianvaria 1842 g.," *Krasnyi Arkhiv*, LXXVI (1936), 146-147; *Postroika i eksploatatsiia*, pp. 6-7.

reality by imperial decree. The Tsar had spoken, and even the men who had opposed him must carry out his orders.

There remained the problem of setting up the government committees which would administer the construction of the railway. Since it was to be built by the government, the services of Dufour and Harkort were no longer required. The Tsar, as a reward for their services, presented each of them with a snuffbox with his monogram and studded with diamonds.[85] Nevertheless, the possibility that Dufour and Harkort might yet be asked to build the St. Petersburg–Moscow Railway was not entirely discounted. It was not until July 30, 1844, when construction at government expense was well under way, that the Benckendorff Commission submitted its final report on Dufour and Harkort's proposals, stating that they had considered the terms offered to them by the Russian government unacceptable.[86]

The administration of the construction of the St. Petersburg–Moscow Railway was taken out of the competence of the Committee of Ministers and the Main Administration of Transport and Buildings because, it is generally supposed, the Tsar felt that these organs of his government had been opposed to the railway and therefore would not fulfill their duties with zeal. However, a contemporary attributed the Tsar's decision partly to the machinations of Count Kleinmichel, who had gained imperial favor by supervising the rapid rebuilding of the Winter Palace after the disastrous fire of 1837, and of General Chevkin. Both men were thought to feel that they could advance their careers if a special committee were created and they could serve as members.[87]

In late January, 1842, Nicholas I set up the committee to supervise the railway's construction. On January 23, he ordered that Colonel Kraft and Mel'nikov, who had also been promoted to the rank of colonel, were to be considered on a mission for him. On January 24 he appointed the special committee under the chairmanship of Grand Duke Alexander Nikolaevich. It was to be intrusted with the giving of all orders in building the railway and would supervise it until its successful completion. In addition

85. *Journal des débats politiques et littéraires*, March 1, 1842.
86. Shtukenberg, p. 313.
87. "Zapiski senatora K. I. Fishera," *Istoricheskii Vestnik*, CXII (1908), 445.

to the Grand Duke, its members were to be: the minister of finance, the minister of the interior, the minister of state domains, Count Toll, Count Benckendorff, Count Orlov, Count Levashev, Count P. A. Kleinmichel, Lieutenant General Destrem, Major General Chevkin, the Duke of Leuchtenberg, Count Bobrinskii. Five members of the special committee were chosen for the construction commission, which was to be under the chairmanship of Count Benckendorff. It was intrusted with the immediate direction and supervision of the construction of the railway. Its members, in addition to Count Benckendorff, were: Count Kleinmichel, Lieutenant General Destrem, Major General Chevkin, the Duke of Leuchtenberg, Count Bobrinskii, Colonel Mel'nikov, Colonel Kraft.[88]

It should be noted that, although the administration of the construction of the railway had been taken out of the competence of the Committee of Ministers and the Main Administration of Transport and Buildings, the membership of the special committee was basically that of the special meeting of the Committee of Ministers of January 13, 1842. There were two notable additions, Count P. A. Kleinmichel, the Tsar's favorite, and the Duke of Leuchtenberg, the Tsar's son-in-law, both of whom were favorably disposed to railways.[89] But Count Kankrin, Count Perovskii, and even Count Toll were also included in the membership of the special committee, in spite of their previous opposition to railways. Nicholas I probably wished to use their knowledge. But they were to serve on a special committee, which the Tsar would feel would be more amenable to his wishes than the Committee of Ministers and the Main Administration of Transport and Buildings, both of which had opposed him previously. Furthermore, they would be serving with convinced partisans of railways such as Bobrinskii, Chevkin, Mel'nikov, and Kraft.

88. Dubrovin, XI, 19-20.
89. P. E. Gronskii, "Ocherk vozniknoveniia i razvitiia zheleznykh dorog v Rossii," *Zapiski Moskovskogo Otdeleniia Imperatorskogo Russkogo Tekhnicheskogo Obshchestva*, IV (1886), 11. Count Kleinmichel was to become head of the Main Administration of Transport and Buildings in August, 1842, after Count Toll's death. In the same month a Department of Railways was created in the Main Administration of Transport and Buildings, which gave Kleinmichel a leading role in the administration of the St. Petersburg–Moscow Railway.

The Tsar had little reason to doubt that his wishes would be carried out efficiently and well.

The special committee met for the first time on January 29. At this meeting the Grand Duke, as chairman, explained to the other members the importance and breadth of the committee's work. The ukase confirming the decisions of the special meeting of the Committee of Ministers of January 13 and the setting up of the special committee and the construction commission was drafted, and Count Kleinmichel and General Chevkin were given the task of drafting the regulations of the special committee and of the construction commission.

On January 30, the construction commission had its first meeting. Preliminary plans were made for surveying the proposed routes of the railway[90] and making exact estimates of construction costs. Mel'nikov and Kraft were intrusted with this task and were given as assistants several young officers of the Corps of Transport Engineers. On the motion of Mel'nikov and Kraft, the American engineer Major George Washington Whistler was to be invited to Russia to serve as consulting engineer for the St. Petersburg–Moscow Railway. Mel'nikov and Kraft had met Major Whistler in 1840 at Springfield, Massachusetts, while he was building the Western Railway (now the New York Central) westward from Boston toward Albany. Mel'nikov and Kraft were of the opinion that of all the engineers they had met in America, Major Whistler had impressed them most with his ability and had given them the fullest and most satisfactory information.[91]

90. The route of the St. Petersburg–Moscow Railway was not finally determined until February, 1843. Contrary to popular belief, Nicholas I did not take a ruler and draw a line between St. Petersburg and Moscow, arbitrarily stating that this line would be the route of the railway. Rather, there was considerable debate among members of the special committee on whether the railway should be built in a straight line, in order to make travel between the capitals faster and to cut down construction costs, or whether the railway should be built via Novgorod, in order not to damage that town's economic interests. The Tsar, having heard arguments on both sides, decided that the railway should be built in a straight line via Volochek and Tver, thus bypassing Novgorod and Torzhok (V. A. Panaev, "Vospominaniia," *Russkaia Starina*, CVII [1901], 35-37; Verkhovskii, pp. 60-61), i.e., the route which he had favored since 1835 (see p. 86, n. 55 above).

91. George L. Vose, *The Life and Works of George Washington Whistler* (Boston, 1887), pp. 28-29. Major Whistler served as consulting engineer of

The minutes of the meeting of the special committee of January 29 and of the construction commission of January 30 were confirmed by Nicholas I on February 1, 1842.[92] On the same day the ukase officially authorizing the construction of the St. Petersburg–Moscow Railway was given to the Senate, which published it on February 6, 1842. The ukase confirmed the decisions of the special meeting of the Committee of Ministers of January 13 and the setting up of the special committee and construction commission under it. The ukase also ordered that three members of the merchant class be chosen to help the special committee and the construction commission in their dealings with merchants. Also the minister of finance was ordered to prepare a special fund, separate from the usual revenues of the Treasury, to build the railway.[93]

Why did Nicholas I desire the building of the St. Petersburg–Moscow Railway enough to order it built as soon as he could convince himself that it would not be a financial disaster when almost all of his government was content to develop canals, at least for the time being? He is quoted by Mel'nikov as saying:

We suffer from excessive distances. I consider the bringing of St. Petersburg and Moscow closer to each other a matter of great importance for the State. Whatever the intentions of Peter the Great were in founding St. Petersburg, time and

the St. Petersburg–Moscow Railway until his death in 1849. He is best remembered for fixing the gauge of the railway at five feet (1,524 mm.), the gauge which has been used by most Russian railways ever since. Major Whistler did not suggest this gauge, which was three and one-half inches broader than that used in Austria and Prussia, to keep the rolling stock of these countries from using Russian tracks in case of invasion, as is popularly believed. Rather Major Whistler thought that railways could be operated more efficiently and less expensively using a relatively narrow gauge, but many Russian engineers wanted a gauge of six feet, like that of the Tsarskoe Selo Railway. Whistler arbitrarily chose a gauge of five feet, which was used on many railways in America, especially in the South, until after the Civil War. Thus the gauge of Russian railways, which even today separates them from those of most of the rest of Europe, was chosen by an American (New York Public Library, Manuscript Division, "Report of George Washington Whistler to His Excellency Count Kleinmichel on the Gauge of Russian Railways," September 9, 1842).

92. Verkhovskii, pp. 56-57.

93. *Polnoe Sobranie Zakonov Rossiiskoi Imperii*, 2nd ser., XVII, No. 15265 (February 1, 1842).

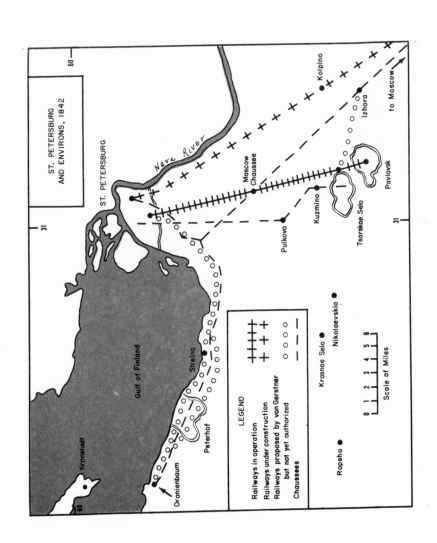

ST. PETERSBURG
AND ENVIRONS, 1842

ST. PETERSBURG

Neva River

Kronstadt

Gulf of Finland

Oranienbaum

Peterhof

Strelna

Moscow
Chaussee

Pulkovo

Kuzmino

Tsarskoe Selo

Pavlovsk

Izhora

Kolpino

to Moscow

LEGEND

Railways in operation
Railways under construction
Railways proposed by von Gerstner
 but not yet authorized
Chaussees

Ropsha

Krasnoe Selo

Nikolaevskia

0 1 2 3 4 5 6
Scale of Miles

m

55

50

circumstances have made St. Petersburg a residence of the Russian Emperors, the main administrative center, and one of the greatest ports of Europe. On the other hand, Moscow by its situation is the natural center of the Empire, the focal point of its internal movement, and of the entire internal life of Russia. Therefore any bringing together of these two capitals has to be accomplished for the good of the Fatherland, *no matter what the expenses may be* [italics mine]. A railway will resolve this question of [how to] bring the capitals together, lessening by nearly three times the time and expense of travel and freight transportation as against ordinary means of transportation. Therefore a railway system between these two points must exist. I have decided to call it into existence against the majority of those whom I call to counsel, and I hope that posterity will justify my decision.[94]

Posterity has justified his decision, but not entirely for the reasons that he would have imagined, since he had no idea of the far-reaching changes that the coming of railways would bring.

To Nicholas I administrative advantages may have seemed to be promised. He did not spare himself in his attempts to inspect every corner of his realm. Since he distrusted the bureaucracy, he tried to make sure that his orders were carried out and that the unwieldy administrative machinery bequeathed by his predecessors functioned properly by serving as his own chief inspector, traveling incessantly and rapidly in a two-wheeled carriage the length and breadth of the empire in an attempt to attend personally to the minutiae of government. To him a railway between the capitals would be a very real convenience. At the committee meeting of February 28, 1835, Nicholas jokingly remarked that it would be nice to be able to travel by railway from St. Petersburg to Moscow in a day in time to dine with Prince D. V. Golitsyn, military governor general of Moscow, and still be able to return by early the next morning.[95] Probably more significant to Nicholas was the fact that the railway would speed

94. *Kratkii istoricheskii ocherk razvitiia i deiatel'nosti Vedomstva Putei Soobshcheniia za sto let ego sushchestvovaniia* (1798–1898) (St. Petersburg, 1898), p. 96.
95. Baron M. A. Korf, "Imperator Nikolai v soveshchatel'nykh sobraniiakh," *Sbornik Imperatorskogo Russkogo Istoricheskogo Obshchestva*, XCVIII (1896), 125.

up correspondence, especially the communication of orders. In a time before telegraphic communication had been established between St. Petersburg and Moscow, faster communication between the capitals would have seemed an important consideration.

Although when von Gerstner had originally proposed railways in Russia, the Tsar had stressed the advantages of the rapid transportation of troops by rail, there is no evidence that he thought of railways as a military necessity because neighboring countries were providing themselves with them. He was probably thinking more about internal security.[96] He did think, however, of military economies that the railway might bring. The Tsar told Mel'nikov that when the St. Petersburg–Moscow Railway had been built he was planning to station most of the Guards Regiments in Moscow, where their maintenance would be cheaper since they could be quickly moved to St. Petersburg by railway.[97] The *Donesenie* also suggested that the expense of provisioning of military forces stationed in and around the capital could be reduced through the use of the railway.[98] There was also the possibility that the expenditures could be cut down by reducing the size of the army as a whole if the St. Petersburg–Moscow Railway was built. In November, 1841, N. S. Mordvinov wrote that if the size of the army was reduced to raise the necessary capital for railways, especially for railways between St. Petersburg and Moscow or Moscow and Riga, Russia's military poten-

96. In addition to seeing the obvious advantage of being able to transport troops rapidly by railway to prevent or quell civil disturbances, Nicholas I probably was very favorably impressed by the suggestion of the *Donesenie* that if the St. Petersburg–Moscow Railway was built, factories could be spread out along the railway, thereby avoiding overly large concentrations of workers in any given area.

In the 1830's the Tsar had become worried about the effect that large concentrations of factory workers in Moscow and other centers might have on the internal order of the empire, especially in the Moscow area. He had created a special committee, which in October, 1840, decided to let the Russian government give exemptions from taxes and other inducements to those who would build factories outside the limits of Moscow (M. K. Rozhkova [ed.], *Ocherki ekonomicheskoi istorii pervoi poloviny XIX veka: Sbornik statei* [Moscow, 1959], pp. 377-378).

97. Virginskii, *Vozniknovenie*, p. 223.

98. "Donesenie," *Krasnyi Arkhiv*, LXXVI (1936), 144.

tialities would not be reduced because the smaller army would be more mobile.[99] The American minister in St. Petersburg, Colonel Charles S. Todd, reported just after the St. Petersburg–Moscow Railway was authorized that he had heard that Nicholas I had gained the consent of his ministers (Todd called them "the nobles") to the railway by promising a reduction in the size of the army. Colonel Todd even felt that the St. Petersburg–Moscow Railway was primarily of military value and of little economic importance.[100]

Although these administrative and military advantages of the railway were not unimportant, so much additional construction would be necessary to insure adequate supervision of distant provinces by the central government and to carry troops swiftly to defend borders thousands of versts apart that the St. Petersburg–Moscow Railway would fill only a very small part of the need. Construction adequate to the need would have to include routes built through areas with little population or economic significance and could be hoped for only at a later time.

The probable economic value of the first railway was the really important consideration, and the one most emphasized by the report of the Benckendorff Commission. Nicholas I himself almost from the beginning had shown interest in the economic value of railways. As early as the summer of 1835, Speransky had reported to von Gerstner that the Tsar looked upon railways with interest and favor because they might aid economic

99. N. S. Mordvinov, "Kapital dlia postroiki zheleznykh dorog," *Arkhiv grafov Mordvinovykh*, ed. V. A. Bil'basov (St. Petersburg, 1901–1903), VIII, 700-701.

100. National Archives, Washington, Foreign Relations Division, Department of State, Diplomatic Dispatches, Russia. Record Group 59, Vol. XIV. Colonel Charles S. Todd to Daniel Webster, January 27/February 8, 1842.

Todd talked to some members of the construction commission who expressed the hope that once the railway between the capitals was completed, railways would be built from Moscow (1) across the Urals to protect Russia from England in India, (2) to the Caucasus and the country beyond the Caspian Sea, (3) to Odessa to facilitate the approach to Constantinople, and (4) to Warsaw. Such railways, in their opinion, would give Russia the ability to move troops rapidly to any frontier and would increase its internal security (*ibid.*, Todd to Webster, February 24/March 8, 1842).

acitvity in Russia.[101] After 1837 he consistently showed great interest in the potential economic significance of railway projects, in addition to their military and administrative value. It will be remembered that he suggested construction of a St. Petersburg–Rybinsk railway, which would have had only economic value.

The fact that the St. Petersburg–Moscow Railway would serve only one part of Russia would not prevent its having considerable economic value. The northwestern part of Russia had a disproportionately large share of the population and trade of the country. Most important for the railway's potential economic value was, however, the fact that as Russia started to change, though slowly, from a natural to a market economy, there was a growing differentiation between the agriculturally rich region south of the Upper Volga and the river Oka and the less fertile but more commercial and somewhat more industrialized area to the north. If rapid and dependable transport of agricultural products (including cattle and perishables as well as grain) to St. Petersburg from this part of "surplus" Russia and to a lesser extent from the Middle and Lower Volga regions was possible, it would produce benefits for the Russian producer, the Russian merchant, and the Russian consumer. The economic value of the St. Petersburg–Moscow Railway would eventually become even greater when additional trunk lines were built from Moscow to the Lower Volga region and through the Ukraine to the Black Sea, areas which were agriculturally very productive. The railway between the capitals could thus be considered the first part of a railway network that would at some time in the future serve to integrate the Russian Empire economically.

The question why Nicholas I decided to have the St. Petersburg-Moscow Railway built at the expense of the state also arises. Such a decision would plainly be in line with the Tsar's usual desire to have all control centralized and in his own hands. Such a decision would also be in keeping with the policy hitherto prevailing in Russia that major transportation facilities were to be built and maintained by the state.

However, until January, 1842, the state had shown a prefer-

101. "Proekt otveta predsedatelia osobogo komiteta M. Speranskogo Fr. fon Gerstneru iiul' 1835 g.," *Krasnyi Arkhiv*, LXXVI (1936), 101.

ence for having private interests shoulder the primary expense of railway building. The means by which the government might obtain money for railways—floating a foreign loan, when servicing the debt was already a burden, imposing an additional tax on the servile population, when taxes in many provinces were often, as it was, uncollectable, or issuing additional currency, just when currency reform was beginning to stabilize the ruble— all seemed undesirable at the time. Apparently resorting to these devices seemed preferable nevertheless because of the possible (and certain) undesirable consequences if Dufour and Harkort took the responsibility for financing the railway.

Probably the most important consideration was that there was the risk that Dufour and Harkort would not be able to raise the necessary capital, especially since the financial crisis of 1841 had reduced the supply of money available on the money markets of Europe. Even in 1839 the capital for the more modest Warsaw-Vienna Railway had been raised with difficulty. It was questionable whether such large amounts of capital could be raised even for a project to be built in Germany or some other Western European country, and many investors would be especially reluctant to invest in an enterprise to be built in Russia.

The failure of Dufour and Harkort to raise sufficient capital would have meant that their project, like von Gerstner's project for a St. Petersburg–Moscow Railway in 1835, would have to be abandoned, which would not have improved the climate of opinion in which to try to build the St. Petersburg–Moscow Railway at another time—or other railways, should other projects be put forth later. Or else the government would have had to supplement capital raised by private means through taking shares of stock, or through loans or outright subsidies, with the result that it might have to supply the major part of the capital for an undertaking directed by others. In such circumstances it would have been better for the government to have built the railway itself.

Also, Dufour and Harkort were planning to raise most of the capital abroad, probably largely in Germany. The headquarters of the company would be located in Leipzig, and effective control would be exercised by non-Russians, although the railway was to be subject to the supervision of the Russian government. And, while increased economic activity and employment resulting from the railway would benefit Russians, the greatest share of the profits would go to foreigners. This, as some Russians pointed out,[102] would in practice levy a heavy tax on Russians in favor of foreigners and would divert funds abroad that were needed for the economic development of Russia.

The official reason given in the ukase of February 1, 1842, for Nicholas I's decision to build the St. Petersburg–Moscow Railway at government expense was that he wished to keep this enterprise, so important for the life of the empire, firmly in the hands of the state in the interest of the public welfare.[103] It would seem not unlikely that the Tsar was influenced in his decision by Count Kankrin. Kankrin had said that if railways had to be built they should not be built by private companies, but from the beginning should be kept in the hands of the government, which would have the public interest at heart.[104]

Other pioneering countries on the Continent were tending to exercise more control and offer much more help to railways; this was the whole trend of the time. Government ownership as

102. "Zamechaniia ministra finansov gr. E. Kankrina na proekt A. Abazy, aprel' 1838 g.," *Krasnyi Arkhiv*, LXXVI (1936), 119; A. Safonov, "Ob ustroistve v Rossii zheleznykh dorog," *Syn Otechestva*, IX (1839), Sec. III, 147.

103. *PSZ*, 2nd ser., XVII, No. 15265 (February 1, 1842). It should be remembered that the Russian government had exercised increasingly strict supervision over the construction and operation of the Tsarskoe Selo Railway (see chap. iv, above, parts 1 and 2). If the St. Petersburg–Moscow Railway was built by the state, the government could go one step further and set its own standards of construction and operation without having to deal with a private entrepreneur, who might be more interested in immediate profits than in efficiency and safety.

Also, if the state owned the railway, it could encourage activities which it deemed especially desirable, for instance, the export of grain via the port of St. Petersburg, by setting advantageously low rates without regard to immediate profits and losses.

104. Graf E. Cancrin, *Die Oekonomie der menschlichen Gesellschaften und das Finanzwesen* (Stuttgart, 1845), p. 96. The fact that both the Tsar and Kankrin agreed that major railways like the St. Petersburg–Moscow Railway should be built by the state did not exclude the possibility that shorter railways might still be built by private enterprise if sufficient capital could be raised and if the terms asked by the entrepreneur were acceptable to the government. However, the government could be expected to follow a very cautious and conservative policy in such negotiations, just as it had with Dufour and Harkort.

opposed to private was being vigorously debated in the French Parliament, and the supporters of construction by the government were using the same argument as Count Kankrin. Only a few weeks before Nicholas I announced his decision, Austria had announced that railways in that nation would be built according to a fixed plan at government expense.[105] It is quite possible that it was Austria's action as well as Kankrin's opinion which influenced Nicholas I in his decision to dispense with the services of Dufour and Harkort, a decision which to many was unexpected and seemed sudden, but which was the logical result of the increasing interest of the Russian government in railways.

105. See below, p. 239, n. 3.

Epilogue

It is impossible not to conclude from the evidence that has been reviewed here that it was Tsar Nicholas I who, with the aid of a few of his more enlightened bureaucrats and courtiers, was responsible for the building of Russia's first railways. But whatever his reasons—administrative, military, or economic—there is no evidence that he was thinking in terms of anything but Russia's existing needs. In this Nicholas I was like most people in the 1830's and 1840's. When he was ordering railways to be built, some countries more economically advanced than Russia, Sweden, for example, had not even considered them. There is no reason to think, because he ordered the building of several railways, that his government, any more than those others, foresaw the industrial competition or the need for the quick movement of troops that railways would bring to Western Europe.

Those few persons who thought in broad terms were usually thinking of the development of agriculture, not industry. Almost all Russians thought that Russia not only was, but always would be, an agricultural country. Von Gerstner, Golievskii, and Murav'ev in the projects they urged upon the government and Safonov in his article in the *Syn Otechestva* all were thinking of linking the black soil regions to Russia's population centers and ports. Murav'ev went to some pains to explain that non-industrial countries needed railways too. The journalist Bulgarin did predict that the St. Petersburg–Moscow Railway would develop the industry of Moscow[1] (as in fact it did), but he did not argue that railways would develop industry in general. V. P. Gur'ev, the advocate of plank roads for northern Russia, had more vision. He suggested that if railways were built in the South coal from the Don and Donets regions could be combined with iron ore from Taman,[2] but such foresight was unusual.

1. F. Bulgarin, "Poezdka v Moskvu vo sne," *Severnaia Pchela*, April 20, 1840, p. 348.
2. V. P. Gur'ev, *Ob uchrezhdenii tortsovykh dorog i sukhoputnykh parokhodov posredstvom kompanii* (St. Petersburg, 1837), pp. 56-57. The prospectus in which he made this observation was published in the same year that LePlay examined the rich iron ore deposits of Krivoi Rog (later

This limited view of the need for railways was the underlying reason for Russia's falling behind other pioneering countries in railway building after its early start, although it must be admitted that the demands with which Russia would be faced in building many lines were especially formidable. Other pioneering countries seemed to become aware of the enonomic and military implications of railways sooner, and several began taking appropriate action about the year 1842. By that year the Russian government had conceded the importance of railways by deciding to build a major railway and taking financial responsibility for it. But Russia did not see, as France did, a traditional enemy approaching its borders with railways, nor, probably, did the possibility of a coming industrial competition seem Russia's concern. By 1842 the general success of railways had brought confidence in their usefulness and financial feasibility to all the pioneering countries, and military and economic considerations led the governments of Prussia, France, and Austria to pass laws acknowledging the state's interest in railways and providing for financial participation by the state in order to get railways built. In each case the government laid down a plan for the country's trunk lines connecting major cities, ports, and frontiers.[3] The passage of these laws marked the end of the era of experimentation and debate in these three countries as Nicholas I's decision of January, 1842, marked the end in Russia. It also marked the end in all these

so profitably worked in connection with the Donets coal fields) and declared them too remote to be profitably exploited.

3. In Austria, by the law of December 21, 1841, four major railways were planned to connect Vienna with all the major areas of the Cisleithanian part of the empire at government expense (*Geschichte der Eisenbahnen der Österreichisch-ungarischen Monarchie* [Vienna, 1898], I, 195-198). In 1842 Prussia planned 1,000 miles of railway and set up a railway fund which was to be used, when necessary, to purchase railway shares, to guarantee the interest on shares, and to advance loans (Hira Jagtiani, *The Role of the State in the Provision of Railways* [London, 1924], pp. 47 ff.). In the same year France passed a law containing a master plan for railway building for the entire nation with the provision that the government would furnish the necessary land and, in co-operation with local authorities, would build the roadbed and structures such as bridges and tunnels for the use of private companies which would provide everything else necessary (Jean Ernest-Charles, *Les chemins de fer en France pendant le règne de Louis-Philippe* [Paris, 1896], pp. 106-108).

countries of a great deal of reliance on private initiative and private financial support in getting railways started.[4]

But before going on to discuss further the railway situation after 1842 it will be advisable to review the activities of the period when railway building was dependent on private initiative and governments either held themselves apart or restricted rather than helped railway construction. During this period, that is, before 1842, Russia fell only slightly behind the other pioneering countries on the Continent whose governments rather discouraged railway building, but far behind the countries whose governments followed a laissez faire policy. Kankrin's and Toll's determined opposition had prevented the government from granting more permissions for railways in Russia proper after the building of the Tsarskoe Selo Railway. This was made easier because railway building in Russia was furthered neither by the interest and support of many small entrepreneurs and of people in general, as it was in England and the United States, nor by the interest of strong international bankers, as it was in parts of Western Europe.

The laissez faire policy followed in England and the United States resulted in wasteful duplication and ruinous competition that was the cause of many failures, but it did get railways built. By 1842 England had three or four times as many miles of railway as any other European country, and the United States had more miles of railways than all of Europe, although some of them were flimsily built. There was no dearth of willing entrepreneurs in England or the United States, and the people were enthusiastic. England had capital, but in America, where there were no large pools of venture capital, the people made up the lack by a pioneering spirit. Whole communities vied with each other in building, small merchants pooled their resources, and local and state governments helped. Even when "railway fever" helped to bring on the Panic of 1837, the people were not discouraged for long. Nothing could present a greater contrast than Russia, with its passive and illiterate peasantry, who could not

4. Unlike the other pioneering countries, Belgium had decided in 1834 that railways would be cheaper, faster, and more dependable than canals, had made a plan calling for a network of railways, and had set out on construction at government expense (Ulysse Lamalle, *Histoire des chemins de fer belges* [Brussels, 1953], p. 26).

have imagined that railways were in any way connected with them, with its small merchant class, whose most enterprising members were regularly siphoned off into government service because of the low prestige enjoyed by the burghers, and with its largely insolvent gentry, who thought of bad roads only as an inconvenience which had to be endured occasionally and which kept serfs and draft animals busy carrying produce to the nearest river landing during the off season. Plainly what happened in the United States could not have happened in Russia, even if the government had been ready with its permission.

In France and Prussia permissions for railways were granted which allowed only a few hundred kilometers of railway line to be built in each country before 1842. So little building was done because the governments did not give permission very willingly. In Prussia the government imposed restrictions and regulations on railway entrepreneurs at every turn. It appeared to tolerate them only because it seemed necessary; the bureaucracy's basic attitude was apparently one of disapproval. The French Parliament debated and wavered, meanwhile granting some permissions, but more than one French entrepreneur gave up when he found the restrictions laid upon him too onerous. France, however, fortunately for the cause of railways, had what Russia lacked, international banking houses with capital to invest and ready to promote railways. Perhaps the reason there was more early building in Germany than in France was that individual Prussians and Saxons invested rather readily in railways, while the French were cautious. The French investor continued apparently to prefer to invest in land or government securities.

But in the years after 1842, in addition to the interest and assumption of responsibility by the governments that has already been mentioned, there was a marked rise in most pioneering countries in popular interest and in willingness to invest in railways. Although nothing like America's bouts with "railway fever" or England's railway mania of 1843–1845 struck the Continent, the people began to want to speculate in railway stock. Even the cautious and thrifty French invested in railways, although during the 1840's half the capital for railway construction in France still came from England.

Private initiative, however, no matter what the popular interest was, had never been able to provide such public utilities as roads and canals on the Continent as it had in England. It is therefore not surprising that governments had to aid in amassing the large amounts of capital necessary to build railways and that much of it had to be obtained from abroad. After all, Western European countries on the Continent still had largely agrarian economies, and savings were not easily accumulated, even if in comparison to Russia it might have seemed so. In Russia's case any large-scale spending would have been less possible except through collective action. For Russia to have kept pace in railway building with Western Europe decisive government action would have been altogether necessary.

Such decisive action was not taken by the Russian government in the years following 1842. Meanwhile whole networks of railways were being built in Western Europe with varying degrees of governmental help. In England and the United States many new routes were being built and old short ones were being merged to allow through trunk lines.[5] Compared to these countries, Russia accomplished little, especially in relation to its total land area. As a result, in the period 1842-1855 Russia fell even farther behind not only England and the United States but also behind those Western European countries in which railway construction had lagged before 1842. By 1855, the year of Nicholas I's death, only 979 versts (653 miles) of railway (including the Warsaw-Vienna Railway in the Kingdom of Poland) were completed and open to traffic. In addition to the Tsarskoe Selo Railway, the St. Petersburg–Moscow and Warsaw-Vienna railways had been completed and the St. Petersburg–Warsaw Railway begun.

Nicholas I must have become increasingly aware of how desirable militarily many railways could be. He must have heard

5. In 1842 in the United States 3,877 miles of railway were open to traffic and in England 1,261 miles. On the Continent, Germany had 683 kilometers, France 559, Belgium 379, and Austria 385.

In 1855 the United States and England still remained world leaders in total length of railways completed, with the United States having 17,398 miles of railways and England 8,054 miles. In Continental Europe the relative increase in railways completed was even greater. Germany had 7,571 kilometers, France 4,641, Belgium 1,072, and Austria 2,315. (Georg Stürmer, *Geschichte der Eisenbahnen* [Bromberg, 1872], I, 33, 38, 78, 90, 137-139, 154-155, 211.)

the same sort of talk concerning the military desirability of railways to Russia's widely separated borders which Colonel Todd reported members of the construction commission as indulging in.[6] A. S. Khomiakov wrote in 1845: "When all other countries are crisscrossed by railroads and are able rapidly to concentrate and to shift their armed forces, Russia necessarily must be able to do the same. It is difficult, it is expensive, but alas, inevitable."[7] Such ideas obviously were current not only among Russians but among foreign observers also, some of whom feared that Russia's ability to concentrate masses of troops on its frontiers in a short time might make it more aggressive toward neighboring countries.[8] Probably it was with military needs in mind that Nicholas I ordered the St. Petersburg–Warsaw Railway to be built as the railway to follow the St. Petersburg–Moscow Railway. But Russia's military needs in transportation were so enormous, its borders were so many thousands of versts apart, that the task must have seemed one that would take years. Meanwhile no one was questioning Russian military might, which was simply taken for granted. It took the Crimean War to make it abundantly clear that if Russia was to keep its place as a great power, it must be able to get troops and supplies to where they were needed as quickly as her neighbors.

Nicholas I also, even if industrialization was not in his mind, could not have failed to realize the advantages railways could bring, if they were built to bring "surplus" and "deficit" Russia together. A system of railways of the sort proposed several times in the late 1830's would increase the usefulness and revenues of the St. Petersburg–Moscow Railway and would bring great economic benefits to many additional areas of the country. The need for such a network of railways was becoming increasingly obvious during the 1840's and early 1850's, as Russia's urban population and domestic trade continued to grow and there was

6. See p. 233, n. 100 above.
7. Quoted in Alexander Gerschenkron, "The Problem of Economic Development in Russian Intellectual History in the Nineteenth Century," in *Continuity and Change in Russian and Soviet Thought*, ed. Ernest J. Simmons (Cambridge, Mass., 1955), p. 25.
8. See, for example, Lawrence Oliphant, *The Russian Shores of the Black Sea in the Autumn of 1852* (4th ed.; London, 1854), pp. 8–9.

an increasing market for Russian products abroad, especially grain exported via Black Sea ports.

Nicholas I probably thought that he was doing everything reasonable to get railways built in Russia. The budget was already burdened with servicing a huge accumulated debt amounting to millions of rubles. Military expenses were exorbitant, far beyond the means of an economically backward country that was still operating largely as a natural economy. During the course of the 1840's, especially great demands were made on Russia's financial resources because of harvest failures and, above all, because of the extraordinary military expenditures incurred in the pacification of the Caucasus and the Russian military intervention in Hungary in 1849. The St. Petersburg–Moscow Railway itself was costing much more than originally estimated.[9] It was being financed by a series of loans floated abroad and from the State Loan Bank and by one issue of notes from the Treasury,[10] all measures, especially the last, distasteful to the state. Moreover, the doubts of the financial wisdom of building railways that had assailed the government before 1842 could not be dispelled finally until the St. Petersburg–Moscow Railway was operating and proving that the *Donesenie's* estimates were reliable and that major railways would not fail financially.[11]

In spite of all these financial problems and still lingering

9. The total cost of the railway, which was 604 versts (403 miles) in length, was 71,872,836 silver rubles (*Sbornik svedenii o zheleznykh dorogakh v Rossii* [St. Petersburg, 1867], I, 87-88).

10. For details, see S. A. Urodkov, *Peterburgo–Moskovskaia Zheleznaia Doroga: Istoriia stroitel'stva* (1842–1851 gg.) (Leningrad, 1951), pp. 92-98.

11. In the first years of its operation the St. Petersburg–Moscow Railway did not realize the anticipated profits. Although from the beginning the volume of both freight and passenger traffic exceeded the original estimates and grew steadily from year to year, revenues were disappointing because freight rates and passenger fares were kept low to encourage the growth of traffic and to make the railway of more benefit to Russia generally. Also costs of operation and maintenance were exceedingly high, partly because of the large number of railway employees and because of the high prices charged by Harrison and Winans for repair and maintenance of locomotives and rolling stock.

Only after a few years, when traffic increased, costs were reduced, and other railways had made connections with the line at Moscow, did the St. Petersburg–Moscow Railway become profitable (J. N. Westwood, *A History of Russian Railways* [London, 1964], pp. 34-36).

doubts, when the Warsaw-Vienna Railway had been completed (in 1848) and the St. Petersburg–Moscow Railway was almost ready to be opened to traffic (in November, 1851), Nicholas did not hesitate to authorize (in February, 1851) the construction of the St. Petersburg–Warsaw Railway, to be built by the state, a railway that was to be 1,043 versts (695 miles) in length. By November, 1853, the first stretch of track, St. Petersburg to Gatchina, 43 versts (28.3 miles) long, was opened to traffic, but further construction was stopped by the outbreak of the Crimean War.[12]

Meanwhile, projects for private construction of shorter railways were also being considered. None of the railways proposed was built before 1855, to be sure, but the government reacted favorably to some proposals. The promoters could not raise enough capital to start construction, because, as before, of the scarcity of capital and the unwillingness of the government to offer enough assistance to attract what capital there was.[13]

By the time Alexander II came to the throne the military and economic necessity of railways was obvious. It was also obvious that railways could sometimes pay for themselves, directly as well as indirectly. By a decree of January 26, 1857, establishing the Main Company of Russian Railways (Glavnoe Obshchestvo Rossiiskikh Zheleznykh Dorog), Alexander II attempted to bring Russia more abreast with other pioneering countries by providing Russia with a railway system which, both in extent and in the routes selected, was similar to those proposed by von Gerstner

12. V. M. Verkhovskii, *Kratkii istoricheskii ocherk nachala i rasprostraneniia zheleznykh dorog v Rossii po 1897 g. vkliuchitel'no* (St. Petersburg, 1898), p. 72.

13. For a detailed discussion of these projects, see I. P. Borichevskii, "Predlozheniia chastnykh lits ob ustroistve zheleznykh dorog postupivshie v G. U. P. S. i P. Z. do 1860 goda," *Zhurnal Putei Soobshcheniia*, XXXIX, kn. I (1863), pp. 148-162, 262-285. The government refused to make the concessions for any great length of time, reserved the right to acquire the railway at any time by buying up the shares, and above all never agreed to give a guarantee higher than 4 per cent, and sometimes offered no guarantee at all. (See P. N. Giatsintov, "Pravitel'stvo i chastnaia zheleznodorozhnaia promyshlennost' v Rossii tsarstvovaniia Imperatorov Nikolaia I i Aleksandra II," *Russkoe Ekonomicheskoe Obozrenie*, No. 8 [1902], pp. 5-8; Public Record Office, London, Foreign Office 65 [Diplomatic and consular reports from Russia to England], Vol. CCCXXII. Andrew Buchanan to the Earl of Aberdeen, No. 45 [St. Petersburg, September 26 (N.S.), 1846].

and others in the 1830's.[14] From this point on the pace of construction accelerated, and a few years later Russia was experiencing its first railway boom. Wherever railways were built production was encouraged. Russia's railway building, unlike that of the United States, where railways were built ahead of population, was for a long time behind its population. It was not until the 1890's that Russia built railways ahead of demand.

The railways that Nicholas I built and the locomotive works that he saw established provided the basis for this further construction. Nicholas I may not have built many versts of railways, but he did bring Russia into the Railway Age. Furthermore, he established the principle, so necessary for a backward country, that the state should take responsibility for the building of railways. If the Tsar neither foresaw nor desired any fundamental changes in Russian life through railway construction, eventually railways were nevertheless to make a valuable contribution to the modernization and partial economic and social transformation of Russia.

14. The Main Company was to complete the St. Petersburg–Warsaw Railway, with a branch from Wilno via Kovno to the Prussian border. It was to build three new trunk lines: (1) Moscow–Nizhnii Novgorod; (2) Moscow–Orel–Kharkov–Theodosia; (3) Orel–Libau (*Polnoe Sobranie Zakonov Rossiiskoi Imperii*, 2nd ser., XXXII, No. 31448 [January 26, 1857]).

Bibliography of works cited

I. Primary sources

A. Laws and statutes

Dnevnik Zakonov Tsarstva Pol'skogo. 70 vols.
Warsaw, 1810–1871.
Polnoe Sobranie Zakonov Rossiiskoi Imperii.
240 vols. St. Petersburg, 1825–1916.

B. Archival sources

1. Russian—*manuscript*

Tsentral'nyi Gosudarstvennyi Istoricheskii Arkhiv v Leningrade.
Fond 1263 (1839), delo 1248, pp. 244-250; delo 1249, pp. 432-441; delo 1250, pp. 384-394; delo 1261, pp. 500-506.

2. Russian—*published*

Dubrovin, N. (ed.). *Sbornik istoricheskikh materialov, izvlechennykh iz Arkhiva Sobstvennoi Ego Imperatorskogo Velichestva Kantseliarii.* 16 vols. St. Petersburg, 1876–1917.

Mel'nikov, P. P. "Poezdka na Volgu," edited by M. Krutikov, *Krasnyi Arkhiv,* LXXXIX-XC (1938), 309-335.

———. "Svedeniia o russkikh zheleznykh dorogakh," edited by M. Krutikov, *Krasnyi Arkhiv,* XCIX (1940), 127-179.

Mordvinov, N. S. "Kapital dlia postroiki zheleznykh dorog," *Arkhiv grafov Mordvinovykh,* edited by V. A. Bil'basov (St. Petersburg, 1901–1903), VIII, 700-701.

———. "Soobrazheniia pri razstroenii rospisa na 1828 god," *Arkhiv grafov Mordvinovykh,* edited by V. A. Bil'basov (St. Petersburg, 1901–1903), VII, 52-126.

———. "Zapiska o chugunnoi doroge," *Arkhiv grafov Mordvinovykh,* edited by V. A. Bil'basov (St. Petersburg, 1901–1903), X, 472-476.

"Pervye zheleznye dorogi v Rossii," edited by M. Krutikov. *Krasnyi Arkhiv,* LXXVI (1936), 83-155. (The individual documents found here are not listed separately in this bibliography but are quoted by title in the footnotes of the text.)

3. Non-Russian—*manuscript*

National Archives, Washington. Foreign Relations Division. Department of State. Diplomatic Dispatches, Russia. Record Group 59, Vol. XIV.

New York Public Library, Manuscript Division. "Report of George Washington Whistler to His Excellency Count Kleinmichel on the Gauge of Russian Railways" (September 9, 1842). (Typewritten copy of the original document in Central State Historical Archives, Leningrad.)

Österreichisches Haus-, Hof-, und Staatsarchiv, Vienna. Letters of Count Karl Ludwig Ficquelmont to Prince Klemens Metternich: 1836, No. 21 (May 5/17); 1839, No. 17 (May 29/June 10).

Public Record Office, London. Foreign Office 65 (Diplomatic and consular reports from Russia to England). Vols. CCLV, CCLXXX, CCCXVI, CCCXXII, CCCXXVI.

C. *Letters, memoirs, and travel accounts*

1. Russian

Del'vig, Baron A. I. *Moi vospominaniia*. 4 vols. Moscow, 1912–1913.

Mal'tsov, S. I. "Iz vospominanii S. I. Mal'tsova," *Zapiski Moskovskogo Otdeleniia Imperatorskogo Russkogo Tekhnicheskogo Obshchestva*, IV (1886), 39-42.

Nikitenko, A. V. *Zapiski i dnevnik* (1826–1877). 3 vols. St. Petersburg, 1893.

Panaev, V. A. "Vospominaniia," *Russkaia Starina*, LXXX (1893), 63-89, 395-412; CVII (1901), 31-66.

Shiman, V. M. "Imperator Nikolai Pavlovich. Iz zapisok i vospominanii sovremennika," *Russkii Arkhiv*, No. 1 (1902), pp. 459-475.

Shumakher, A. D. "Pozdnye vospominaniia," *Vestnik Evropy*, CXCVI (1899), 89-128.

Sushkov, A. "Vospominaniia o grafe K. F. Tole," *Chteniia v Imperatorskom Obshchestve Istorii i Drevnostei Rossiiskikh pri Moskovskom Universitete*, LV (1865), 206-221.

Viazemskii, Prince P. A. "Krushenie tsarskosel'skogo poezda," *Polnoe Sobranie Sochinenii* (St. Petersburg, 1879), II, 276-281.

"Zapiski senatora K. I. Fishera," *Istoricheskii Vestnik*, CXII (1908), 56-78, 426-465, 825-845.

2. Non-Russian

Aus den Reisetagebüchern des Grafen Georg Kankrin, ehemaligen kaiserlich russischen Finanzministers, aus den Jahren 1840–1845. 2 parts. Braunschweig, 1865.

Custine, Marquis de. *Russia.* 2nd ed. 3 vols. London, 1854.

Maxwell, John S. *The Czar, His Court, and People.* New York, 1848.

New York Public Library, Manuscript Division. Patton Collection. Letters of Major George Washington Whistler: to Major William G. McNeill (London, July 15 [N.S.], 1842); to General Joseph H. Swift (St. Petersburg, December 19 [N.S.], 1845).

Oliphant, Lawrence. *The Russian Shores of the Black Sea in the Autumn of 1852.* 4th ed. London, 1854.

D. Contemporary books and journal articles

1. Russian

"A. A." [A. V. Abaza]. *Mysli moskovskogo zhitelia o vozmozhnosti uchredit' obshchestvo na aktsiiakh dlia sooruzheniia zheleznoi dorogi ot S. Peterburga do Moskvy.* St. Petersburg, 1838.

Atreshkov (Ostreshkov-Tarasenko), N. *Ob ustroenii zheleznykh dorog v Rossii.* St. Petersburg, 1835.

"Budushchnost' zheleznykh dorog," *Moskovskii Nabliudatel',* XI (1837), 475-483.

Bulgarin, F. "Patrioticheskii vopros: mogut li sushchestvovat' v Rossii chugunnye dorogo i budut li oni polezny," *Severnaia Pchela,* October 12, 1836, pp. 930-932.

———. "Poezdka v Moskvu vo sne," *Severnaia Pchela,* April 20, 1840, pp. 347-348.

"Chugunnye dorogi," *Biblioteka dlia Chteniia,* VIII (1835), Sec. III, 106-120.

"Chugunnye dorogi," *Zhurnal Obshchepoleznykh Svedenii,* I (1834), 307-309.

"Chugunnye dorogi i parovye pushni," *Syn Otechestva,* CI (1825), 309-314.

"Chugunnye dorogi v Amerike," *Biblioteka dlia Chteniia,* VI (1834), Sec. VII, 23-28.

Destrem, M. "Obshchie suzhdeniia ob otnositel'nykh vygodakh kanalov i dorog s koleiami i prilozhenie vyvodov k opredeleniu udobneishego dlia Rossii sposoba perevozki tiazhestei," *Zhurnal Putei Soobshcheniia,* kn. XXI (1831), 1-90.

"Eshche pis'mo iz Moskvy o zheleznoi doroge," *Severnaia Pchela,* May 9, 1839, pp. 403-404.

Fon Giubental, K. V. "Prizimaticheskie dorogi, vmesto zheleznykh, v Rossii," *Severnaia Pchela,* March 9, 1839, pp. 215-216.

Gersevanov, "O vodianykh i sukhoputnykh soobshcheniiakh v Rossii," *Syn Otechestva,* IX (1839), Sec. III, 125-137.

Gorlov, I. *Obozrenie ekonomicheskoi statistiki Rossii.* St. Petersburg, 1849.

Gur'ev, S. "O perenosnykh zheleznykh dorogakh, ustraivaemykh pri krepostiakh i arsenalakh," *Gornyi Zhurnal,* II, kn. VI (1834), 569-574.

Gur'ev, V. P. "Mysli o pervoi kompanii zimnikh dorog v Rossii," *Biblioteka dlia Chteniia,* XXXI (1838), Sec. IV, 1-17.

———. *Ob uchrezhdenii tortsovykh dorog i sukhoputnykh parokhodov v Rossii posredstvom kompanii.* St. Petersburg, 1837.

"Izvestie o sukhoputnom parokhode, ustroennom v ural'skikh zavodakh v 1833 godu," *Gornyi Zhurnal,* II, kn. V (1835), 445-448.

Korf, Baron M. A. "Imperator Nikolai v soveshchatel'nykh sobraniiakh," *Sbornik Imperatorskogo Russkogo Istoricheskogo Obshchestva,* XCVIII (1896), 101-283.

"Mashina vymyshlennaia g. inzhener-mekhanikom Puadebardom dlia vvozki sudov s velikim gruzom vverkh protiv techeniia bol'shikh rek," *Syn Otechestva,* XV (1814), 59-66.

Mel'nikov, P. P. "Opisanie v tekhnicheskom otnoshenii zheleznykh dorog severo-amerikanskikh shtatov," *Zhurnal Putei Soobshcheniia,* II, kn. I (1842), 19-85; kn. II, 95-197; kn. IV, 285-374; III, kn. I, 1-70; kn. II, 85-156.

———. "Zheleznye dorogi v Bel'gii," *Zhurnal Putei Soobshcheniia,* I, kn. I (1841), 1-28.

———, and Kerbezd, S. V. "Ob otnositel'nykh vygodakh razlichnykh sistem vnutrennykh soobshchenii," *Zhurnal Putei Soobshcheniia,* III, kn. III (1840), 206-227.

250

"Moskovskii Zhitel'." "Pis'mo iz Moskvy o kolomenskoi zheleznoi doroge," *Severnaia Pchela*, November 20, 1839, pp. 1051-1052.

"Mysl' russkogo krestianina-izvozshchika o chugunnykh dorogakh i parokhodnykh ekipazhakh mezhdu Peterburgom i Moskvoiu," *Zhurnal Obshchepoleznykh Svedenii*, III (1835), 177-178.

Nebol'sin, G. P. *Statisticheskoe obozrenie vneshnei torgovli Rossii.* 2 vols. in 1. St. Petersburg, 1850.

Neskol'ko slov o zheleznykh dorogakh v Rossii. Moscow, 1836.

"O chugunnoi doroge v Kolyvanskikh zavodakh," *Otechestvennye Zapiski*, VII (1821), 173-179.

"O chugunnykh dorogakh i parovykh koliaskakh," *Gornyi Zhurnal*, II, kn. IV (1832), 137-153.

"O parovykh povozkakh," *Syn Otechestva*, CXXXI (1830), 378-380.

"O vygodakh, dostavliaemykh kanalami, rekami i zheleznymi dorogami dlia perevozki i splava tiazhestei," *Zhurnal Obshchepoleznykh Svedenii*, I (1834), 52-54.

"O zheleznoi doroge iz S. Peterburga v Moskvu," *Severnaia Pchela*, May 30–June 1, 1838, pp. 475-476, 479-480, 483-484.

"O zheleznoi doroge mezhdu Peterburgom i Moskvoiu," *Severnaia Pchela*, July 2, 1838, pp. 587-588.

Odoevskii, V. F. Letter to M. S. Volkov (May 4, 1837) in *Russkaia Starina*, XXVIII (1880), 804.

Pel'chinskii, V. O. *sostoianii promyshlennykh sil Rossii do 1832 g.* St. Petersburg, 1833.

"Pervaia poezdka na parokhode iz Peterburga v Kronshtadt i obratno v 1815 g." *Syn Otechestva*, XXVI (1815), 37-40.

Pravdin, A. *O zheleznykh i tortsovykh dorogakh v Rossii.* Moscow, 1838.

Review of Franz Anton von Gerstner, *O vygodakh postroeniia zheleznoi dorogi iz Sanktpeterburga v Tsarskoe Selo i Pavlovsk* (St. Petersburg, 1836), in *Teleskop*, XXXIII (1836), 278-285.

Review of N. Atreshkov (Otreshkov-Tarasenko), *Ob ustroenii zheleznykh dorog v Rossii* (St. Petersburg, 1835), in *Biblioteka dlia Chteniia*, XIII (1835), Sec. VI, 38-47.

Review of V. P. Gur'ev, *Ob uchrezhdenii tortsovykh dorog i sukhoputnykh parokhodov v Rossii posredstvom kompanii* (St. Petersburg, 1837), in *Biblioteka dlia Chteniia*, XXIII (1837), Sec. V, 21-56.

Safonov, A. "Ob ustroistve v Rossii zheleznykh dorog," *Syn Otechestva*, IX (1839), Sec. III, 138-151.

Shcheglov, N. "O zheleznykh dorogakh i preimushchestvakh ikh nad obyknovennymi dorogami i kanalami," *Severnyi Muravei*, Nos. 1-2 (1830), pp. 4-5, 14-15.

"Stimbot na Neve," *Syn Otechestva*, XXIV (1815), 210-219.

Zheleznaia doroga ot S. Peterburga do Tsarskogo Sela I Pavlovska. St. Petersburg, 1837.

"Zheleznye dorogi v Germanii," *Otechestvennye Zapiski*, XI (1841), Sec. VII, 12-13.

Ziablovskii, E. *Rossiiskaia statistika.* 2nd ed. 2 vols. St. Petersburg, 1842.

2. Non-Russian

Cancrin, Graf E. *Die Oekonomie der menschlichen Gesellschaften und das Finanzwesen.* Stuttgart, 1845.

Falk, Johann Peter. *Beiträge zur topographischen Kenntnis des russischen Reichs.* 3 vols. St. Petersburg, 1785-1786.

Gerstner, Franz Anton von. *Bericht über den Stand der Unternehmung der Eisenbahn von St. Petersburg nach Zarskoe-Selo und Pawlowsk.* Leipzig, 1838.

——. *Berichte aus den Vereinigten Staaten von Nordamerika über Eisenbahnen, Dampfschiffahrten, Banken und andere öffentliche Unternehmungen.* Leipzig, 1839.

——. *O vygodakh postroeniia zheleznoi dorogi iz Sanktpeterburga v Tsarskoe Selo i Pavlovsk.* St. Petersburg, 1836.

——. *Pervyi otchet ob uspekhakh zheleznoi dorogi iz Sanktpeterburga v Tsarskoe Selo i Pavlovsk.* St. Petersburg, July 26, 1836.

——. *Vtoroi otchet ob uspekhakh zheleznoi dorogi iz Sanktpeterburga v Tsarskoe Selo i Pavlovsk.* Moscow, October 7, 1836.

——. *Third Report on the Railroad from St. Petersburg to Zarscoe-Selo and Pawlowsk.* St. Petersburg, January 29, 1837.

Kreeft, Christopher (trans.). *First Russian Railroad from St. Petersburg to Zarscoe Selo and Pawlowsk.* London, 1837.

Mueller, Ferdinand H. *Historisch-geographische Darstellung des Stromsystems der Wolga.* Berlin, 1839.

Sandars, Joseph. *A Letter on the Subject of the Projected Railroad between Liverpool and Manchester.* 5th ed. Liverpool, 1824.

Wittenheim, Otto, Baron von. *Über Russlands Wasserverbindungen wie solche bis zum Jahre 1830 bestanden und seitdem bis jetzt vermehrt oder verändert worden.* Mittau, 1842.

E. *Contemporary newspapers and periodicals quoted but not listed above.*

1. Russian

Aziatskii Vestnik (St. Petersburg) 1825.
Journal de St. Pétersbourg (St. Petersburg) 1838–1839, 1841–1842.
Kommercheskaia Gazeta (St. Petersburg) 1840.
Moskovskii Telegraf (Moscow) 1826.
Sibirskii Vestnik (St. Petersburg) 1819.

2. Non-Russian

Journal des débats politiques et littéraires (Paris) 1842.
Mechanics' Magazine (London) 1831, 1836–1837.
Railway Magazine and Annals of Science (London) 1837.
Railway Times (London) 1839–1840, 1842.
Times (London) 1839, 1842.

II. Secondary sources

A. *Russian*

Bogachev, I. N. *Sekret Bulata.* Sverdlovsk, 1957.

Boiko, F. I. *Parovozy promyshlennogo transporta.* 3rd ed. Moscow, 1957.

———. *Zamechatel'nye russkie mekhaniki Cherepanovy.* Sverdlovsk, 1952.

Borichevskii, I. P. "Predlozheniia chastnykh lits ob ustroistve zheleznykh dorog, postupivshie v G.U.P.S. i P.Z. do 1860 goda," *Zhurnal Putei Soobshcheniia,* XXXIX, kn. I (1863), 127-162, 262-285.

Bozherianov, I. N. *Graf Egor Frantsevich Kankrin, ego zhizn', literaturnye trudy i dvadtsatiletniaia deiatel'nost' upravelniia Ministerstvom Finansov.* St. Petersburg, 1897.

Brandt, A. *Ocherk istorii parovoi mashiny i primeneniia parovykh dvigatelei v Rossii.* Vol. XXIII of *Sbornik Instituta Inzhenerov Zheleznodorozhnogo Transporta.* St. Petersburg, 1892.

Chuprov, A. I. "Pervaia zheleznaia doroga v Rossii," in *Iz proshlogo russkikh zheleznykh dorog*. Moscow, 1909.

——. *Zheleznodorozhnoe khoziaistvo*. 2 vols. Moscow, 1910.

Danilevskii, V. V. "Pervaia chugunnaia doroga, postroennaia na Altae v 1806–1809 gg.," *Trudy Leningradskogo Industrial'nogo Instituta*, I, No. 4 (1939).

——. *Russkaia tekhnika*. 2nd ed. Leningrad, 1948.

Findeisen, N. F. *Pavlovskii muzykal'nyi vokzal: Istoricheskii ocherk (1838–1912 gg.)*. St. Petersburg, 1912.

Giatsintov, P. N. "Pravitel'stvo i chastnaia zheleznodorozhnaia promyshlennost' v Rossii v tsarstvovaniia Imperatorov Nikolaia I i Aleksandra II," in *Russkoe Ekonomicheskoe Obozrenie*, No. 8 (1902), pp. 1-46.

Gronskii, P. E. "Ocherk vozniknoveniia i razvitiia zheleznykh dorog v Rossii," *Zapiski Moskovskogo Otdeleniia Imperatorskogo Tekhnicheskogo Obshchestva*, IV (1886), 7-37.

Iatsunskii, V. K. "Promyshlennyi perevorot v Rossii," *Voprosy Istorii*, No. 12 (1952), pp. 48-70.

"Istoricheskoe obozrenie putei soobshcheniia i publichnykh zdanii s 1825 po 1850 g.," *Sbornik Imperatorskogo Russkogo Istoricheskogo Obshchestva*, XCVIII (1896), 530-591.

Kargin, D. I. *Nachalo signal'nogo dela na nashikh zheleznykh dorogakh*. Moscow, 1922.

——. "Podgotovitel'nyi period k postroike nashei pervoi magistral'noi zheleznoi dorogi mezhdu stolitsami," *Tekhnicheskii Zhurnal Narodnogo Komissariata Putei Soobshcheniia*, Nos. 9-10 (1923), pp. 406-421.

Katikman, A. A. *"Chugunka" v vozraste 100 let*. Leningrad, 1925.

Kislinskii, N. A. *Nasha zheleznodorozhnaia politika po dokumentam arkhiva Komiteta Ministrov*. 4 vols. St. Petersburg, 1902.

Kliuchevskii, Vasilii. *Peter the Great*. Translated by Liliana Archibald. New York, 1961.

Kratkii istoricheskii ocherk razvitiia i deiatel'nosti Vedomstva Putei Soobshcheniia za sto let ego sushchestvovaniia (1798–1898). St. Petersburg, 1898.

Kratkii istoricheskii ocherk razvitiia vodianykh i sukhoputnykh soobshchenii i torgovykh portov v Rossii. St. Petersburg, 1900.

Larionov, A. M. *Istoriia Instituta Inzhenerov Putei Soobshcheniia Imperatora Aleksandra I-go za pervoe stoletie ego sushchestvovaniia, 1810–1910*. St. Petersburg, 1910.

Liashchenko, Peter I. *History of the National Economy of Russia to the 1917 Revolution*. New York, 1949.

Meien, V. F. *Rossiia v dorozhnom otnoshenii*. 3 vols. St. Petersburg, 1902.

Migulin, P. P. *Russkii gosudarstvennyi kredit (1769–1899)*. 3 vols. Kharkov, 1899–1904.

Ministerstvo Finansov. *Ministerstvo Finansov, 1802–1902*. 2 vols. St. Petersburg, 1902.

Mokrshitskii, E. I. *Istoriia vagonnogo parka zheleznykh dorog SSSR*. Moscow, 1946.

Oppengeim, K. A. *Rossiia v dorozhnom otnoshenii*. Moscow, 1920.

Polievktov, M. A. *Nikolai I: biografiia i obzor tsarstvovaniia*. Moscow, 1918.

Postroika i eksploatatsiia Nikolaevskoi Zheleznoi Dorogi (1842–1851–1901 gg.): Kratkii istoricheskii ocherk. St. Petersburg, 1901.

Rozenfel'd, I. B. "Ocherki istorii zheleznodorozhnogo khoziaistva v Rossii," *Zhurnal Putei Soobshcheniia*, II (1917), 8-45.

———. *Pervaia zheleznaia doroga v Rossii*. Petrozavodsk, 1925.

Rozhkova, M. K. (ed.). *Ocherki ekonomicheskoi istorii Rossii pervoi poloviny XIX veka: Sbornik statei*. Moscow, 1959.

Rudchenko, P. I. *Guzhevye i vodnye puti*. St. Petersburg, 1904.

Salov, V. V. "Nachalo zheleznodorozhnogo dela v Rossii, 1836–1855," *Vestnik Evropy*, CXCVI (1899), 221-268, 580-626.

Sbornik svedenii o zheleznykh dorogakh v Rossii. 3 parts. St. Petersburg, 1867.

Semevskii, M. I. *Pavlovsk: ocherk istorii i opisanie, 1777–1877*. St. Petersburg, 1877.

Seredonin, S. M. *Istoricheskii obzor deiatel'nosti Komiteta Ministrov*. 5 vols. St. Petersburg, 1902–1905.

Shcherbatov, A. P. *General Fel'dmarshal kniaz' Paskevich: ego zhizn' i deiatel'nost'*. 7 vols. St. Petersburg, 1888–1904.

Shtukenberg, A. I. "Iz istorii zheleznodorozhnogo dela v Rossii: Nikolaevskaia doroga mezhdu Peterburgom i Moskvoiu," *Russkaia Starina*, XLVI (1885), 309-322; XLVIII (1885), 309-336; XLIX (1886), 97-128.

Sokolov, A. I. *Nakanune 100-letiia: Pervaia russkaia zheleznaia doroga v proshlom.* Leningrad, 1925.

Sokolovskii, E. *Piatidesiatiletie Instituta i Korpusa Inzhenerov Putei Soobshcheniia.* St. Petersburg, 1859.

Strumilin, S. G. *Istoriia chernoi metallurgii v SSSR.* Vol. I. Moscow, 1954.

Tanenbaum, A. S. *Vasilii Petrovich Gur'ev i ego idei o dorogakh dlia avtomobilei.* St. Petersburg, 1902.

Tengoborskii (Tegoborski), Ludwik. *Commentaries on the Productive Forces of Russia.* 2 vols. London, 1855.

Tonkov, R. R. "K istorii parovykh mashin v Rossii," *Gornyi Zhurnal,* II (1902), 168-186.

Urodkov, S. A. *Peterburgo-Moskovskaia Zheleznaia Doroga: Istoriia stroitel'stva (1842–1851 gg.).* Leningrad, 1951.

Vasilevich, K. V. *Pochta v Rossii v XIX veke.* Moscow, 1927.

Velikin, B. *Peterburg-Moskva: iz istorii Oktiabr'skoi Zheleznoi Dorogi.* Leningrad, 1934.

Verkhovskii, V. M. *Kratkii istoricheskii ocherk nachala i rasprostraneniia zheleznykh dorog v Rossii po 1897 g. vkliuchitel'no.* St. Petersburg, 1898.

Virginskii, V. S. *Dzhordzh Stefenson, vydaiushchiisia angliiskii inzhener-izobretatel'.* Moscow, 1956.

———. *Russkie izobretateli Cherepanovy: sozdateli pervoi parovoi rel'sovoi dorogi v Rossii.* Moscow, 1953.

———. *Vozniknovenie zheleznykh dorog v Rossii do nachala 40-ykh godov XIX veka.* Moscow, 1949.

———. *Zamechatel'nye russkie izobretateli Frolovy.* 2nd ed. Moscow, 1952.

———. "Zheleznodorozhnyi vopros v Rossii do 1835 goda," *Istoricheskie Zapiski,* XXV (1948), pp. 135-168.

———. *Zhizn' i deiatel'nost' russkikh mekhanikov Cherepanovykh.* Moscow, 1956.

Zhitkov, S. M. *Biografii inzhenerov putei soobshcheniia.* 3 vols. St. Petersburg, 1889–1902.

Zlotnikov, M. "Ot manufaktury k fabrike," *Voprosy Istorii,* Nos. 11-12 (1946), pp. 31-48.

B. *Non-Russian*

Blum, Jerome. "Transportation and Industry in Austria, 1815–1848," *Journal of Modern History,* XV (1943), 24-38.

256

Briavoinne, Natalis. "Sur les inventions et perfectionnements dans l'industrie depuis la fin du XVIII-e siècle jusqu'à nos jours," in *Mémories couronnés par l'Académie Royale des Sciences et Belles-lettres de Bruxelles*, XIII (1838).

Ernest-Charles, Jean. *Les chemins de fer en France pendant le règne de Louis-Philippe*. Paris, 1896.

Gerschenkron, Alexander. "The Problem of Economic Development in Russian Intellectual History in the Nineteenth Century," in *Continuity and Change in Russian and Soviet Thought*. Edited by Ernest J. Simmons. Cambridge, Mass., 1955.

Geschichte der Eisenbahnen der Österreichisch-ungarischen Monarchie. 3 vols. Vienna, 1898.

Hodges, Theodore B. "The Iron King of Liège: John Cockerill." 2 vols. Unpublished Ph.D. dissertation, Columbia University, 1960.

Hungerford, Edward. *The Story of the Baltimore & Ohio Railroad, 1827–1927*. 2 vols. New York, 1928.

Huyer, R. "Die Budweis-Linzer Pferdeeisenbahn," *Mittheilungen des Vereins für Geschichte der Deutschen in Böhmen*, XXXI (1893), 75-92, 157-183; XXXII (1894), 77-88, 170-193.

Jagtiani, Hira. *The Role of the State in the Provision of Railways*. London, 1924.

Lamalle, Ulysse. *Histoire des chemins de fer belges*. Brussels, 1953.

Die Leipzig-Dresdner Eisenbahn in den ersten 25 Jahren ihres Bestehens. Leipzig, 1864.

Matthesius, Oscar. *Russische Eisenbahnpolitik im XIX. Jahrhundert, 1836–1881*. Inaugural dissertation, Berlin, 1903.

———. "Verkehrswesen und Verkehrspolitik in Russland bis zum Jahre 1835," *Archiv für Eisenbahnwesen*, No. 5 (1903), 933-980.

Monas, Sidney, *The Third Section: Police and Society under Nicholas I*. Cambridge, Mass., 1961.

Pintner, Walter M. "Count Kankrin's Administration, 1823–1844." Unpublished Ph.D. dissertation, Harvard University, 1962.

———. "Government and Industry during the Ministry of Count Kankrin, 1823–1844," *Slavic Review*, XXIII (1964), 45-62.

Portal, Roger. "Das Problem einer industriellen Revolution in

Russland im 19. Jahrhundert," *Forschungen zur Osteuropäischen Geschichte*, I (1954), 205-216.

Repczuk, Helma. "Nicholas Mordvinov (1754–1845): Russia's Would-Be Reformer." Unpublished Ph.D. dissertation, Columbia University, 1962.

Riasanovsky, Nicholas V. *Nicholas I and Official Nationality in Russia, 1825–1855*. Berkeley, 1959.

Smiles, Samuel. *George and Robert Stephenson: The Locomotive*. Vol. V of *Lives of the Engineers*. New York, 1905.

Stürmer, Georg. *Geschichte der Eisenbahnen*. 2 vols. Bromberg, 1872.

Tesnière, Lucien. "Les antécédents du nom russe de la gare," *Revue des études slaves*, XXVII (1951), 255-266.

Vose, George L. *The Life and Works of George Washington Whistler*. Boston, 1887.

The Vulcan Locomotive Works, 1830–1930. London, 1931.

Warren, James H. G. *A Century of Locomotive Building by Robert Stephenson and Co., 1823–1923*. Newcastle-on-Tyne, 1923.

Westwood, J. N. *A History of Russian Railways*. London, 1964.

Young, Robert. *Timothy Hackworth and the Locomotive*. London, 1923.

Index

Abaza, A. V., 164-169, 207, 210, 211
Accidents. *See* St. Petersburg–Tsarskoe Selo Railway, operation of
Advantages of railways, 165, 173, 214; administrative, 202, 204-205, 231-232; economic, 74, 179 n., 203, 204, 211, 214, 233-234; military, 74, 75, 82, 87; military economies, 232-233
Agriculture and agricultural products, 37-43, 179 n., 187, 211, 214, 238
Alexander I, 6, 21-22, 66, 67, 81, 190
Alexander II, 202 n., 245-246; as Grand Duke, 60, 225, 226, 227
Alexandrovskii state factory, 51
America, 8, 66-67, 67 n., 94, 97, 156, 168 n., 177, 201, 203, 213, 230 n. *See also* United States
Archangel, 5, 7, 17
Astrakhan, 13, 34

Baader, Josef von, 67
Baird, Charles, 19-20, 51, 52, 53 and n., 110
Baltimore and Ohio Railroad, 68
Bankers and Banking: international bankers, 105, 109, 240, 241; Russian bankers, 91, 105; state banks, 105, 130 and n., 131, 184, 186, 195, 244. *See also* Dufour and Harkort, bankers; Harman and Company, London; Pereire, Emil; Rothschild family
Barges, 18-20, 34, 214
Benckendorff, Count A. K., 81, 89, 135, 163, 167, 210 and n., 211, 225, 228
"Benckendorff Committee" and "Commission." *See* Committees to consider project for St. Petersburg–Moscow Railway; Report of "Benckendorff Commission"
Bestuzhev, A., 69
Bludov, Count D. N., 81, 154, 167
Boatmen. *See Burlaki*
Bobrinskii, Count A. A., 97, 103, 141, 169, 205, 207, 210, 212, 225, 228
Boiko, F. I., 46, 59
Brandt, A., 50
Brunel, Isambard Kingdom, 112 n., 202
Brussels–Antwerp Railway, 204
Budweis–Linz Railway. *See* Linz–Budweis Railway
Bulgarin, F., 159 n., 179 n., 238
Burlaki, 18, 19, 33

Canals, 4, 5; and Alexander I, 6; and Nicholas I, 7-9; and Paul I, 6; and Peter I, 5, 6. *See also* names of individual canal systems
Cancrin, Count E. F. *See* Kankrin, Count E. F.
Capital, extinction of. *See* State policy concerning railways, revision to state, question of
Capital, raising of. *See* Financing of railways
Carting industry, 27, 36-37, 82, 137 n., 177, 182
Catherine II, the Great, 22 n.
Cattle trade, 42-43, 217

Caucasus, 171, 174, 244
Cession of land. *See* St. Petersburg–Tsarskoe Selo Railway, construction of; State policy concerning railways
Cession of private land, difficulties in, 117-118, 126, 152-153, 199
Charters. *See* Privileges, terms of
Chaussées, 22, 24, 25, 30, 31, 35, 36, 37. *See also* Moscow *Chaussée*
Cherepanov, E. A., 50, 52, 53, 54
Cherepanov, M. E., 50, 52, 53, 54, 55, 56, 57, 58, 60
Cherepanov railway, 55, 56, 60, 112
Chernigov, 40 n., 170
Chernyshev, Count A. I., 81, 225
Chevalier, Michel, 180
Chevkin, Major General K. V., 73, 206, 210-211, 212, 215, 225, 227, 229
Chuprov, A. I., 96 n.
Cockerill, John, 113, 114, 155-156, 165
Commerce. *See* Trade
Committee of Ministers, 23, 111, 127, 130, 154, 171, 173, 174, 175, 184, 206, 210, 225, 226, 227
Committee to consider Abaza's project, 167; report of, 167-168
Committees to consider project for St. Petersburg–Moscow Railway: "Benckendorff Committee" (Committee for the preliminary preparation and consideration of a project for a railway from St. Petersburg to Moscow), 210-211; committee to negotiate terms with Dufour and Harkort, 211-212; "Benckendorff Commission" (Commission on the construction of a railway between St. Petersburg and Moscow), 213, 220-233; review committee of Main Administration of Transport and Buildings, 221-222; other opinions offered and requested, 222-224; reply of "Benckendorff Commission" to review committee, 224; written opinions offered, 225; decision at Committee of Ministers meeting, 226. *See also* Report of "Benckendorff Commission"
Committees to consider von Gerstner's project: commission of Main Administration of Transport and Buildings, 78-80; committee of State Council members, 81-84; special committee, 84-99
Committees to oversee construction of St. Petersburg–Moscow Railway: special committee, 226, 227-229; construction commission, 226, 228, 229, 233 n.
Corps of Mining Engineers, 73, 206
Corps of Transport Engineers, 6, 201, 202, 229
Cost of Russian railway construction: St. Petersburg–Tsarskoe Selo Railway, 129, 131-132, 161; Warsaw–Vienna Railway, 200; St. Petersburg–Moscow Railway, 244 n.
Cracow, Republic of, 200 n.
Custine, Marquis A. de, 25
Customs duties, freedom from. *See* State policy concerning railways

Danilevskii, V. V., 46
Dargomyzhskii, A. S., 139
Darlington, 3. *See also* Stockton–Darlington Railway
Del'vig, Baron A. I., 169
Demidov factories and mines, 50, 53, 54, 56, 57, 60, 110
De Riddel, railroad promoter, 163
Destrem, General M., 66 n., 87, 221, 222, 225, 228

Deviatin, A. P., 205 and n., 212, 220, 222
Diligences, 29-31, 36, 177
Donesenie. See Report of "Benckendorff Commission"
Dufour and Harkort, bankers, 104, 207-210, 212-213, 224-225, 227, 235
Duke Alexander of Württemberg Canal, 7, 12 n., 17

Economic results of railways: not realized, 63, 178, 239; becoming apparent, 243-244
Elizaveta, steamship, 20 n.
El'manov, I. K., 162
Elton, Lake, 50 n., 175 n.
Engineers, 133. See also Foreign personnel, names of individual engineers
Equipment, railway. See Locomotives; St. Petersburg–Tsarskoe Selo Railway, construction of
Ermolov, General A. P., 167
Estimates. See St. Petersburg–Moscow Railway

Factory and mine railways, 47-49 and n., 56, 60
Feigen, E. I., 163-164
Ficquelmont, Count Karl, 74, 103, 169, 176, 177, 181, 186, 193
Financial feasibility, 65, 82, 83, 159 n., 181; of Tsarskoe Selo Railway, 85-86, 88; of Warsaw–Vienna Railway, 196; of St. Petersburg–Moscow Railway, 86-87, 91, 161, 167-168
Financing of railways: difficulty in Russia in, 91, 105-107, 235, 245; considerations in use of foreign capital in, 82, 235-236
——, St. Petersburg–Tsarskoe Selo Railway: raising of capital, 97-98, 105-106, 108-109; loans from the state, 129-131
——, Warsaw–Vienna Railway: by a stock company, 197-198, 199; by subsidy from the state, 199; by the Treasury, 200
——, St. Petersburg–Moscow Railway: von Gerstner's inability to raise necessary capital, 91; by the Treasury, 226; means open to the state, 235; means used by the state, 244
Foreign personnel, 6, 110, 115, 133, 140, 143, 144, 220
Forests, depletion of, 43, 182, 206, 214
Franz I, Kaiser, 67, 72 n., 73, 78
Frolov, K. D., 47, 50
Frolov, P. K., 47, 48, 49 and n., 57
Frolov railway, 47-49
Fulton, Robert, 19

Gamaleia, I., 50 n.
Gamaleia, N. M., 70, 71
Gascoyne, Charles, 47, 51
Gatchina, 22, 245
Gauge of railways, 55, 112 and n., 113 and n., 198, 230 n.
Gentry. See Nobility
Georgian Military Road, 22 n.
Gerstner, Franz Anton von, 16, 46, 60, 65, 132, 208, 245; early career, 71 n.; and the Linz–Budweis Railway, 72-73, 91 n., 94 n.; arrival in Russia, 73-74; and first proposal, 74-78; and official request for a privilege, 80; and concessions, 80 n.; and request for permission to build experimental railways, 85, 92; and negotiations with special committee, 85-93, 98-99;

and his *Mémoire*, 87; and the search for capital, 89, 91, 97-98; surveys made by, 89, 93; his prospectus, *O vygodakh*, 89, 93-97; concessions made by, 80 and n., 89 n.; financial backing obtained by, 97-98; agreement with Tsarskoe Selo Railway stockholders, 109-110; orders of railway equipment by, 110-115; criticism of Obvodnyi Bridge construction, 118; driver on opening run, 127; departure from Russia, 146; death, 146; character of, 157

——, other proposals: measures to improve Tsarskoe Selo Railway, 146-149; second "experimental" railway, 149-152; Moscow–Kolomna Railway, 153-155; factory to produce rails, 155-156; overall plan, 156

Glinka, M. I., 139

Golievskii, A., 169, 170-171

Golitsyn, Prince D. V., 23, 89, 153-154, 164, 231

Government aid, government construction, government policy. *See* State aid; State construction; State policy

Grain supply. *See* Agriculture and agricultural products; Moscow, provisioning of; St. Petersburg, provisioning of; Trade, objects of

Guarantees of dividends for stockholders. *See* State policy concerning railways, guarantees

Gur'ev, V. P., 17, 27, 32, 162-163, 238

Gzhat River, 13, 17, 170

Hackworth, Timothy, and Company, 113

Harkort, Friedrich, 178

Harkort, Gustav. *See* Dufour and Harkort, bankers

Harman and Company, London, 197

Harrison, Eastwick, and Winans, American firm, 51, 61, 244 n.

Highways. *See* Roads

Horse-drawn railways, 47, 56, 66 n., 72, 73, 122, 128; suggested, 165, 171, 179, 198, 207

Hübenthal, K. V. von, 162

Industry and railways, 3, 179 n., 203, 214-215, 238

Institute of Mining, 47

Institute of Transport Engineers, 6, 78, 133, 201

Intelligentsia, 178

Iron: exports of, 10; transport of, 14, 43; areas supplying, 43; cost of, 43-44, 111; use of Finnish, 44; distance from coal reserves, 44; customs duties on, 77 n., 111; increase in output of, 110 n. *See also* Metallurgical industry

Izhora, 148, 149

Joint stock companies. *See* Stock companies

Journal articles on railways. *See* Mel'nikov, Major P. P.; Opinion on railways, press

Journals, technical: *Journal of Mining*, 57; *Journal of Transport*, 204

Jurburg, 198 n.

Kama River, 13-14, 27

Kankrin, Count E. F., 23, 68, 81, 84, 108, 167, 196, 205 n., 210, 228; quoted, 183; general political and economic views, 184, 186-187; on legislation concerning stock companies, 183 n.; on private banks, 105; on steamboats, 182 n.; on railways, 82, 85, 130, 182-187, 198 n., 225, 236 and n.

Kazan, 13, 14, 74, 75, 171
Kerbezd, S. V., 202, 221
Khomiakov, A. S., 178; quoted, 243
Kiselev, Count P. D., 206, 225, 228
Kleinmichel, Count P. A., 227, 228 and n., 229
Kolomna, 153. See also Moscow–Kolomna Railway, proposed
Kolomna Railway. See Moscow–Kolomna Railway, proposed
Kolyvano–Voskresenskie factories, 47-50 passim
Korf, Baron M. A., 83, 84
Kraft, Colonel N. O., 91 n., 201, 210-211, 215, 227, 228, 229
Kramer, Benedict, 97
Kronstadt, 19, 20 n., 51, 148, 149
Krüdener, Baron, 67
Kuzmino, 120, 124, 127

Labor, 115-116, 133, 198
Lad'ia. See Barges
Ladoga Canal, 6 n., 8, 9
Land, cession of. See Cession of private land, difficulties in; St. Petersburg–
  Tsarskoe Selo Railway, construction of; State policy concerning railways
Leipzig–Dresden Railway, 207
Leuchtenberg, Duke of, 228
Levashev, Count V. V., 225, 228
Libau, 194, 198 n., 246 n.
Linz–Budweis Railway, 72-73, 75, 78, 79, 84, 85, 91 n., 94 n., 109, 129, 132,
  143 n., 157, 201
List, Friedrich, 160, 178
Liverpool–Manchester Railway, 3, 55, 66 n., 68, 74-75, 87, 96, 112, 132,
  180, 204
Loans to railways. See State policy concerning railways
Locomotives: first in Russia, 50; production of in Russia, 61; ordered by
  von Gerstner, 112, 113; Stephenson locomotives, 57, 58 and n., 59 and
  n., 60, 66 n., 113, 122-127 passim, 144; Cockerill locomotive, 113, 122;
  Hackworth locomotives, 113, 122, 123, 124, 155; Vulcan locomotives,
  113, 125, 143, 144
——, Cherepanov locomotives: difficulties with, 54; descriptions of, 54-55;
  originality of, 56-58; compared to Stephenson locomotives, 58-60; lack
  of support for more building of, 60-61
London-Birmingham Railway, 132
Ludwig, King of Bavaria, 4 n.
L'vov, Colonel, railway manager, 144
Lyons–St. Etienne Railway. See St. Etienne–Lyons Railway
Lyons–Marseilles Railway, proposed, 196 n.

Main Administration of Transport and Buildings, 7, 66 n., 87, 99, 103, 130,
  152, 188, 190, 205, 227, 228 n.; rejections of railway projects, 69, 70-71,
  170-171; Commission to consider von Gerstner's project, 78-80; Com-
  mittee to review "Benckendorff Commission" report, 221-222
Main Company of Russian Railways, 245, 246 n.
Mal'tsov, S. I., 68 and n., 73, 201
Manchester. See Liverpool–Manchester Railway
Mariinskii Canal System, 6, 7, 17, 33; course of, 6 n.; improvements on, 7,

8; goods carried on, 11; time to traverse, 11; quantity of goods carried on, 12

Mauthausen, 72 n., 78
Mednyi (Copper) Mine, 53, 56
Mel'nikov, Major (later Colonel) P. P., 78, 83, 103, 163, 183, 201, 210-211, 215, 222, 227, 228, 229; career, 201-202 and n.; journal articles, 204; report on America, 203-204; report on Belgium, 204-205; difficulty in getting a hearing, 205-206
Menshikov, Prince A. S., 225, 226
Merchants, 40-41, 107, 169, 210
Metallurgical industry, 43-44, 74, 91 n., 110-111, 155-156, 165, 204, 216
Metternich, Prince Klemens, 64
Michael Pavlovich, Grand Duke, 99, 100, 119-120, 124, 136
Military necessity of railways: not realized, 239; becoming apparent, 243
Mine railways. See Factory and mine railways
Mittau, 155
Mordvinov, Admiral N. S., 176, 232
Morshansk, 15, 32, 71
Moscow: access to by water, 7; extent of river traffic to and from, 15-16; population of, 16; provisioning of, 16, 40; as a road center, 26
Moscow Chaussée, 16, 22, 26, 86, 87, 89, 94, 136, 148, 207, 215, 218, 221; described, 24-25
Moscow–Kolomna Railway, proposed, 16, 113, 153-155, 164, 225
Moskva River, 7, 15, 16, 19, 32, 153, 154
Msta River, 6 n., 8, 9, 216
Murav'ev, N. N., 169, 171-175

Nebol'sin, G. P., 37, 42-43
Nekrasov, N. A., "The Railway," 133
Neva River, 6 n., 9, 21
Nicholas I, 7, 47, 127 and n., 130, 131, 135, 151-152, 154, 164 and n., 171, 188, 189, 194, 196, 220-221, 224, 225, 226, 227; quoted, 124, 179, 190-191, 201, 230-231; and canals, 7-9; and roads, 22-25; interest in engineering and technological innovations, 23, 24, 67 and n., 163; attention to trifles, 24, 99, 100, 231; attitude toward railways, 63, 64-65, 160, 181, 190-192, 197; early interest in railways, 67-69, 78; desire for the St. Petersburg–Moscow Railway, 74, 102, 161; negotiations with von Gerstner, 74, 78, 80, 81, 82, 86, 87-88, 90, 91, 92, 99; preference for small committees, 81; and state policy on railways, 83; negotiations with founders of the Tsarskoe Selo Railway, 99-100; and support of the Tsarskoe Selo Railway, 134, 141; his suggestion of a railway between St. Petersburg and Rybinsk, 178-180; relationship with Kankrin, 190 and n.; motives for railway building, 230-234; motives for state construction, 234-237; primarily responsible for railway construction, 238; contribution to railway construction, significance of, 246. See also Railways, reasons for little construction of in Russia
Niemen River, 69 n., 198 n.
Nizhnii Novgorod, 14 and n., 32, 33, 75, 97, 153, 211
Nizhnii Novgorod Fair, 4, 12, 14 and n., 218, 221
Nizhnii Tagil factories and mines. See Demidov factories
Nobility, 107, 176-178
Nordbahn, Kaiser Ferdinands–, 194 n., 198, 199

264

Pravdin, A., 159 n.

Press opinion. *See* Opinion of railways

Privileges, terms of: granted to Charles Baird, 20, 80; granted to diligence companies, 29, 30; asked by von Gerstner, 75-78; as altered, 80 n., 89 and n., 90 n.; offered by special committee, 90 n., 91 n., 92–93; granted to founders of Tsarskoe Selo Railway, 100 n., 101, 102 n.; granted to Warsaw–Vienna Railway Company, 195-196; asked by Dufour and Harkort, 208-209; offered by "Benckendorff Committee," 212

Projects, railway: Bestuzhev, Volga–Don Rivers, 69-70; Gamaleia, Morshansk to mouth of Tsna, 70; von Gerstner, network, especially St. Petersburg–Moscow, 75-78; von Gerstner, experimental railways, 76, 85-86, 92; von Gerstner, extension to Izhora, 148-149; von Gerstner, Moscow–Kolomna, 153-155; von Gerstner, Riga–Mittau, 155-156; de Riddel, St. Petersburg–Odessa, 163; anonymous, Volga–Don Rivers, 163; Feigen, St. Petersburg–Tver–Rybinsk with extension to Moscow, 163-164; Abaza, St. Petersburg–Moscow, 164-168; Golievskii, network, 170-171; Murav'ev, network, 171-175; Nicholas I, St. Petersburg–Rybinsk, 178-180; Paskevich–Steinkeller, Warsaw–Vienna, 194-195; Bobrinskii and Abaza, Rybinsk–Moscow *Chaussée*, 207; Dufour and Harkort, St. Petersburg–Moscow, 208-210

Proposals for railways: Lake Elton–Volga River, 50 n.; Tver–Novgorod or St. Petersburg, 66 n.; Niemen River–Windau, 69 n.; extension of St. Petersburg–Moscow to Nizhnii Novgorod or Kazan, 75, 97; Moscow to Odessa or Taganrog, 75, 97, 156; capitals with Odessa and Kazan, 159 n.; St. Petersburg–Moscow via Novgorod, 159 n.; network, 175 n.; Warsaw–Nizhnii Novgorod, 198 n.; Jurburg–Windau or Libau, 198 n.; Moscow–Kharkov–Alexandrovsk, 211; Nizhnii Novgorod–Moscow–Warsaw, 211. *See also* Projects, railway

Railways in other countries, 74, 142 n., 156, 168 and n., 191, 204, 213-214, 217; comparisons with Russia, 3, 75, 106, 131-132, 133-134, 143 n., 178, 215-216, 238, 240-241, 242 and n.; government participation in construction of, 64, 196 n., 236-237, 239 and n., 240, 241, 242; comprehensive planning by governments for construction of, 3, 160, 204-205, 239 and n. *See also* individual names of railways

Railways, reasons for little construction of in Russia: limited objectives, 238, 239; financial burdens of state, 244; Crimean War, 245

Rasputitsa, 29, 35

Rates. *See* St. Petersburg–Tsarskoe Selo Railway, operation of; State policy concerning railways

Regulations (*polozhenie*). *See* Privileges, terms of

Report of "Benckendorff Commission," 213-220; reviews of, 221-224

Revenues, opinions on importance of passenger as opposed to freight, 173, 180, 183, 192, 202, 203, 211, 213, 218

Reversion of railways to state. *See* State policy concerning railways

Riddel, de. *See* De Riddel

Riga, 10, 11, 41 n., 155, 174, 175 n., 232

River traffic, 13-18. *See also* names of individual rivers

Roads: lack of in Austria and Prussia, 5; and Alexander I, 21-22; and Peter I, 21 n.; and Catherine II, 22 n.; and Nicholas I, 22-25; plan for a network in Russia, 24; character of in Russia, 26; use of in Russia, 26-28; limitations of in Russia, 34-37. *See also* Chaussées; Moscow *Chaussée*

Rothschild, Baron Solomon, 199
Rothschild family, 105
Routes. *See* Projects, railway; Proposals for railways
Rybinsk, 6 n., 11, 12, 32, 33, 42, 163-164, 179, 207, 214; commercial importance of, 16-17

Safonov, A., 175 and n.
St. Etienne–Lyons Railway, 96, 132, 134, 180
St. Petersburg: population, 9, 10, 40, 168 n.; provisioning of, 10, 11, 15, 16, 38-40; exports of, 10-11; imports of, 11; as a road center, 26
St. Petersburg–Moscow highway. *See* Moscow *Chaussée*
St. Petersburg–Moscow Railway, 55, 61, 74, 133, 161, 169; project of Dufour and Harkort, 208-210; terms offered by state, 212; refusal of terms, 213; further consideration of by state, 213-226; estimates of construction costs, 215-217, 221, 222, 226; estimates of revenue, 217-219, 221, 222; estimates of maintenance and operating costs, 220, 221, 222; estimates of profit, 220, 221, 222, 223; decision to build, 226; operating and maintenance costs of, 244 n.; revenues of, 244 n.; profits of, 244 n. *See also* Committees to consider von Gerstner's project; Committees to oversee construction of St. Petersburg–Moscow Railway; Projects, railway, Abaza; Projects, railway, von Gerstner; State construction of railways in Russia
St. Petersburg–Peterhof Railway, proposed, 92, 96, 113, 121, 149-152, 156
St. Petersburg–Tsarskoe Selo Railway, 4 n., 55, 161; proposed, 76, 85, 92; prospectus for, 89, 93-97; government conditions for privilege for, 92-93; company formed for construction of, 97-98; authorized, 100, 102; privilege for, 100 n., 101, 102 n.; trial runs, 121-122, 123-124, 125, 126-127; formal opening, 127; regular service, 128; reasons for high cost, 132; patronage of Nicholas I, 134; as first segment of St. Petersburg–Moscow Railway, 148 and n.; proposed extension to Izhora, 148-149; significance, 157-158
—, construction of: administration of, 109; auxiliary buildings, 119; bridges, 118-119; cost of, 131; delays in, 117-119; embankments, 117; equipment, 110, 112-115, 123 n., 126, 143-144; foreign personnel, 115; labor for, 115-116; land, acquisition of, 116, 117-118, 126; land, clearance and drainage of, 116; rails, 110-112; roadbed, 120-121; stations at St. Petersburg, 94, 99, 119, 126, 146-147; station at Moscow *Chaussée*, 119; station at Tsarskoe Selo, 119; station at Pavlovsk, 119-120; construction of track, 120-121; gauge of track, 112. *See also* Iron; Locomotives; Metallurgical industry
—, operation of: accidents, 139, 140-141; attractions provided, 136, 138-139, 140 and n., 141; classes of travel, 128 and n., 136, 142; costs, maintenance and operating, 143 and n., 144-145; foreign personnel, 143-144; police supervision, 99 n., 100, 135, 148; profit, 134, 142, 145-146; rates, 136, 142 and n.; revenues, 143, 145; schedules, 128, 138, 139 and n., 140, 142, 145; signal system, 140; volume of traffic, 128, 134, 135-136, 138, 143 n.
St. Petersburg–Warsaw Railway, 242, 243, 245
Schedules, train. *See* St. Petersburg–Tsarskoe Selo Railway, operation of
Shcheglov, N., 66 n.
Shtukenberg, A. I., 157
Siberia, 174

Tengoborskii, Ludwik, 38, 43, 44; quoted, 37
Tikhvinskii Canal System, 6 and n., 17, 32, 179-180, 218; course of, 6 n.; improvements on, 8; time to traverse, 12; nature of goods carried on, 12-13; higher cost of use of, 12
Todd, Colonel Charles S., 233 and n.
Toll, Count K. F., 60, 87, 88, 99, 100, 173, 182, 198 n., 205, 210, 220, 225; rejections of projects, 70-71, 164, 167, 171; and von Gerstner's project for St. Petersburg–Moscow Railway, 78, 79-80, 84-85; committee membership, 81, 84, 167, 228; early attitude toward railways, 83; opposition to Moscow-Kolomna Railway, 155; opposition to Murav'ev's project, 174; opposition to St. Petersburg–Moscow Railway, 206, 226; adverse report on Murav'ev's project, 172-173; adverse report on Nicholas I's project, 179-180; adverse report on report of the "Benckendorff Commission," 222-223; importance of opposition of, 181-182, 190, 191; his views in general, 187-189
Torzhok, 86 n., 165, 215, 225, 229 n.
Trade, 9-10, 168 n.; objects of, 9, 10, 11, 167, 172, 175 n., 194 n., 219; effect of poor transport on, 41-43. See also Merchants; Nizhnii Novgorod Fair
Transport: need for improved, 3-5; effect of inadequate, 38-44; government responsibility for, 63, 241-242. See also Canals; Carting industry; Main Administration of Transport and Buildings; Roads; Waterways
Transport and Buildings Administration. See Main Administration of Transport and Buildings
Travel, road, 28-29. See also Diligences
Tsarskoe Selo, 94, 95, 101, 102 n., 119, 122-127 passim
Tsarskoe Selo Railway. See St. Petersburg–Tsarskoe Selo Railway
Tsna River, Tambov Province, 15, 32, 71
Tsna River, Tver Province, 6 n.
Tula, 15, 211
Tver, 6 n., 32, 33, 163, 214, 218, 229 n.; commercial importance of, 17-18

United States, 41 n., 143 n., 177, 191, 246. See also America
Urodkov, S. A., 46

Valdai Hills, 206
Vasil'chikov, Prince I. V., 225
Vitebsk, 40 n., 113, 170
Virginskii, V. S., 46, 47, 48, 56, 58, 59, 61, 68; quoted, 57
Vokzal, origin of Russian word, 136 n.
Volga River, 9, 21, 32, 33, 34, 154, 201, 216, 219; value and kind of goods carried and areas served by, 13-15, 16-18
Volga–Neva water systems, 33, 64, 172, 219, 221. See also Mariinskii, Tikhvinskii and Vyshnii Volochek canal systems
Volkhov River, 6 n., 216
Volkonskii, Prince P. M., 81, 82, 225
von Gerstner, Franz Anton. See Gerstner, Franz Anton von
Vronchenko, F. P., 212, 225
Vulcan Locomotive Works, 113, 125
Vyshnii Volochek Canal System, 5, 17, 18, 32, 33-34, 66 n., 164, 218; course

of, 6 n., 7; improvements on, 7, 8-9; goods carried on, 11; time to traverse, 11; quantity of goods carried on, 12

Vyskii Factory, 53, 54, 55, 56

War: in Caucasus, 244; Crimean, 243, 245; in Hungary, 244; Napoleonic, 5, 6 n., 7, 50 n.; with Persia, 87; in Poland, 87; with Turkey, 87

Warsaw, 170, 171, 211

Warsaw–Vienna Railway, 104, 193-200, 201 n., 212

Waterways, Russian, 9; limitations of, 31-32, 34; good features of, 31; Count Toll's emphasis on, 187-189. *See also* Barges; Canals; River traffic; Steamboats; individual names of canals and rivers

Whistler, Major George W., 36, 58 n., 158, 229 and n.

Winans brothers. *See* Harrison, Eastwick, and Winans, American firm

Windau, 69 n., 194, 198 n.

Winter Palace, 227

"Winter roads," 15, 17, 34, 67 n., 162, 167, 169 n., 188, 219; advantages of, 27-28; limitations of, 36

Württemberg, A. F., Duke of. *See* Duke Alexander of Württemberg Canal

Yartsev, A. S., 47

Zaplyvy, 8

Zmeinogorsk Mine, 47, 48, 49